BUCKET
~ TO ~
GREECE

Volume 16

V.D. BUCKET

Copyright © 2024 V.D. Bucket
All rights reserved.

No part of this publication may be reproduced, distributed, or transmitted in any form or by any means, including photocopying, recording, or other electronic or mechanical methods, without the prior written permission of the publisher, except in the case of brief quotations embodied in critical reviews and certain other noncommercial uses permitted by copyright law.

All names have been changed to spare my wife embarrassment.

Editor: James Scraper
Proofreader: Alan Wood
Cover Designer: German Creative
Interior Formatting: The Book Khaleesi

Other Books in the Bucket to Greece Series

Bucket to Greece Volume 1
Bucket to Greece Volume 2
Bucket to Greece Volume 3
Bucket to Greece Volume 4
Bucket to Greece Volume 5
Bucket to Greece Volume 6
Bucket to Greece Volume 7
Bucket to Greece Volume 8
Bucket to Greece Volume 9
Bucket to Greece Volume 10
Bucket to Greece Volume 11
Bucket to Greece Volume 12
Bucket to Greece Volume 13
Bucket to Greece Volume 14
Bucket to Greece Volume 15

Bucket to Greece Collection Vols 1-3
Bucket to Greece Collection Vols 4-6
Bucket to Greece Collection Vols 7-9
Bucket to Greece Collection Vols 10-12

Bucket to Greece Short 1
Bucket to Greece Short 2

Chapter 1

A Plague of Ticks

"What do you reckon's got your Marigold's knickers in a twist this time?" Planting her legs wide apart, Violet Burke supported her considerably bulbous frame on her mop whilst positing the question in response to the blood curdling scream emanating from the Bucket master bedroom. "I bet it's one of them gecko things."

"I don't know. Last week I caught Marigold screaming the kitchen down whilst battering the living daylights out of a handful of lime leaves with her shoe; she'd mistaken them for a lizard."

"It sounds as though your Marigold needs to get her eyes tested," Vi opined, peering at me intently over the top of her rectangular spectacles.

"In her defence, leaves and lizards are both green. I'd left the leaves out to defrost ready to add to a Thai curry. After Marigold had clobbered them, I had to bin them. Such a waste, it's impossible to get them over here."

"You should have just slung them in the pot anyway, lad."

"I didn't dare risk contaminating the curry with bacteria from the sole of Marigold's shoe."

"Well, 'Appen it's just as well that you binned them. You don't want to be eating leaves, lad. It's bad enough the way you tuck into them horrible bitter weeds."

"*Horta* is rich with antioxidants…"

"It's rich with all sorts of crap if those blasted goats have been doing their business in the greenery. Next thing you know, you'll be turning into one of them accidental vegetarians…"

Vi's words were interrupted by another frantic scream from the bedroom, prompting the two of us to belatedly leap into action. Marigold had cried wolf one time too many of late for us to bother taking her hysterical whelps too seriously.

As I could have predicted, Marigold was balanced precariously on a chair in the bedroom, her face flushed in vexation. Pointing at the bed, she shrieked, "Do something, Victor. We have an infestation of miniscule spiders. I've a feeling they could be those venomous scorpions."

Apparently, Marigold was seeing things. The only obvious thing despoiling our bed was my wife's pampered imported domestics; sprawled out languidly, paws in the air, their heads no doubt shedding hair all over my pillow. Quite why they always seemed to choose my pillow over that of my wife, remained one of life's little mysteries.

"Open your eyes, Victor. The quilt is a hotbed of spiders," Marigold insisted.

"You felt you had to climb on a chair for a spider," my ever-practical mother scoffed. "You need to get some mucky fat down your gullet, lass, to toughen you up."

It struck me that mucky fat had a myriad of uses, at least according to my mother: only yesterday she had promised a good dollop of the greasy concoction would put some much needed-hairs on Doreen's chest and advised Spiros to use it to put the shine back on his best leather undertaking shoes. There again, actual shoe polish tended to be appropriated as an all-purpose hair dye around these parts.

I reflected that unlike Marigold, it would take more than a spider to throw Violet Burke into a tizzy. My mother remained blithely oblivious to the look on Marigold's face, a look I interpreted as a passionate desire to tip a bowlful of said mucky fat over her mother-in-law's head.

Moving closer to the bed, I was able to identify three small black dots that did indeed resemble miniature spiders; moving at speed, their glossy black bodies stood out in sharp relief against the delicate hue of the sky-blue duvet cover. Scooping them up in a tissue, I held them at arm's length as I dashed to the bathroom and flushed them down the toilet, adding a generous dose of bleach in the hope of poisoning any of them that may have mastered the art of swimming. Returning to the bedroom, I assured Marigold it was safe to come down from the chair.

"They weren't spiders, darling. They were ticks," I revealed. "The cats must have brought them in."

"Ticks?" Marigold visibly paled. "But the cats hardly ever venture outdoors. How on earth have they managed to pick up ticks?" The usual indulgent look she graced the cats with had been replaced with one of definite sourness as she stared at her precious felines: anyone would think they had deliberately become infested just to wind her up.

"Perhaps Pickles brought ticks indoors and these two caught them off him," I suggested.

"Or more likely, Cynthia's vile cat has been infiltrating the house again via the balcony and spreading its ticks around. That mutant cat has a malicious streak," Marigold mused.

"That certainly sounds plausible," I agreed, having ejected the trespassing Kouneli only the day before.

"Or it could be down to Guzim," Marigold pondered.

"How so?" I asked incredulously. "It's a bit of a stretch to go blaming Guzim for the cats having ticks."

"Well, he must have allowed the ticks to breed in the garden. Or maybe the cats caught them from that rabbit of his."

"Doruntina hasn't been anywhere near your cats," I assured her. "We're going around in circles with this blame game. We must check the cats…"

"You want to give them cats a good going over with one of them nit combs," Vi interrupted.

"They haven't got nits, they've got ticks," I pointed out.

"Or 'Appen a good brushing would get rid of the pests…like this." Without further ado, my mother grabbed hold of Catastrophe. Rudely awakening it from its nap, she used the reluctant feline to demonstrate the art of a good brushing.

"That's my hair brush." Marigold's screech morphed into words of dismay. "My silver backed Victorian hair brush. I'll have to bin it now."

"You wouldn't catch me brushing my hair with a second-hand brush that had been used by them Victorians," Vi said. "I 'Appen to know they weren't big on shampoo."

"That's because it wasn't invented back then," I schooled my mother.

"I'll have to boil wash all the bedding now," Marigold grumbled. "Perhaps you could examine the cats' hair for ticks, Victor."

"Fur, not hair," I muttered under my breath.

"Just the thought of finding a tick on one of my darlings is absolutely horrifying," Marigold continued.

"You don't half make a song and dance about nothing, lass. Back in the war, we had to contend with a sight more than ticks but you didn't see me getting a dose of the heebie-jeebies."

Ignoring Vi, Marigold turned to me. "Are you sure they weren't baby scorpions?"

"Ticks do resemble spiders…" I began

"How many legs did they have?" Vi demanded.

"I didn't get close enough to count them." Marigold shook her head as though the very idea of counting legs was preposterous.

"Like spiders, ticks have eight legs," I said. "They are classified as arachnids rather than insects, even though they aren't actually spiders."

"*Arachni* is Greek for spider, Victor, yet you're insisting that those things weren't spiders." Marigold seemed determined to have the last word.

"I wish they had been spiders rather than ticks," I said with a heavy sigh. "Once a tick attaches itself to one of your cats, it can suck so much of their blood that the tick's whole body becomes engorged. The tick can remain attached for up to four days, leaving the cat susceptible to tick borne diseases such as tularaemia, babesiosis, and Lyme disease…"

"Lyme disease," Marigold repeated before splaying her hand in front of her gaping mouth, her eyes bulging in shock.

"Then of course, we are at risk of tick bites if we catch ticks from your cats. If we have the misfortune to be allergic to tick bites, our lips could swell up or we may come out in hives."

Marigold visibly shuddered at the prospect of developing an unsightly rash along with an unflattering trout pout.

"Cooee, anyone home?"

"Not again. Doreen was here only yesterday," I complained.

"Victor, really. Play nice," Marigold instructed before calling out, "We're in the bedroom, Doreen. Come on through."

"Hello, Mrs Burke, Victor…" Doreen greeted, sparing the two of us from the air kisses she lavished on Marigold. To my surprise, Doreen had Milton in tow. Following hot on her heels, Milton projected the image of a faithful lapdog. Marigold's face dropped at the sight of our elderly neighbour: undoubtedly, my face bore a similar expression, irritated by both Doreen and Milton barging into our bedroom and turning it into Piccadilly Circus.

"I say, old chap, glad to catch you at home…" Milton's words tailed off; catching sight of Violet Burke, he sucked in his stomach and visibly blushed, his rheumy eyes taking on a look of puppy-dog adoration.

"Did you want anything in particular?" I asked Milton, my tone uninviting.

"Wanted to bend your ear about a book related matter, old chap."

"Porn really isn't my thing," I reminded Milton, wishing he'd find someone else's ear to bore.

"Erotica, old chap, erotica," Milton corrected me. "Your advice has steered me right in the past."

I was grateful to Doreen when she spoke over Milton, asking, "What was that you were just saying about Lyme disease as we came in?"

"It's just dreadful, absolutely dreadful." Marigold paused for dramatic effect. "The cats have somehow got ticks. Victor was just saying that ticks can transmit diseases to the cats."

"Not just to cats. Ticks can pass diseases to humans too," I clarified, much more comfortable with the subject of communicable diseases than Milton's smut. "Lyme disease is transmitted by ticks via the bacterium known as Borrelia burgdorferi…"

"Bergdorf," Doreen interrupted, a look of confusion on her face. "I thought that was a posh shop."

Being easily amused, Milton brayed with laughter at Doreen's comment.

"Bergdorf Goodman is a luxury department store in Manhattan," Marigold trilled. "I'd love to go there for a shopping spree but I've never been able to persuade Victor."

"It's bad enough hanging around outside the ladies' changing rooms in Marks and Sparks, without flying all the way to the Big Apple for you to make merry with my credit card," I said.

"Nasty business, ticks, what," Milton opined. "Suffered a positive plague of the blighters during my time in Kenya. Drove the goats crazy. You'd best keep an eye on your chickens, old chap. Once they latch on, your hens might stop laying."

"'Appen your chucks will be needing a good going over with a nit comb too, lad," Vi suggested.

"Course, your chickens could well make a meal of the old ticks, what. One way to get rid of the blood-sucking scallywags," Milton guffawed.

Marigold shuddered at the thought of our egg source tucking into a meal of ticks. No doubt the old adage 'you are what you eat' had sprung to mind. I reflected that from a purely selfish perspective, I could imagine myself welcoming the idea of my chucks being tick-ridden: it would prevent Marigold, once and for all, from threatening to bung my feathered friends in the oven.

"'Appen I'd best keep my Petey away from the hen house. And Marigold, you'd best keep your mangy cats away from my Petey…"

"My cats aren't mangy," Marigold protested whilst visibly keeping a suitable distance from her darling pets.

"Course they are, what with being riddled with ticks. I don't want my Petey catching anything communicable from yours. My Petey's what you'd call right sensitive," Vi said.

"There's no denying your cat is a bit of a diva," I observed.

"Having that dopey Doreen knock up a matching sun bonnet to go with Petey's coat doesn't sound so daft now, does it, even though you scoffed at the time?"

"I am right here, Mrs Burke," Doreen bravely piped up, visibly bridling at my mother's insult.

Ignoring Doreen, Vi gloated, "'Appen I was psychic, kitting out Petey in cat clothes. There'll be no ticks attaching themselves to my Petey when her fur is well under wraps."

"You said you clothed Petey to stop it from shedding," I pointed out.

"'Appen I did. It's right annoying to have to start sweeping up cat hair in the *apothiki* after I come home from a hard day's charring. Still, dressing the cat has come in handy for protecting my Petey from blood sucking insects."

"Ticks aren't insects, they are arachnids," I reminded her.

"I always think of blood sucking ticks as being

like vampires," Doreen interjected. "Do you suppose they spend their days lounging around in coffins, only to emerge after dark?"

Surprisingly, even though Doreen isn't generally known for her sparkling wit, I found myself chuckling at her comment.

"I can pop over to the pharmacy for you, old chap," Milton offered. "Ticks must be drowned in rubbing alcohol or eucalyptus oil, what, only thing for them. Just fill up a jam jar with the stuff and drop any ticks into it, what."

"I don't like the sound of a jar full of dead ticks cluttering up my bedside table," Marigold said with a shudder.

"You won't be saying that, old girl, if you find one of the critters crawling up your body for a bloodthirsty feast in the middle of the night."

"Well, luckily there's no need to go to such disgusting lengths. Victor has already flushed them down the loo," Marigold apprised Milton.

"That won't do, won't do at all, old girl." Marigold sent a scathing look in Milton's direction, his reference to her as an old girl never failing to rile her up. "No good trying to flush the blasted things down the lavatory. Flushing a tick won't kill it; the little cooties are darn near indestructible. They'll reappear after being flushed, what, then float on their backs looking up at you, what."

"I can't say I fancy one of them staring up at me

when I'm on the khazi," Vi said, her face involuntarily gurning her disgust.

"I'll pop out now for a bottle of the old rubbing alcohol…no bother at all, what," Milton volunteered. If he was trying to ingratiate himself in my mother's good books with his offer, he failed miserably, Vi's expression indicating she held him in no more esteem than a tick drowning in a jam jar.

"I say, old chap, bit embarrassing, what. I seem to be a bit short of the old readies."

As Milton scurried off on his mission with a couple of notes from my wallet, Marigold turned to me. "As soon as Milton returns with the rubbing alcohol, you'll have to check if those three ticks you flushed earlier are hanging around in the toilet bowl. If they are, you'll have to scoop them out and kill them properly. Just the thought of them crawling up the pan is enough to give me nightmares."

"Can you imagine one of them creeping up and latching onto your bum, lass?"

Seeing the colour draining from Marigold's face, I scolded, "That's not helping, Mother."

"It's all right for you, lad. You can just point down."

"Must you be so vulgar, Vi?" Marigold complained. "We do have company."

"Company. What company?"

"Doreen."

"Doreen's hardly what you'd call company. She's never away from the place," Vi gibed.

"I really think we need to take the cats up to the vet at once, Victor," Marigold said, suddenly decisive. "If by chance they've already been bitten, they may be suffering."

"You'll have to take them up on your own," I dared to say. "I have other plans for this morning."

"You'll have to cancel them, Victor. How am I supposed to cope with two tick-ridden cats on my own? You know how heavy they are when they're in their cat carriers. I'll give the vet a bell now."

I hadn't even received any wages from this year's repping season yet and Marigold was already squandering my money on expensive veterinary bills.

As Marigold disappeared to make the call, my mother gave me a hand to strip the bedding in preparation for a good boil wash. When Marigold returned, she announced that the vet couldn't see the cats until the next day, unless it was an emergency. "For some reason, he didn't think ticks were urgent. What are we supposed to do with the cats today?"

"Appen you could spray them with vinegar. Your Barry swears by the stuff," Vi suggested.

"They won't appreciate getting a mouthful of vinegar when they lick themselves," Marigold said.

"'Appen they'll like it a sight more than having

their blood sucked out." My mother does love to have the last word.

"I'll leave you to it. I'm already late for meeting Barry," I said, edging towards the door.

"That's just typical," Marigold said crossly. "Leaving me alone to cope with infested cats."

"You aren't on your own. You have Doreen and my mother."

"Well, don't forget that we're hosting the expat dinner party this weekend," Marigold piped up as I tried to sneak away. "We have to decide which country's cuisine to feature before you start planning your menu."

"This is the first I've heard of it. You could have given me a bit more notice," I grumbled.

"Honestly, darling. Sometimes I think you never listen to a word that I say…I must have mentioned it at least a dozen times."

"Rubbish," Vi scoffed. "You only volunteered to do it earlier this morning when Moira Strange called to say she'd have to cancel her turn to host this weekend because she's flying back to England with her ears."

For once, lost for words, Marigold turned a guilty shade of puce.

"I tell you what, lad. I'll take charge of the cooking for your dinner party but I'll do it up here," Vi volunteered. "I reckon I've been invited to enough of the things that it must be my turn to play hostess, only there's not enough room in my place."

"I'll take you up on that offer, Mother," I said hastily, allowing Marigold no chance to object. "You do realise you're meant to cook something foreign?"

"'Appen since we live in a foreign place, good old British food ought to count as foreign."

"Bunging a tinned Fray Bentos in the oven doesn't count as cooking," Marigold jeered.

Chapter 2

The Technically Redundant Ruin

Keen to avoid Milton returning with isopropyl alcohol and, no doubt, some rather lame rubbing innuendos, I made a hasty exit, heading on foot up to the old ruin that Barry and I had jointly purchased to convert into two holiday apartments. Since the actual physical renovation of said ruin was now finally complete bar all the whistles and bells, I reflected that the term ruin was technically redundant. I made a mental note to refer to the transformed house as rental apartments in future, at least until Barry and I could come up with a name for them that we could both agree on.

V.D. BUCKET

A brief, light summer shower just before dawn had unleashed a mixture of intoxicating scents from the wild herbs in the fields and olive groves. I found the distinctive aroma of mint refreshing, whilst the heady tang of sage and thyme in the air inspired ambrosial culinary thoughts. The gentle tinkle of goats' bells serenaded my stroll on the uphill path, though recalling Milton's warning about tick infested goats, I made a point of keeping a precautionary distance. I mentally compared the goats' bells to the common medieval practice of kitting out lepers with bells to warn of their presence.

The last time I'd been to the rental apartments, Barry had been concentrating on tackling the snagging list. The rest of us had each mucked in, utilizing our particular skill sets. Cynthia, persuaded to slap a paint brush around, had revealed a hidden talent for textured painting, whilst Marigold had promoted herself to head of garden design, even getting her hands dirty in-between bossing Guzim around. Doreen developed a stiff foot from all the pedalling she'd been doing on her sewing machine; knocking out cushion covers, pillow cases, and duvet covers from repurposed fabric had saved a small fortune on the interior soft furnishings bill. Amazingly, I had come up with a cunning wheeze to put a curb on Marigold's extravagant tendencies, finally managing to convince her that her insistence on purchasing new would eat into any funds that could be better allocated towards future mini-breaks. Admittedly, I had shamelessly manipulated my wife, knowing that even a hint of any savings made might go towards a luxury weekend away, would keep her profligate tendencies in check.

Although I had been rebuffed with contemptuous snorts when it came to my getting down and dirty with any actual DIY, I had not been completely idle, shouldering the burden of ensuring the rentals complied with all the relevant Greek health and safety requirements. Spiros and Vangelis had proved themselves invaluable when it came to assisting me in securing an essential EOT licence from the *Elliniko Organismo Tourismo*, the Greek Tourist Organisation.

I had it on good authority that a number of Greeks, along with some foreign second-home owners down on the coast, illicitly rented out their houses without securing a vital EOT certificate. Rather than admitting they simply had no intention of declaring any rental income to the tax authorities, they used the lame excuse that doing things by the book involved negotiating the inevitable bureaucratic nightmare of running frantically from pillar to post in search of pointless rubber stamps.

Although Spiros had initially suggested we follow their example and conduct our business under the table, I had resolutely refused: I am far too law-abiding to cut a single corner, fearing it could well come back to bite me in the proverbial. It was only when Spiros' good friend Bill, whose hospitality we had enjoyed during our second honeymoon, was fined an exorbitant sum for failing to secure an essential EOT licence for a number of his holiday lets, that Spiros saw the sense in my insisting on keeping everything above board.

Obtaining the EOT certificate had involved getting our hands on a Fire Certificate confirming the apartments were furnished with the requisite number of fire extinguishers and essential Emergency Exit lighting. There were sighs of relief all round when we were finally granted the Health Certificate relating to the sewerage system, reminding me of the necessity of sticking up signs warning the tourists that it was verboten to flush loo roll down the toilet. As for the final piece in the certification process, Spiros had urged me to pester the accountant relentlessly until the tax office issued the necessary certificate declaring that neither Barry nor I had any unpaid taxes outstanding.

In addition to chasing up paperwork pertaining to all the necessary licences, I had taken on the task of promoting the apartments to prospective holiday makers. A tad behind schedule, we hoped that the apartments would be in a fit state to welcome our first visitors within the next fortnight. Having already missed the first few weeks of the tourist season, it was imperative that the apartments started earning their keep pretty sharpish. Unfortunately, despite all my best efforts, we had yet to receive a single bite.

Approaching the apartments, I was impressed with the progress made in the garden: as Violet Burke had observed, it looked bloomin' beautiful. It was a pity any potential holiday makers electing to stay in the apartments wouldn't be able to appreciate the striking naked men orchids since they had finished for the season. Instead, they would be impressed with Marigold's handiwork in accentuating the typically Greek theme of a blue and white garden, achieved by planting sky-blue plumbago adjacent to white bougainvillea. The deep blue of the newly painted wooden shutters added to the unmistakably Greek motif.

"Mr Victor, *edo*." Looking around, I spotted Blat leaning against the freshly pointed stonework of the downstairs apartment, enjoying a cigarette break. As a labourer, he had gone above and beyond, not only taking great pride in his work but dedicating many hours outside the normal working day to our project. Although Blat appreciated the security that accepting a full-time job in the building business jointly owned by Barry and Vangelis offered him, he still harboured fanciful dreams of moving to England.

"Blat, good to see you," I greeted him, suppressing the snort that the smug image of Tony

Blair's larger-than-life head emblazoning Blat's tee-shirt prompted. Recalling it must be almost a month since I had dropped Blat's latest letter to the British prime minister in at the post office, I asked, "Any word yet from Tony Blair?"

"The great Tonibler is much the busy. He has been to visit the great George Bush in the great White House," Blat informed me, impressing me with the way that he had his finger on the pulse of current events in the UK and across the pond. It reminded me that since Sali Berisha had replaced Fatos Nano as the prime minister of Albania, I had somewhat let my interest in Albanian politics slide. Marigold assured me that despite Berisha's perfectly coiffured hair-do, boasting not so much as a single lacquered strand out of place, Fatos' replacement did not meet the description to qualify as very handsome. Memorising the phrase book phrase 'your prime minister is very handsome' had initially sparked my interest in the premier of the neighbouring country, the phrase now indelibly fixed in my brain: *o prothypourgos sas einai poly omorfos.*

"And how is young Tonibler," I asked, enquiring about Blat's son.

"He is much the busy with the studies," Blat replied.

"The school holidays are about to start," I reminded Blat, wondering how Tonibler planned to keep himself occupied for the thirteen-week break.

"Ask the boy if he fancies coming along when I rep on Pegasus next week. Captain Vasos says Tonibler is welcome any time."

"The great captain is most kind."

"Victor." Looking up, I spotted Barry gesturing for me to join him in the upstairs apartment.

"I must get back to work," Blat said, extinguishing his cigarette butt underfoot before pocketing it in his overalls. "The Mr Barry need me to demolish the outside toilet and then to tile the new patio."

"It will certainly improve the outlook to be rid of that eyesore," I said.

"Eyesore?" Blat queried, clearly unfamiliar with the term.

"Something ugly. A blot on the landscape," I explained.

"The outside toilet is the palace compare to the ones in rural Albania," Blat opined. Recalling the slum of a bathroom at Guzim's humble Albanian dwelling which I had visited back in January, I was inclined to agree. Nevertheless, palace or eyesore, Barry and I had agreed that the outdoor lav must go.

Approaching the outside stairs leading to the upstairs apartment, I was relieved to see that Guzim, despite his constant grumbling, had done an excellent job of hacking down the prickly pear plants that had previously attacked any visitors heading towards the entrance. Although a natural deterrent against burglars, I doubted paying guests would welcome being poked and prodded by prickly spikes.

The upstairs of the former ruin had been transformed from the dusty and derelict space that had been a magnet for pigeons, into a welcoming self-contained apartment boasting a comfortable and stylish open-plan living room and kitchen, along with a separate bedroom and an ensuite bathroom. The view over the rear garden would be most enticing once Blat had finished bulldozing the monstrosity of the outdoor loo.

"It's all looking good, Barry," I greeted my brother-in-law.

"We need to get the signs done," Barry reminded me. "There's two of them need doing; one for the gate and one for at the end of the lane to direct the guests. We have to come up with a name for the apartments."

Barry had originally agreed with my suggestion that we name the apartments Marigold. However, Cynthia had thrown a strop at the news, demanding that Barry name the apartments after her rather than his sister. In order to appease both our wives, I had decreed that perhaps we should plump for a name more typically Greek.

"Any more thoughts on a name?"

"I've been thinking," Barry confirmed. "How about we combine both of our wives' names in an effort to keep them both happy?"

"That's a thought. Cyn…Gold," I posited.

"That's terrible. How about Thia…Marg?

"But that just means Aunty Marg in Greek and neither of us have got one of them."

"I've got it," Barry declared. "Mar…Ia."

"You do realise that's just Maria, you dipstick."

"Oh, yeah. I can't see Cyn being happy if we go naming them after a random Maria. I'll have to put my thinking cap on and see if I can come up with something more suitable."

Changing the subject, I asked, "How's the snagging list going?"

"I need Marigold to go into town to buy some light fittings," Barry replied.

Bridling at the thought of the extra expense, I had to admit that bare lightbulbs hardly projected the plush ambiance we were aiming for.

"We've got to take the cats up to the vet tomorrow so we can sort out the light fittings whilst we're there," I volunteered. "Anything else that you need us to pick up?"

"Fittings for the bathrooms: towel holders and soap dispensers. Have a look and see what else is needed. And kettles for both apartments. We can't claim to be upmarket if we expect our guests to boil a pan of water on the hob for a brew."

"I'll give Marigold a quick call and ask her to bob over and compile a list. It probably needs a woman's eye to identify any missing touches," I acknowledged, recalling that kettles had not really been a thing during the many visits we had made to Greece as holidaymakers, a pan plonked down on a slow heating hob generally having to suffice for an early morning brew.

"Well, just don't let Marigold get too carried away in town," Barry warned.

"I'll steer her towards somewhere cheap," I promised, admiring the apartment's transformation. I would certainly consider the accommodation more than satisfactory for a holiday, not to mention a tad more upmarket than the norm. When Marigold and I had holidayed in Greece over the years before our move, we had rarely found accommodation offering such luxuries as shower cubicles or kitchens fitted out with cafetieres and cheese knives.

"You need to pull your finger out and find us some bookings," Barry pressed.

"I'm working on it. I'm sure the standard of accommodation will secure us lots of return bookings."

"That's as maybe but a return on nothing is still nothing." The stern frown accompanying Barry's pragmatic words aged him, the stress of our joint venture already responsible for the streaks of grey around his temples.

"Cynthia promised to print off some posters at work advertising the apartments. We're going to stick them up around the village, in the shop, *kafenion* and taverna," I said, practically shouting my words to compete with the sound of Blat swinging a mallet against the shabby wooden structure housing the outdoor toilet. "Tourists that discover the village are always bemoaning the lack of somewhere to stay. I'm sure we'll soon have some bookings."

Making no effort to disguise the scepticism written all over his face, Barry continued with the laborious task of grouting the ensuite tiles whilst I stepped outside on the balcony to call Marigold. No sooner had she agreed to pop over to compile a list of missing essentials, I received a call on my mobile. After the call, I was delighted to be able to announce to my brother-in-law that we had secured our very first booking, although it was a bit of an anti-climax when I admitted it was for August, two months hence. Apostolos, the local barber, had requested one of the apartments for his sister-in-law and her husband, admitting his wife may well commit sororicide if forced to give the pair houseroom in their own home. Apparently, Apostolos' wife's citified sister had pretensions and expected a more luxurious environ than her sibling's rustic village home.

"Mr Barry..." Blat's cry was almost drowned out by the sound of a sudden explosion. Barry and I immediately rushed to the balcony, stunned at the sight of Blat lying flat on his back next to the half-demolished toilet structure, clutching what appeared to be a long-barrelled shotgun. As Blat hauled himself to his feet, the side of his face smudged black with what I assumed was gunpowder, he reassured us, "Is all okay. I find the *toufeki* bury under the toilet."

"*Toufeki*?" I questioned.

"I think it's pretty self-explanatory that a *toufeki* must be a gun," Barry guessed. "And an antique by the look of it."

"What on earth was it doing being buried under the toilet structure?" I queried.

"Perhaps the owner didn't have a permit," Barry hazarded.

"Well, it was pretty irresponsible of whoever buried it to leave it loaded with live ammunition," I observed.

"What do you suppose we should do with it?" Barry asked as the pair of us headed outside. Joining Blat, I offered the labourer a steadying arm whilst Barry relieved him of the deadly weapon, almost staggering under the weight of the dated contraption. Whistling in admiration, Barry declared, "Phew, it's a beauty. Look at this walnut stock."

"It is very old," Blat observed, rubbing his blackened face.

"What on earth was it doing lying around in the

toilet?" I asked. "And how come neither of you noticed it when you used it?"

"It was under the toilet, not in it. Under the earth floor," Blat clarified.

"So, not easily accessible," I mused, wondering who had hidden it there.

"It is the enigma what it do there," Blat said, puffing up with pride as he repeated, "The enigma. The Tonibler teach me that word."

"Your son has a remarkable vocabulary for one so young," I praised, aware from chatting to the boy that his linguistic skills were way in advance of the basic English language he was taught in school. Without wishing to sound swollen-headed, I believe that my influence and encouragement has had some bearing on Tonibler's mastery of linguistics.

"What should we do with it?" Barry repeated. "We can't just leave it lying around and I can't take it home. Cynthia would have a meltdown. Anastasia is at the age where she gets into everything."

"Perhaps we should hand it in at the police station," I suggested.

"But it might be worth a few bob," Barry posited. "It is a beauty."

"Well, I for one don't fancy spending time in a Greek prison cell for being caught in possession of an illegal weapon."

"Hang on, it might not be illegal," Barry piped up. "There are some numbers carved into the side. I seem to recall Kostis saying something about each gun being issued a number corresponding to its licence. I'll give Spiros a quick call, see what he suggests we should do with it."

"Good idea," I concurred, smiling at the irony of the local undertaker being the first person we thought of consulting about a lethal weapon squirreled away under an outside toilet.

Chapter 3

Dog Vomit Slime Mould

Spiros told Barry that we should head over to join him in the *kafenion* as he wanted to cast his eye over the gun before deciding what we should do with it. I must confess to a certain relief knowing that Spiros had no intention of leaping to an impulsive decision regarding the unearthed weapon, rather choosing to give the matter the full force of his weighty consideration.

Parking the builder's van at the back of the *kafenion*, we decided against entering the premises with all guns blazing. Instead, we hid the shotgun beneath Barry's building supplies, ensuring the vehicle was tightly secured. Taking the short cut through the courtyard, we were immediately confronted by Doreen's rapidly expanding collection of decorative tat. Increasingly torn between the expectations of his primarily elderly male clientele, that the *kafenion* should serve as a traditional male only establishment, and the modern demand for equality, Manolis had high hopes that the courtyard could become an oasis for women. Doreen, given carte blanche by Manolis to spruce up the courtyard, or what he insisted on referring to as the lady-garden until someone explained the embarrassing connotations, had gone completely over the top, seemingly incapable of putting the brakes on her new-found junkaholic addiction.

Whilst Doreen's simple remit had been to create a rustic seating area adorned with colourful pot plants, she had got rather carried away. In no small part egged on by Marigold, Doreen's obsession with beautifying the courtyard saw her turn into a newly minted shopaholic with extravagant tendencies. Fortunately, for Manolis' wallet, the bulk of Doreen's spree centred on second-hand junk, or, as she preferred to describe it, quaint and quirky bric-a-brac, a sizeable proportion of said tat having been rescued from the local bins. Doreen had demonstrated a previously untapped entrepreneurial streak, managing to keep her own hands clean by paying Milton in cat food to comb through the rubbish to rescue anything she considered kitsch that might be worth salvaging.

After splashing out on a set of ludicrously expensive wind chimes, Doreen had butted heads with Violet Burke. My mother scoffed at Doreen, complaining the chimes made a right old din, a sentiment I happened to share. Despite Doreen's natural reluctance to stand up to Violet Burke, she stood her ground, sounding like some new-age hippie as she defended her purchase by proclaiming the chimes symbolised good luck whilst radiating positive energy. Doreen insisted they weren't just any old rubbish picked up from Lidl, declaring that a far-flung sect of monks had fashioned the chimes in the finest aluminium that radiated dulcet melodic tones at the first hint of a breeze. Choosing to sit on the fence rather than offend her friend, Marigold disclosed to me in confidence that she loathed the racket emitted by the costly wind chimes, opining that they were probably cobbled together in China, most likely by slave labour.

"Ouch." Weaving our way through reclaimed jugs brimful with plastic flowers, scattered throughout the courtyard, Barry proved he really did have a head like a sieve when he almost knocked himself out as his head collided with an old colander hanging from the wall. Recognising a cracked container hosting a plant as an old chamber pot harbouring a suspect stain, I gave it a wide berth. Since I had last ventured through the courtyard, Doreen had further filled up the space by adding an eclectic mix of garden statues. Eschewing the typical choice of Greek statues such as the ever-popular Aphrodite and Aristotle, Doreen had plumped for some rather garish models of roosters and hedgehogs, not to mention a large squirrel clutching an oversized nut. I was only surprised that she hadn't gone all out and created a vulgar display of garden gnomes.

Walking into the *kafenion* with Barry, I was inclined to agree with the general sentiment in the village that the two brothers had done a great service to Meli in reopening their grandfather's establishment. It provided a welcome spot to partake of coffee in good company; in addition, it was a convenient venue to hide out in when the likes of Doreen and Milton were littering my home, certainly an improvement on Barry's musty, frog-infested shed. Moreover, despite Manolis' initial reservation about how Doreen's makeover of the courtyard would go down with his male clientele, most of the die-hard bachelors welcomed her efforts, admitting it gave the place a woman's touch, something notably missing from their own homes. I quite envied the ones that were hard of hearing since they were able to adjust the volume on their hearing aids to avoid the constant clangour from the wind chimes.

Now, just past noon, the place was buzzing, many of the elderly gents in the village killing an hour or two whilst savouring a coffee and anticipating Blerta's dish of the day. Engaging Blat's wife, Blerta, to come in for a couple of hours each morning to prepare food for the brothers to simply heat up and serve at lunchtime had been another savvy move on Manolis' part. Additionally, it had provided Blat's family with the security of a regular wage packet on top of his earnings from labouring and the money Blerta contributed through charring and ironing.

"Oh, for goodness' sake. I came here to escape my mother," I muttered to Barry as I spotted Violet Burke scrubbing the kitchen sink.

"Well, at least you can be satisfied that the cleanliness of the place will live up to your exacting standards," Barry chortled.

"*Ela, Victor, Barry. Elate mazi gia enan kafe,*" Spiros called out, inviting us to join him for a coffee. Although the place was busy, Spiros had elected to sit alone, no doubt appreciating the need for privacy when we discussed the unearthed shotgun.

Accepting Spiros' invitation, Barry only narrowly avoided coming a cropper, slipping on the newly mopped and still wet floor.

"You really ought to put up a 'Wet Floor' sign

to comply with health and safety regulations, Mother," I admonished. Violet Burke had clearly been slopping her mop around irresponsibly with a total disregard to the dangers a wet floor presented, blithely contravening the Liable Premises Law as it pertained to foreseeable hazards.

Spinning around, my mother gave me the evil eye whilst barking, "Take it up with the management," before stomping into the *apothiki* for more cleaning supplies.

"It seems I can't get away from my mother today," I complained. "She was cleaning at mine earlier and now she's followed me here."

"To be fair to the Violet, she was the here before you," Spiros pointed out before shouting over to Manolis and placing an order for three coffees. From the state of his stubble, I surmised Spiros had a burial free day. His outfit of jogging trousers paired with a grubby white undershirt exposing his greying chest hair, indicated he was letting things slide on the personal grooming front whilst his wife was away. I supposed that without Sampaguita around to remind him, Spiros was blithely oblivious that his bushy eyebrows were in need of a good trimming.

"Do you want to see the gun now?" Barry asked. "It's in my van."

"After the coffee." Spiros clearly didn't consider the matter to be urgent.

"Have you heard from Sampaguita?" I asked. Following the recent fire that fatally incinerated Haralambos, the retired corrupt agricultural policeman for whom Sampaguita served as a paid carer, Spiros' Filipina wife had decided to take the opportunity to visit her three grown-up children back in the Philippines before taking up a new position in the village on her return. Even though Haralambos had been far from an ideal employer, Sampaguita had taken his death hard, the nature of his demise being particularly horrific.

"Yes, we speak on the telephone," Spiros confirmed. Lacking his usual bonhomie, his tone indicated he was missing his wife.

"Perhaps you should get my mother to come round and give your place a good bottoming before Sampaguita returns," I suggested. I doubted that Spiros would lift a finger around the house whilst he had the place to himself; poor Sampaguita would no doubt return to a scene of utter domestic chaos.

"That is the good idea. I ask her now," Spiros said as Vi trudged out of the *apothiki*, weighed down with Vim and bleach. Turning on the charm, Spiros called out, "*Violet mou*. Can you to clean my the house before the Sampaguita return?"

"As if I haven't got enough on my plate already with cleaning for half the village. I could do with another pair of hands…"

"It is for the Sampaguita," Spiros wheedled,

knowing full well that Violet Burke had a soft spot for his wife.

"Aye, okay. I'll try and squeeze you in seeing as it's for the lass," Vi promised.

"You are the life belt, Violet," Spiros complimented.

Sidling up next to my chair and planting a hand on my shoulder, Violet Burke uttered one word.

"Faggots."

"What on earth are you talking about, Mother?"

"Faggots, mushy peas and trifle," Vi said as though it was self-explanatory.

"Not all one plate, I hope," Barry quipped.

"For that fancy dinner party your Marigold wants me to do the cooking for."

I bit my tongue, certain that Marigold really didn't want Violet Burke doing the cooking for the upcoming expat dinner party: in her own inimitable way, my mother had simply bulldozed her way in. Still, it suited me fine to have Violet Burke doing the cooking since it would let me off the hook. Moreover, whatever else one could say about my mother, her cooking was decidedly more edible than that of the other expats in the village.

"What is the faggots?" Spiros asked.

"They're like British meatballs," Vi replied.

"Ah, like the Greek *keftedakia*," Spiros said.

"Not really. They're made out of offal," I added.

"Offal?" Spiros queried.

Unable to immediately conjure up the Greek

word for offal, I compromised with tripe. "*Patsas.*"

"*Patsakeftedes.* You foreign have the strange food," Spiros observed, looking none-too impressed at the thought of meatballs fashioned out of tripe.

"You do know that Marigold won't let you serve up faggots, Mother."

"I wish she would," Barry said longingly. "I'm quite partial to a nice faggot."

"Your Marigold can keep her nose out. I'm going to do a traditional British menu and that's the end to it. If your Marigold can't be arsed to knock up a trifle, I'll do a nice spotted dick."

Intercepting the question posed by Spiros' raised eyebrows, Barry explained, "It's a pudding, not the sort of spotted dick you have to get ointment for from the pharmacy."

"You should see your faces. Dead gullible, the lot of you," Vi declared with a gruesome cackle, nudging me in the ribs so violently I almost fell off my chair. "I'm pulling your legs, lads. I know your Marigold would have kittens if I served up faggots. 'Appen I'll knock her socks off with some fancy French recipe. I'll have a thumb through them cookery books of yours, Victor, and rustle up something to do your Marigold proud."

Whilst I tried to determine if my mother was speaking in jest or being serious, before I could get to the bottom of it Vi was distracted by her mobile ringing. Retrieving her phone from the pocket of her pinny, Vi clamped it to ear. "What? What? Hang on a minute. I'll have to take you outside. I can't hear diddly-squat in here."

No sooner had my mother disappeared outside than Doreen put in an appearance. Making a bee-line for the kitchen, she and Manolis started kissing and canoodling, putting on a quite unnecessary public display of affection that was greedily lapped up by the pensioner clientele living vicariously. Whilst I considered their loved-up display with possible hygiene risks totally unsuitable for a *kafenion* kitchen, I had to admit that the pair of them looked happy together, Manolis definitely having a mellowing influence on Doreen.

I reflected that it really was beyond time for Doreen and Norman to think of divorcing. Even though the pair of them still lived in the same house, Doreen had moved on with Manolis and, according to Athena, who had witnessed it with her own eyes, Norman had been spotted sharing a trolley with another woman in Lidl. To say that Marigold was exasperated by Athena's lack of details and her inability to put a name to Norman's alleged squeeze, is an understatement. Even though it would undoubtedly put Doreen's nose out of joint, I would put good money on my wife badgering Norman to bring his new lady friend to the upcoming expat dinner party. I must confess to just a frisson of interest myself, wondering what sort of woman would be prepared to saddle herself with the sort of dreary bore who collected traffic cones for a hobby.

"Have a look at this, Victor. I thought it would be right up your street." I almost jumped out of my skin as Doreen crept up behind me, thrusting a photograph of what appeared to be a rancid yellow sponge oozing something of a mucilaginous nature, under my nose. "Manolis took this picture in Texas when he had an outbreak of dog vomit slime mould. As soon as I saw it, I thought of you."

"Dog vomit slime mould made you think of Victor." Barry could barely control his mirth.

"It reminded me of how he's always going on about putrescent washing up sponges," Doreen elaborated. "It does bear an uncanny resemblance to a grubby sponge."

"The Manolis take the photograph of what his dog puke up?" Surveying the image, Spiros scrunched his nose in disgust.

"Oh, no, you've got the wrong end of the stick," Doreen trilled. "Dog slime vomit is a fungus that grows in rotting logs and mulch piles."

"Well, that's just scintillating, Doreen." Barry's obvious sarcasm was lost on Doreen, and, in my opinion, completely uncalled for. Personally, I thought it was the most interesting thing to ever come out of Doreen's mouth.

"Actually, Doreen, dog vomit slime mould isn't

a fungus," I corrected. "Technically it is classified as an amoeba. It likes to feast on bacteria…"

"You mean it's alive?" Barry asked with a shudder.

"Does it to glow in the dark?" Spiros asked, snatching hold of the photograph. "It look like something from the horror movie."

"It's actually quite harmless, although it isn't the sort of thing you'd welcome growing inside your air conditioner."

"Is that even a thing?" Barry asked, deferring to my superior knowledge of all things hygiene related.

"Yes, indeed. It can sprout in units with inadequate drainage. Not good for the chest if you're breathing it in, but generally harmless in the wild."

With a wide grin on her face, Violet Burke re-entered the *kafenion*. Looking extremely pleased with herself, she declared, "Eh, lad. 'Appen I've only gone and got you a booking for one of them snazzy new apartments of yours."

All thoughts of dog vomit slime mould were eliminated from my mind at this remarkable news.

"You've got me a booking," I repeated incredulously. Despite shelling out a small fortune on an advertising campaign, it hadn't elicited so much as a sniff of interest thus far. Even though I had told myself it was early days, I must confess to being just a tad worried by the lack of reservations.

"We can sort out my commission later," Vi threatened before filling me in on the potential booking. "You remember that time you and your Marigold went gadding off on that rock…"

"Monemvasia," I confirmed. "It was a delightful break, so considerate of Marigold to arrange it. I fail to see what it has to do with the apartments though?"

"If you'd shut your gob for once instead of talking the hind leg off a donkey, I'd tell you. Remember, I stopped at yours…"

"And rented out the *apothiki* on the sly…"

"Well, 'Appen it's a good job that I did. That pair of top-drawer poshies that stopped at mine only want to have another break in Meli…"

"We can't be letting the new apartment to dogs," Barry objected. "Perhaps you're confusing the place with kennels, Vi."

"Dogs? What are you wittering on about, you dopey lad?"

"You're the one that brought up Poshies…"

"Posh Hooray Henry types," Vi clarified.

"Oh, right. I thought you were on about a breed of dogs…" Barry spluttered.

"You daft 'apeth. I was on about the posh pair that stopped at mine. Course, they fancied stopping at mine again but I can't be turfing Petey out to make room for them, not when she's just got settled."

"Petey?" Barry queried.

"Her cat," I clarified.

"I told them all about that wreck you've done up, and talked it up for you. Anyhow, they've decided they want to stop there."

"Toby and Felicity," I said, their names indelibly etched on my brain after my run in with them in the *apothiki* on my return from Monemvasia, my mother having brazenly rented it out behind my back. "When were they thinking of?"

"They fly in this Sunday. They haven't booked anywhere to stay yet...Toby's going to call me back in a bit to see if they can have it."

"But it will be at least another week to ten days before everything is ready for paying guests," I said.

"Not so fast, Victor," Barry challenged. "With all the cash we've shelled out on that place, we'd be daft to turn down an actual booking. I reckon if we pulled out all the stops, we could have the place ready for this weekend."

"I reckon we can all muck in together to get it shipshape," Vi encouraged.

"If we put in the hours, me and Vangelis can get the snagging list sorted in time," Barry decreed.

"And I'm happy to give Marigold a hand with the soft furnishings that still need finishing," Doreen volunteered. "It will be quite fun getting it just so."

"And I won't say no to a spot of overtime to make sure the place is sparkling," Vi said, pointedly adding as she looked at me, "I don't know what use you'll be when it comes to the finishing touches…"

"Victor would probably be more help keeping out of the way," Barry chuckled. "Just joking, Victor. The garden still needs some work doing."

"Well, if everyone is happy to muck in and we pull out all the stops, I suppose we could have the place ready by Sunday," I conceded, feeling a frisson of excitement at the thought of our very first paying customers settling into our luxurious accommodation.

"That's settled then," Barry seconded.

"Mother, you can go ahead and tell Toby and Flick that the place is reserved for them," I said, discreetly whispering the going rate in her ear. Whilst everything had been set up legally with nothing hidden from the taxman, I didn't want my neighbours gossiping about our financial arrangements.

From the corner of my eye, I caught Kyrios Stavropoulos openly eavesdropping on our conversation whilst badgering Manolis to translate for him. The communistic pensioner had recently invited me to drop the Kyrios when addressing him, telling me to call him Stavros. Despite pressing me to address him more informally, I was still in the dark as to whether Stavros was his first name or a nickname derived from shortening his surname.

"Stavros say you are crazy doing up that old house to rent out to holiday makers," Manolis said.

Half-an-hour earlier, with not the whiff of a booking in place, I may have been inclined to agree with him. Now, with the prospect of an actual reservation on the horizon, I was confident that Barry and I had made the right decision by investing in the restoration of the rundown property. Perchance if Toby and Flick had a memorable stay, they would be happy to promote the apartment by recommending it to friends and family: there is nothing more effective than word of mouth in spreading the word. From what I recalled of their posh BBC accents, they were likely to move in top-drawer circles. I would infinitely prefer a bunch of appreciative snobs than any old riff-raff.

"And why does Stavros think we are crazy?" I asked. "It is likely to be a sound investment."

"I agree with you," Manolis said. "But Stavros say you are crazy to think you can make money by charging tourists to stay there. He says he is eighty-two years old and never he waste the money on the holiday."

"That's because he's a parsimonious old commie," Barry butted in.

Ignoring Barry, Manolis continued to translate Stavros' unfiltered opinions. "Stavros says it is the terrible thing to sleep in the strange bed. He sleep all his life in the same bed and never to sleep in another: in the war, he sleep on the ground. Stavros says the holidays are terrible things. He say, 'If I went away on the holiday, I would have to speak to strangers in the strange *kafenion*.' He wants to talk with people he knows, not the mystery people."

"Well, it's a good job that not everyone is as insulated and short-sighted as Stavros... remind him that Greece relies on the tourist trade to fill the coffers," I urged.

"And tell Stavros that we were both strangers to him when we first moved to Meli but he's happy enough to talk to us now," Barry added.

"Yes, but the Stavros says you are not really strangers because you live in the village. If you lived in town, he would consider you foreigners and not want to speak to you." Manolis appeared to have bought into the old pensioner's logic.

"So, does Stavros consider the Greeks that live in town to be foreigners?" I asked.

"Yes," Manolis confirmed, rolling his eyes as though it was self-evident before ducking back behind the counter.

"Don't look now," Barry hissed, elbowing my arm so violently that my coffee sloshed into my saucer.

"Oh, for goodness' sake," I spluttered, spotting Milton in the doorway, eyeing the patrons before zoning in on me and heading in my direction. Until this moment, I had always considered the *kafenion* a sanctuary, the local porn-merchant too strapped to splash out on such unnecessary extravagances as coffee.

"Why have Milton's hands turned blue?" Barry blurted, watching intently as the white-haired pensioner limped slowly towards our table.

Chapter 4

The Worst Opening Sentence

"You've got to be kidding me. Milton looks like a serial killer. What on earth has he got on his hands?" Unable to control his laughter, Barry's Adam's apple visibly wobbled as he spoke.

"He appears to be wearing fine latex gloves," I observed.

"Remember that weirdo in the hospital when we visited Litsa?" Barry prompted.

Nodding in agreement, my mind flashed back to a day back in March when we had done a spot of hospital visiting, calling in to see Litsa after she'd had the misfortune to take another tumble. The pair of us had been fascinated by the abnormally tall, painfully thin son of the elderly woman in the hospital bed next to Litsa, said son continually delving into a box of disposable blue latex gloves.

After turning a cold-shoulder on our greeting, he continued to studiously ignore us, his superior air dismissing us as nothing more than a couple of plebs. Seemingly oblivious to our stares, his face took on a look of intense concentration as he snapped a pair of translucent blue gloves into place before wiggling his fingers in front of his eyes. I could only assume he was inspecting the latex with a laser stare to ensure there were no microscopic holes that may allow random germs to penetrate. Even though I felt a visceral loathing for his snobbish stance, I must admit to a grudging admiration for his meticulous adherence to hygiene.

After spraying some reddish contusions on his mother's legs with a blast of something icy, he meticulously peeled off the latex gloves before scouring his hands in the bathroom. Returning to the bedside, he made a total song of dance of donning yet another pair of identical blue gloves and vigorously shaking the spray can again. I might have compared his ministrations to those of an undertaker preparing a corpse, but such a comparison would only sully Spiros' professionalism. My good friend certainly treated his charges with a great deal more warmth than weird glove man exuded whilst ministering to his mother.

Milton finally reached our table. "I say, old chap. Dropped the rubbing alcohol off at yours. Your good lady wife said that I would find you in here."

I made a mental note to have words with my wife on my return. In her desperation to be rid of Milton, Marigold had happily thrown me under the bus and landed me in it.

Making no effort to conceal a sneer, Barry prodded, "What's with the creepy gloves, Milton?"

"Thought it best to take Victor's advice and glove up before rummaging through the rubbish, what."

"Are your finances so bad that you need to resort to dumper diving?" Barry asked.

"Something in the bins caught my eye, old chap. I thought Doreen might appreciate it, what." As Milton replied, he pulled what appeared to be a lump of rather mucky grey stone out of his carrier bag. "If my eyes don't deceive me, this thing is an ornamental stone dog. Hard to credit what some folks are happy to toss away, what."

"Looks like a Cockapoo to me," Barry said. "But it's missing an ear."

"And a paw," I added, thinking there was a reason why someone's old rubbish should stay in the bins.

"I thought if Doreen painted it gold, it might bear a passing resemblance to Waffles, what."

"Waffles is a Goldendoodle, not a Cockapoo," Barry said. "Still, I might be able to rustle up an old tin of orange paint. It may still have a bit of life in it, if you stir in some turps."

"I say, that's mighty generous of you, old chap," Milton gushed; snapping the latex, he reminded me again of creepy hospital glove man. "I'll leave any painting to Doreen though; she's more of an eye, old chap."

"You really ought to give that dog a good rubbing down with bleach before bringing it in here where food is served," I advised as Doreen approached, oohing and aahing in delight at Milton's find.

"I'll give it pride of place in the courtyard once it's cleaned up and painted," Doreen cooed as Milton removed a stray strand of something looking suspiciously like egg-smeared spinach from the stone dog.

"Just off to the little boys' room to dispose of these gloves, what," Milton announced before shuffling off.

"I'll send you a nice coffee over on the house when you get back," Doreen called after him.

"Must you encourage him?" I muttered under my breath.

Stavros and his old cronies didn't bother lowering their volume as they audibly sniggered in Milton's wake, "*Aftos einai o palios anoitos pou grafei vromika vivlia.*" There was certainly truth in their words, 'that's the old fool that writes dirty books.' Fortunately for Milton, his inability to translate a word of Greek left him blissfully ignorant that he was considered a figure of fun.

About to bring up the issue of the hidden gun to Spiros, the undertaker pre-empted me by launching into a doleful lament about how much he was missing Sampaguita. Barry and I slapped on suitably sympathetic expressions as Spiros admitted he was pining for his absent wife. His lament became ever more plaintive when he turned to the subject of Sampaguitas' cooking.

"I not to have the good meal since the Sampaguita leave," Spiros grizzled.

"You seemed to be enjoying the meal you were tucking into at the taverna the other evening," Barry pointed out.

"It is not the same as the Sampaguita home-cook food. I miss her the *feta sto fourno me meli*..."

"Baked feta with honey," I translated.

"I miss the Sampaguita's *pastitsio*, her the *papoutsakia*, her the *moussaka*. I even miss her the *tiganites akrides*."

"You miss her fried grasshoppers?" Surprise was evident in my tone since I had always assumed Spiros only tucked into the Filipino delicacy under sufferance.

"Not the eating the *akrides*," Spiros admitted. "But I miss the Sampaguita to sing in the kitchen when she to cook them."

"Well, it will be the height of the grasshopper season when Sampaguita returns," I said in an effort to cheer up the undertaker. His grimace indicated I had failed. Since Spiros was clearly missing a home-cooked meal, I decided to invite him over to dine with me that evening. I would cook one of the dishes he had mentioned he was missing.

Spotting Milton shuffling back towards our table, I quickly extended an invitation to Spiros, telling him that Marigold was out for the evening and he should come over; I would cook for the two of us. *"Spiro, i Marigold einai exo apopse, ela kai tha mageirepso gia tous dyo mas."* My use of Greek was deliberate. If Milton got wind of a free meal being on the cards, he was likely to gate-crash and inveigle his way to a seat at my dining table.

"Alla ochi akrides." Spiros responded by saying 'but no grasshoppers.'

"Ochi ena," I confirmed, saying 'Not a one.

Not bothering to check that Doreen was well out of earshot, Milton confided in a raspy voice, "Just ran into Norman testing out aftershave in the pharmacy, what." Despite finishing his sentence with a pregnant pause, Milton's statement failed to provoke the interest he clearly expected to follow his words. It was only when he continued to speak that he managed to get a rise out of us. "I expect the old chap wants to smell good when he brings that young floozy of his along to the expat dinner party at yours."

"Norman has a young floozy," Barry spluttered. Having made no attempt to moderate the volume of his words, my brother-in-law attracted a withering look from Doreen who was still sharing the marital home with her estranged husband.

"Athena did report that she spotted Norman in Lidl with a woman," I mentioned. "There was no mention of her being a young floozy though."

"What is the floozy?" Spiros asked.

"I'm not sure it translates," I replied, thinking that *'omorfi* gynaika' or 'beautiful woman' lacked the essential spirit of floozy whilst *'porni* or 'prostitute', seemed a tad extreme if not downright slanderous. Sticking her two penn'orth in, Violet Burke's unhelpfully blunt translation of 'tart' left poor Spiros none the wiser.

"It appears that Norman may have another woman," I explained.

As Spiros' unruly eyebrows levitated towards his hairline, I imagined he was allowing them to speak on his behalf. Knowing full well that I would never hear the end of Marigold's nagging if I didn't prod Milton for more details about Norman's burgeoning love life, I nevertheless remained shtum whilst weighing up my options. I decided that on balance, Marigold would probably consider

Milton to be an unreliable narrator on the subject of Norman's apparent romance. If my wife wanted more in-depth information, she could grill the local purveyor of porn herself.

Slamming a coffee down in front of Milton, Doreen scowled. Since he had openly gossiped about her still-husband, she was clearly regretting offering him a freebie. Completely oblivious that he had stuck his size nines in his mouth, Milton took a loud slurp of his beverage before changing the subject.

"I've been trying to get hold of you, old chap. Wanted to let you know that 'Delicious Desire' has only gone and been shortlisted for a gold star literary award."

"I didn't realise the Booker handed out awards for comedic porn," I scoffed, the din of Barry's guffaw practically drowning out my words.

"Erotica, old chap, erotica," Milton corrected.

"Well, don't keep us in suspense. Just how much is this glittering literary award going to set you back?" I just knew that the hapless pensioner had fallen prey to another scam. Milton certainly had form: during the course of our acquaintance, he had been fleeced by con artists posing as Liberian orphans and milked by a dodgy literary agent.

"A hundred quid," Milton admitted. "But it's perfectly legit, old chap; just a small cash outlay to cover the competition fee."

Rolling his eyes, Barry pointed out, "A hundred nicker would buy a lot of cat food."

Scratching his head, Spiros snorted, "The Milton is to pay in woman underwear."

"Not knickers, nicker." Barry's correction did nothing to dispel Spiros' confusion.

"Nicker is slang for English pounds," I explained to Spiros before telling Milton, "You really shouldn't have sent any money off. There are all sorts of dodgy outfits preying on gullible folk like you, doling out spurious prizes that no one has ever heard of."

"I've heard of the Booker," Barry piped up.

"Yes, but I can guarantee that Milton's porn isn't in the running for anything remotely prestigious. It will be some meaningless accolade simply designed to part fools from their money."

"Milton says his book has been shortlisted," Barry reminded me. "Perhaps there is a cash prize that would dwarf the entrance fee."

"I very much doubt it," I scoffed.

"There's no financial gain, what. The prize is a certificate and a gold star to put on my cover," Milton sheepishly admitted. "Darn, I should have consulted you, old chap, before posting the cheque off; you never steer me wrong. Too late now, what. They've only gone and cashed the cheque."

"There is one literary contest that your book

could take a prize in," I mulled, recalling a particular competition that Milton's porn might actually stand a chance in. "Not only is it free to enter; it offers a cash prize."

"You can't seriously think that Milton's smut might be in the running for a real prize," Barry sniggered.

"He could give the Bulwer Lytton contest a go," I said. "They offer an award for the worst opening sentence. I seem to recall the opening of 'Delicious Desire' was pretty dire, though I expect there's a great deal of competition."

Chapter 5

Elephants' Feet

Finally making our escape from Milton, Barry and I headed outside with Spiros, the undertaker eager to cast his eyes over the gun we had uncovered and proffer his seasoned advice. Before he had even clapped eyes on the gun, Spiros took charge; opining I was such a stickler for the law, he gave me short shrift, pronouncing it would be better all round if I was not involved in any capacity. Even though I pointed out that said gun had been discovered on my land, Spiros was not for budging, refusing to help unless I cleared off. Accepting my marching orders, I left Barry and

Spiros to it. I must confess to a frisson of relief: guns, particularly potentially illegal ones, aren't really my thing.

Strolling back through the village at a leisurely pace, my mind wandered to the evening's menu. Deciding to rustle up a home-made *moussaka* for my Greek guest, I ran the list of necessary ingredients through my mind. Drinking in the spectacular vista, I marvelled as always at the sheer beauty of my surroundings, the stunning sea view beyond the leafy lanes a far cry from our old cul-de-sac back in Manchester.

Pondering if I had enough ground cinnamon to do justice to the creamy bechamel sauce that would top my *moussaka*, I was distracted by an overwhelming scent of cheap perfume assaulting my olfactory senses. Since there wasn't another soul around, it was rather bizarre to say the least.

A sudden hiss was followed by the single word, "Victor." Recognising Norman's voice, I looked around in vain, failing to spot the traffic cone bore anywhere. I found it more than a tad unnerving to be confronted by his disembodied voice.

"Behind here," Norman hailed in an over-exaggerated whisper, his head popping into sight on the other side of the hedgerow. The sickly stench grew overpowering, indicating Norman was indisputably the source of the nauseating aroma.

"Norman, what on earth are you doing lurking

in a field?" Noticing the angry red patch barely disguised by his comb-over, it struck me that since he didn't have the good sense to don a sun hat, he'd be in for a spot of painful peeling later.

I couldn't help but notice a definite slur to Norman's words as he confided, "I was hiding from that John Macey fella. He's a terrible bore."

The words kettle, pot and black ran through my mind as I looked around for any sign of John Macey. I was even less in the mood for making mindless small talk with Macey than I was with Norman.

"You can come out of there, Norman. It appears that the coast is clear."

"Thank goodness. If I have to hide out of sight any longer, my elephants' feet will burn to a crisp."

"Choux pastry is tricky at best," I concurred, twigging that Norman must be referring to ginormous, chocolate topped cream puffs rather than the clodhoppers of an actual elephant. I must confess to being rather partial to the odd elephant's foot myself. However, with my dismal reputation when it came to pastry, I had never attempted to rustle them up. "It's not very clever to come out for a walk when you've left cakes in the oven."

"I had to clear my head," Norman said, the slur in his words even more evident at close quarters. "That invitation from your wife rather threw me."

"An invitation from my wife?" I parroted, wondering what fresh hell awaited me now.

"For the expat dinner party this coming Saturday. Marigold was most insistent that I bring my lady friend along…"

"Your lady friend?"

"Well, they were Marigold's words." Squirming with embarrassment and avoiding my eye, Norman elaborated. "I met this woman at that taverna; you know the one where your mother showed that Greek fella how to knock up a decent English Sunday roast. We got chatting and found we were both in the same boat…"

A deep sigh followed Norman's words, his exhaled breath carrying the distinctive fumes of *Metaxa*. Continuing to avoid my eye, he looked decidedly shifty as he nervously nibbled the cuticle on the side of his thumb.

"The same boat," I encouraged. It really was like pulling teeth getting Norman to talk freely about anything other than traffic cones, cakes or house prices.

"Both separated."

"Ah, indeed," I said, wondering if Violet Burke knew about this latest development. My mother could be quite contrary. She may well be up on Norman's love life but find it simply too boring to gossip about even though her daughter-in-law finds even the hint of a possible love match, riveting.

"We've had a couple of dates…though dates is probably too strong a word…yes, definitely too strong. We've met up a couple of times. I certainly wouldn't describe it as a courtship. Her husband left her for another woman but at least he doesn't rub her nose in it: he had the decency to conduct his affair back in England."

Finding the words 'conducting an affair' and 'decency' an odd combination, I detected a hint of a gripe from Norman. Certainly, Doreen had gone out of her way to rub his nose in her carryings on with Manolis.

"Truth to tell, I'm not sure I'm up for being part of a couple again. I'm definitely not ready to take things public yet," Norman continued. "I've no idea how Marigold even got wind of it."

"Athena spotted you in Lidl with a woman and conclusions were drawn."

"Athena? I'm being spied on by a woman I never heard of." Norman's tone was most put out.

"Athena, the local hairdresser…"

"Oh, I know who you mean. The woman who turned Doreen blonde, made her look like mutton dressed as lamb. Doreen's fooling no one. Everyone knows she's concealing the grey."

The fact that the few strands of Norman's remaining hair were all decidedly grey appeared to elude him. His hair really could do with a generous application of Grecian 2000.

"I think going blonde quite suits Doreen," I found myself saying, unable to resist taking the contrary position to Norman.

"Well, at least this woman I've met doesn't try to pretend she isn't grey."

"The woman that you're not sure if you're dating?"

"It's early days. Anyway, Marigold's invitation rather threw me for six. To be perfectly honest, I'm a bit out of my depth when it comes to women and I'm not even sure if I particularly like this woman I've met. She seems to be making all the running. I'd even go so far as to say that I think she's pursuing me."

Biting my tongue, I didn't give voice to my opinion that Norman was most surely deluded. He was hardly what one would call a catch. "Well, that vile aftershave should scare her off."

"Is it too much?"

"You smell like a tart's boudoir."

"Milton suggested I slap it on when I ran into him in the pharmacy earlier."

"Since Milton had been rifling through the bins, I imagine his sense of smell was completely shot." I couldn't help wondering if Norman's overly liberal use of aftershave was a desperate attempt to cover the smell of the booze. He might have been better gargling with the stuff.

"So, what do you think, Victor? Should I bring this woman along on Saturday or will it send too strong a signal?"

Why Norman always insisted on asking my advice on the dating scene was quite beyond me. I'd been out of the game ever since Marigold and I tied the knot, thirty-nine years ago.

About to advise him that inviting a new woman into our social circle may well lead her to believe that Norman was indeed keen, I reflected that ever the matchmaker, Marigold would have my guts for garters if I discouraged Norman. Not wishing to get on my wife's bad side, I advised Norman, "I'd say bring her along. It wouldn't do any harm to show Doreen that you're moving on."

"That's a good point. She's forever rubbing my nose in her new relationship with Manolis. Funny thing is, I quite like the fella."

"There you go then. Perchance if Doreen and this new woman of yours hit it off, you'll be able to enjoy cosy double dates," I suggested.

"Steady on. I'd rather keep well clear of Doreen…"

"Must be a tad difficult when you're still living under the same roof."

"Difficult doesn't begin to describe it. Well, I'd best be on my way. Those elephants' feet won't walk out of the oven themselves," Norman declared before plodding away.

Relieved to be free of the necessity of making mundane chatter, I resumed my stroll home, my heart sinking when the frantic ringing of a bicycle bell alerted me to my mother's approach. Inwardly cursing, I considered running into Violet Burke three times in one day to be a tad excessive. Occasionally, I can go as long as three days without being confronted with the reality of my mother living under my feet.

Turning around, I watched Violet Burke wobbling determinedly towards me with all the precision of a targeted missile. Without a second thought, I threw myself into the hedgerow in a desperate attempt to avoid a nasty collision: there was no way I would be anything but the loser against the combined weight of my mother's formidable frame and her bicycle.

Coming to an inelegant stop, my mother barked, "I clean forgot to tell you before…I need you to stop by at mine to give me a hand with that video machine thingy. It started chewing up that Tracy last night."

"It chewed up Tracy?" I parroted in confusion, picking some nasty thorns from the seat of my slacks.

"That lass that went upstairs and didn't come back down for a decade."

"I'm afraid you've lost me, Mother."

"You know the one, the devil spawn of that Deirdre that used to carry on with Mike Baldwin. She's only gone and got herself knocked up."

Belatedly, I experienced a light bulb moment: it appeared my mother was twittering on about her favourite soap, 'Coronation Street.'

"Deirdre Barlow is pregnant?"

"Don't be daft lad. It's her daughter Tracy what's up the duff by that Steve McDonald fella. It's a mystery to me how he manages to get all that female attention. He's hardly what you'd call a Gregory Peck type. Anyhow, you need to fix it."

"And what exactly do you expect me to do about it? Do you want me to write a stern letter to the television company complaining about the storyline?" I didn't bother to hide the sarcasm in my tone.

"Don't be so wet, lad. I've already said, I need you to fix the video thingy. You might as well bob in and do it now else you'll only go forgetting about it."

"Fixing things is really Barry's forte rather than mine," I argued.

"Aye, but unlike you, Barry's up to his ears in work at the moment," Vi stubbornly persisted, ushering me into the *apothiki*.

"So, how about it, lad? Have you given it any more thought?"

Addressing my backside, my mother had me at a distinct disadvantage. It was typical of her to try and take advantage whilst I was on my hands and knees, attempting to sort out the tangled cables behind her television and video recorder.

"Have I given what any more thought?" As usual, I had no idea what my mother was prattling on about.

Sighing heavily, Violet Burke wheedled, "Any more thought to letting young Kevin stop at the new apartments?"

"I already gave you a resounding no the last time you asked," I reminded her. "The idea of renting out the apartments to tourists is to make some money, not to give freebies to young Kevin and his bridezilla."

The very thought of Chardonnay Billings sullying one of the new apartments with her slovenly ways was not open for discussion. As for that little whipper snapper, Tyrone, I could only imagine the trail of destruction he would leave in his wake.

"But the lad deserves a nice honeymoon."

"Not at my expense," I snapped, repeatedly pressing the eject button to no avail. "You can stop your cajoling, Mother. It is not going to happen."

The way that Violet Burke was trying to persuade me reminded me of the relentless pressure she'd subjected me to when she'd needed a plus one to accompany her to back to Warrington for the social event of the season, the wedding of Kevin, the son of her best friend Dot, to that Chardonnay Billings trollop. Violet Burke had tried every trick in the book to wear me down, ranging from bullying to bribery, before turning on a nauseating charm offensive that I could see right through.

As she continued to labour the point, I resolved to stay firm and refuse to give in this time. It was bad enough that she had bested me over Kevin's nuptials: after weeks of endless arm-twisting, I had ended up accompanying her to England for Kevin's spring wedding to Chardonnay, a decision I regretted to this day.

"'Appen you need a nice cup of tea, lad. I'll chuck a proper bag in it for you, none of that twig muck. I'll even throw in a bickie." It struck me that if Violet Burke was resorting to bribery, she needed to up the ante: a cup of tea and biscuit would hardly cut it.

As my mother adjourned to the kitchen to make a brew, I was finally rewarded by the video recorder spewing out a mangled video cassette, a long trail of plastic tape leaving the cassette attached to the machine. Cluelessly gawping at the twisted strands of magnetic tape, I remembered how Violet Burke had managed to sucker me in the last time, resulting in the pair of us taking a flying trip back to England for the social event of the year. I could still recall the conversation we'd had, as clear as crystal.

"So, Kevin is marrying that tongue-pierced sket that pushes a trolley around Tesco in her pyjamas?" I had clarified. Having quite taken to Dot when she had holidayed in the Bucket household, I imagined that her son must be scraping the barrel, taking on Chardonnay and that little tyke, Tyrone.

"Who else would the lad be marrying? She reckons he knocked her up and now she's got her claws into him, proper like."

"It takes two to tango."

"'Cor, you never tire of stating the bleeding obvious."

Priding myself on original thought, my mother's words cut me to the quick. Stating the obvious was a trait shared by my wife and my brother-in-law, not by me.

"Can't you go to the wedding as Dot's plus one?" I'd asked.

"Don't be daft, lad. Dot will be doing her mother-of-the-groom act."

"I really don't fancy traipsing back to England for the sole purpose of rubbing shoulders with that vulgar Billings' clan."

"Aye, it's a right old trek and no mistake. And we'd have to have somewhere to stay. I knew I shouldn't have let you talk me into giving up that council flat…"

"Don't tell me you'd rather be chucking money away on rent and council tax for a property that's sitting empty? You couldn't wait to get shot of the place. Remember all that trouble you had with your neighbour. What was her name again? The woman in the shiny polyester tracksuit who accused me of being your toy boy."

"Edna Billings."

"Of course." I couldn't believe her name had even momentarily slipped my mind: we were after all discussing her granddaughter, Chardonnay Billings.

"So, why on earth are you lamenting giving up the flat next door to Edna Billings when you can't abide the woman? And why would you want to celebrate the wedding of her granddaughter?"

"Who said I wanted to celebrate that little scrubber getting wed?" Vi's contrariness confused me.

"Why else are you badgering me to escort you to her wedding?"

"Because Dot wants me there to have some numbers on Kevin's side. I've known the lad since he was knee high to a grasshopper and Dot expects a bit of moral support. It's not easy for her, having her Kevin intermingling with such gobby, coarse sorts. Dot told Kevin that that Chardonnay might have got herself knocked up by someone else. Dot wants her Kevin to go on that Jeremy Kyle show and have Chardonnay do one of them lie detector tests…"

"A DNA test might be more useful," I advised.

"Anyhow, Dot says even though her Kevin is besotted with the lass, he refuses to go on the telly because he's right camera shy. Mind you, Chardonnay was all for it. She fancied getting famous."

"Infamous, more like it. You'll have to go on your own," I had declared, knowing full well that this certainly wouldn't be the last I'd hear of it. Indeed, it was only the beginning of a relentless campaign for me to accompany Vi back to England to serve as her plus one at the wedding. Suffering under my mother's barrage of rather ineffectual persuasion, I stood my ground, refusing to even contemplate attending what I was certain would turn out to be a nightmare experience.

When Violet Burke realised that I was having no truck with the wedding, she resorted to some none-too-subtle bribery comprising a humongous home-made steak and kidney pie with perfectly puffed-up pastry to rival the best Fray Bentos could offer. As the pie slipped effortlessly down my gullet, Vi turned to dirty tactics, threatening to dob me in to Marigold by revealing that I had scarfed forbidden food with a dangerously high cholesterol content.

"Do your worst, Mother," I had protested. "The fact of the matter is that flying to England is an expense I could well do without at the moment. The renovation project has rather stretched all my resources. Maybe once it's paying for itself…"

"I can hardly tell young Kevin to postpone his wedding until you're turning a profit," Vi countered.

"It's going to have to be a no, at least on my part," I said firmly, not bothering to conceal the relief I felt in having a ready excuse to avoid the sort of vulgar knees-up I mentally conjured up for any event involving the Billings' clan. "I've already put the kibosh on Marigold's plans to fly back to England for a visit with Geraldine. After scuppering Marigold's trip due to a cash flow problem, I can hardly justify flying to England myself." For once I felt confident that I had won an argument with my mother. However, I had overlooked Violet Burke's propensity for always having the last word.

"Aye, lad, but going back to England for the wedding will be my treat. I managed to stash a tidy sum aside over the winter, teaching that pal of yours how to cook."

"Pal?" I queried.

"Takis, you daft apeth."

"You can hardly take credit for teaching him to cook. I rather imagine he picked up the basics at that fancy culinary school he attended."

"Well, he paid me enough doing Sunday roasts for me to squirrel enough away to splash out and treat you."

Inevitably, my mother had eventually worn me down and I had ended up attending the wedding. If there is one certainty in life, it is that Violet Burke is the mistress of getting her own way.

As my mother returned with two mugs of PG Tips, I felt my resolve harden. Pre-empting another barrage of her pleas that I should host the newly married couple for free in one of the new apartments, I launched into a counter argument.

"Mother, I really can't see that pair of young lovebirds from the council estate deriving any enjoyment from being stuck in the middle of nowhere surrounded by pensioners. They'll want a lively place with discos and cheap beer on tap, somewhere like Faliraki on the Island of Rhodes, or even better, Benidorm."

Taking the wind right out of my sales, Vi said, "'Appen you're right, lad." To say I was taken aback by Violet Burke's meek acquiescence is an understatement. No doubt this wouldn't be the end of the matter, but for now I had apparently won this round with comparative ease.

Slurping her tea, my mother caught sight of the spools of unwound tape. An angry glint shone in her eyes as she demanded, "What the fork have you done to my video, you useless lummox?"

Chapter 6

Too Spicy for a Rabbit

Arriving home, I discovered Marigold applying mascara at the kitchen table, a dodgy practise which I considered particularly unhygienic in light of my intention of cooking up a *moussaka* in the vicinity. Claiming she dare not set foot in the bedroom to apply her makeup, Marigold demanded I give it a thorough once over to ensure not a single tick remained.

"You just caught me. I'm off to the apartments to compile a list of things we need to pick up in town tomorrow before our first paying guests arrive." The glint in Marigold's eye denoted her excitement at the prospect of a spontaneous spending spree. "Speaking about the apartments…I was chatting to Geraldine earlier. She's only gone and got herself a new man."

"Another one!" I exclaimed, hoping that Geraldine had been the one to place the long-distance phone call. "But what on earth has that got to do with the apartments?"

"Well, she's thinking of bringing him over when she next visits…"

"We could always say that we'll be away. Anything is preferable to enduring the likes of Ashley mark two cluttering up the spare bedroom," I groaned, recalling Geraldine's last serious fling, the nylon haired suitor obsessed with samples of sexually transmitted diseases. Ever since Ashley's visit, I had been unable to tolerate the sight of a cauliflower cheese.

"That's why I was wondering about putting them in the apartments rather than risk giving houseroom to another Ashley type."

Ruminating on Marigold's suggestion, I could see the appeal.

"That's actually a good idea," I said. "It puts some distance between us whilst adding to the rental coffers."

"Don't be ridiculous, Victor. We can't possibly charge Geraldine. She's my best friend," Marigold objected, a withering look accompanying her words.

"The apartments are for paying customers, not free-loaders." I could see myself heading towards bankruptcy if my mother and wife both got their way, demanding I loan out the apartments for free to all and sundry.

"Well, if you insist on being so petty, you'll just have to put up with Geraldine's new beau in the house."

"Fine," I churlishly agreed. With a bit of luck, Geraldine and her new squeeze would have parted ways before she next came over to visit. I knew from experience that Geraldine's relationships tended to lack endurance.

Waving the mascara wand in the air, Marigold peered into the magnifying mirror. "Keep this under your hat, darling, but Doreen confided that Norman is back on the booze again."

About to confirm that I had smelled it myself, I decided to keep my own counsel. If I mentioned running into Norman, Marigold would be sure to interrogate me about his lady friend. Since I hadn't even thought of acquiring a name to dangle to satisfy my wife's curiosity, no good would come of spilling the beans about my recent encounter with Norman.

"Now, don't forget that you'll have to fend for yourself this evening, darling. Do you think you'll manage? I'm off for a girls' night in at Sherry's."

Despite the fact that I do most of the cooking in

the Bucket household, I still felt it very considerate of Marigold to worry about my fending for myself.

"I hadn't forgotten your girls' night," I assured my wife. "I've invited Spiros to join me for dinner. With Sampaguita being away, he's missing a home-cooked meal. I'm going to whip up a traditional *moussaka*; we've already got a glut of plump purple aubergines in the garden."

"You're making me jealous. You know how I adore your *moussaka*. No one makes a *moussaka* like you, Victor, not even the Greeks."

"I think it's down to my liberal use of cinnamon…"

"It's the topping, it's so much lighter and creamier than the usual stodge," Marigold positively gushed. "As much as I'm looking forward to an evening of good company, I expect that I'll come home hungry. You know what Sherry is like. She thinks haute cuisine involves slinging a load of Lidl's finest frozen into the oven; mini *tyropitakia* and *spanakopites*, along with those dreadful mini pizzas, are about all she can manage."

"And the cheese pies and spinach pies will likely be burnt to a crisp with frozen fillings," I added with a sympathetic wince.

"Sherry didn't seem to pick up anything useful from attending your cookery classes. I'm supposed to take something along. I was thinking along the lines of a dip…"

"Well, I was planning to whip up two *moussakas*, one for this evening and one for the freezer. Why don't you take the second one along to Sherry's? She'd only need to heat it up in the oven. Even Sherry can't bodge that."

"That sounds perfect. You're so good to me, darling." Even though Marigold sounded nothing but genuine, I couldn't help but wonder if I'd been played, her excessive flattery a cunning ploy to butter me up. At the very least, she'd got out of concocting a dip.

"Well, with the amount of wine that usually flows at your girls' gatherings, you'll be in need of something substantial to soak up the alcohol," I quipped, somewhat distracted by a loud scraping sound. I didn't want to draw attention to the sudden noise in case Marigold got even more paranoid about any lingering ticks.

"It's the cats," Marigold volunteered as the sound of scratching intensified to a level that couldn't be ignored. "I decided to shut them in the spare bedroom until the vet gives them the all clear. Probably best if you feed them in there, dear."

I reflected that it really wasn't like Marigold to banish her precious imported domestics to the dog house. Her aversion to ticks must be off the scale.

"Right, I'm off," Marigold announced, just as the telephone rang.

Answering the phone, I immediately identified

the horsey bray as belonging to Sherry and hastily passed the receiver to my wife. Trilling down the line, Marigold shooed me away. Grabbing a wicker basket, I caught my wife's attention, informing her as I made my escape, "I'm off to pick some aubergines so I can start work on the *moussaka*."

Waving me away, Marigold began jabbering away with Sherry, all thoughts of making a move to the apartments blown out of the window.

The garden looked glorious in the June sunshine. Surveying my terrain, I swelled with pride at the abundance of produce, the result of my extensive labour. Naturally, I gave a mental nod to Guzim since, admittedly, he had done the bulk of the work; weeding, watering, planting, and manuring with nary a word of complaint. Although the latter point isn't strictly true, I have learnt to turn a deaf ear to Guzim's constant grizzling and grumbles.

Approaching the nectarine tree which we'd planted during our first year in Meli, I ducked my head to avoid being slapped in the face by the fruit. The branches were bent under the weight of the shiny red nectarines, their smooth skins hinting at their luscious peachy centres. Impulsively, I decided to gather the ripest of the offerings and knock them up into a crumble. Both Marigold and my mother enjoy a good crumble, Vi's preference to have the dessert smothered in custard. I would be interested to see how Spiros reacted to the classic British pudding.

Moving over to the vegetable patch, I bent low to pluck eight purple aubergines from the plants. In my opinion, a good *moussaka* can never have too many aubergines. Most of the tavernas add sliced potatoes along with the aubergines, but it is aubergine slices all the way in the Bucket household; there's just something about the way in which they soak up the elixir of extra virgin olive oil in the preparation that makes my version of the dish so temptingly moreish, together with my preference for adding a more than generous measure of cinnamon powder not only to the creamy bechamel topping, but to the beef sauce. Although either lamb or beef can be used in the base, I tend to find ground beef to be less fatty than lamb.

I was mightily impressed by the patch of rosy red radishes growing next to Marigold's herb garden; gleaming in the sunshine, they had to be the biggest yet. Recalling Barry's passion for pickled radishes, I decided to pickle some up for my brother-in-law.

Gathering several large bunches of the root vegetable, I wondered if Spiros would appreciate an appetiser of roasted radishes. Experimenting with the dish the previous summer, I had surprised myself with how utterly delicious they were. Sliced thinly, seasoned and tossed in olive oil, roasting the radishes not only caramelised the miniature vegetables but transformed their flavour from their usually peppery bite to delectably sweet. It never ceases to amaze me how a spot of kitchen experimentation can result in either the most mouthwatering discoveries or completely inedible disasters, the prickly pear curry being a case in point of the latter.

Tossing the radishes into my basket, I almost jumped out of my skin when Guzim sneaked up behind me, his guttural Albanian accent tinged with a peevish edge as he grunted, "*Min parete ola ta rapanakia.*" Considering they were my radishes, his churlish demand, 'don't take all the radishes', struck me as a bit of a cheek.

Ignoring the whine in Guzim's voice, I explained that I was going to pickle them, asking if he would like some pickled radishes. "*Pao na ta toursi. Thelete toursi rapanakia?*"

"*Ochi. Miso ta rapanakia.*" Saying no, he hated radishes, Guzim emphasised his disdain by spitting on the ground.

Since our conversation rather dragged on, I will ditch our long-winded, mangled Greek dialogue and report the rest in English.

"If you hate radishes, why on earth are you insisting I leave some?"

"Because Doruntina loves them."

"Surely they are too spicy for a rabbit?"

"She likes the tops…"

"Here, take the radish greens," I offered, yanking the red cruciferous veggies free from their leafy tops. Realising it wasn't like Guzim to be hanging around in my garden in the early afternoon, I asked him why he wasn't working.

"I am working. I work for the Kyria Yiota."

Struggling to conjure up the Greek word for skiving, I held my tongue, letting my sceptical expression do the talking. It would take a more remarkable man than the Albanian shed dweller to master lurking in my garden whilst at the same time working at Yiota's place.

Worn down by Guzim's stubborn silence in the face of my obvious incredulity, I posited, "Are you on a break?"

"No, I finish. The Yiota want me to start at two."

Consulting my watch and wondering if Guzim had been downing the Amstel, I asked, "How can you be finished if you're due to start in half-an-hour."

"I finish. I am the exhausted," Guzim insisted. "I start the work at two in the dark."

"Yiota had you working before dawn?"

"She fix the outside light so I can to pick the *vlita*. She want it freshly picked to sell at the market."

As Guzim's words sank in, I felt a twinge of envy that Yiota would be manning the market stall without me. I always thoroughly enjoy taking a turn as the Del Boy of Meli up at the market. Glad to hear that Guzim had found work locally, I hoped such early starts would not become the norm. Ever since Guzim had written off his tatty old moped back at the start of the year, I had been inconvenienced on an almost daily basis. Whenever Guzim went looking for work down on the coast, he left Meli at an unspeakably early hour, hoping to either thumb a lift or to catch the early morning bus if no one stopped to pick him up. This necessitated me, rather than Guzim, mucking out the chickens and giving them their breakfast, which was rather akin to keeping a dog and barking myself.

"Have you got an early start with Yiota tomorrow?"

"No..."

"Are you working down on the coast tomorrow?"

"No..."

"Good. So, you'll be able to see to the chickens in the morning. That's a weight off my mind. I didn't fancy doing that before driving up to town."

"You're driving up to town," Guzim parroted.

"Yes, indeed. The cats have got ticks so a visit to the veterinarian is in order. I do believe that Mrs Bucket has secured us an early appointment."

"I can't feed the chickens. I have to get the early bus to town." Adding the 'early bus' to his announcement was a tad superfluous since the early bus was in fact the one and only bus.

"Why are you going to town?" Admittedly my direct question was a tad blunt, if not incredulous. Guzim made it his life's work to avoid going to town. Along with beaches, he wasn't keen on built up areas.

"To get my new wheels."

"New wheels?"

"One of my friends is leaving Greece for good and returning to Albania on the bus. He give me the good price for his moped. I meet him at the bus station at two the afternoon tomorrow to collect it. It will be good to have my own wheels again."

After making the exhausting journey to Albania back in January, albeit in the comfort of Spiros' hearse, I could well imagine a moped wouldn't be the ideal form of transportation for the long and arduous trip.

"Well, make sure you wear a helmet on your head this time. We don't want you getting concussion again."

"I could feed the chickens tomorrow if you give me the ride to town," Guzim wheedled.

"Done," I agreed with barely any hesitation. Although Marigold would no doubt throw a strop at the news that the Albanian shed dweller would be cadging a lift, self-interest won out. If I bundled Guzim into the Punto, I would be spared dealing with the chickens at the crack of dawn. Since he would presumably be returning to Meli on his new wheels, we wouldn't have to put up with Guzim's company for the return journey.

"The garden up at the apartments still needs some work if you fancy a spot of overtime," I offered.

"I do it later. Now, I need sleep." Peering into my basket, he asked if I was planning to knock up an aubergine curry. His insatiable appetite for curry showed no sign of abating.

"I'll do one next week," I promised before heading back to the house with my garden bounty.

I reflected that if Guzim had his way he would dine on curry for breakfast, luncheon and dinner. Considering it would be easier all round if I simply gave him the recipe or invited him to attend my cookery classes over the winter, I realised my idea was a non-starter. In Guzim's chauvinistic mind, no normal red-blooded male would be caught dead rustling up something in the kitchen. I'm pretty sure that paying his gardening wages is the only thing preventing Guzim from calling me a sissy.

Chapter 7

Moussaka, Pickled Radishes, and Crumble

After making my escape from Guzim, I returned to the house to discover Marigold still gabbing away to Sherry. Doing one of her Sybil Fawlty impressions, my wife cooed, "Oh, I know…I know," down the telephone line. Hurriedly hanging up with a guilty look, Marigold announced, "Sherry wants to go to the garden centre so I told her that she's very welcome to come up to town with us tomorrow."

"You might have consulted me first," I said in exasperation. "I've just agreed to give Guzim a lift up to town tomorrow."

"Without consulting me first," Marigold volleyed back. "You'd better have a word with him…"

"I've just had several…"

"Well, you'll need to have several more, Victor. If you insist on bringing Guzim, you'll need to make sure he wears something clean otherwise we'll be breathing in the stench of chicken manure all the way up to town."

"Those words would probably be better coming from you, darling. You know how deferential he is towards you."

"I'm not sure my Greek stretches to chicken poop."

"*Skata kotopoulou*," I helpfully translated. "I don't know how you expect me to squeeze Guzim and Sherry in the back of the Punto with two cats. I suppose something will have to go in the boot."

"I don't think it's legal to transport Albanian gardeners in the boot." Marigold eyes twinkled with amusement at the thought of stuffing Guzim in the boot.

"I was thinking about the cats," I clarified with a chuckle.

"You're not putting my precious darlings in the boot." A scathing look replaced Marigold's twinkle. "Guzim will just have to balance their cages on his knee."

"I'll sedate them before the off," I promised, wishing I could sedate both Guzim and Sherry too.

It would certainly ensure a more peaceful journey if the two of them were out for count.

Dropping a peck on my cheek, Marigold stated she was finally off to the apartments to make her list. With the cats locked in the spare bedroom and my wife gone, I had the place to myself, the perfect opportunity to don my chef's hat and blast George Gershwin's 'Porgy and Bess' at full volume.

Deciding to tackle the pickled radishes first, I took some glass jars and gave them a thorough wash in hot soapy water before popping them into a hot oven to ensure they were sterilised to within an inch of their lives. Next up on my agenda was preparing the brine since it would take time to cool, an easy process achieved by heating white vinegar and water seasoned with sea salt and cane sugar. Once the sugar and salt were dissolved, I set the brine aside to cool. Once cool, I would pour it over the sliced radishes, adding mustard seeds and whole black peppercorns to the jars.

Using a mandoline to ensure uniformity of size in my slices, I divided the sectioned vegetables between the jars. I smiled to myself as I worked, knowing how much Barry would appreciate my efforts. His attachment to anything pickled was boundless. I would put a jar aside for Spiros to give to his wife on her return from the Philippines since Sampaguita had a weakness for anything spicy.

Tapping my feet in tune to 'I Loves you Porgy',

I began to slice the aubergines prior to shallow frying them in olive oil. After much experimentation, I had found that the whole kerfuffle of salting the aubergine slices to eliminate any bitterness prior to cooking, to be an unnecessary step that I could confidently skip. Most likely it is advisable to salt the aubergines if one is using less than fresh veggies of unknown provenance, but I am intimately acquainted with the *melitzanes* procured from the Bucket garden, their flavour subtly sweet rather than bitter.

Thanks to the generosity of the villagers, there was no need to ration the oil: I had a positive abundance of the stuff donated by Nikos, Yiota, Spiros, Vangelis and sundry neighbours. Additionally, I still had the remains of a five-litre tin of oil gifted to me from Panos; due to sentimental reasons, I was reluctant to empty it. Every time I picked up the tin, I smiled at the recollection of Panos telling me, "You are as beautiful as the goddess Aphrodite," as he diligently practised his studied English chat up lines on me, prior to trying them out for real on Violet Burke.

Whilst the aubergines absorbed the oil, I made a start on the beef sauce, sauteing minced beef with onions and adding pressed garlic to the mix. Chucking a glass of red wine in the pan, I further seasoned the meat with a heaped tablespoon of ground cinnamon, a couple of bay leaves, a squirt of tomato paste, a tin of chopped tomatoes, and a dash of Worcestershire sauce. Although the savoury condiment isn't remotely Greek, I find it enhances most dishes. With the sauce simmering on the stove, I prepared the bechamel topping, adding my signature touch of two sliced mozzarella balls to the mix, making a mental note not to mention the addition of an Italian cheese to Spiros. The only drawback to a good *moussaka* is the amount of washing up it produces; by the time I was finished, I would have three large mucky pans to deal with.

Leaving the bechamel on a low heat and giving it the occasional stir, I set about preparing the fresh nectarines for a couple of crumbles by combining the chopped fruit with cinnamon, brown sugar and lemon juice. With the nectarines basting in their juices, I dug out two large baking dishes and set about layering the aubergines and beef sauce, ladling the sauce over the vegetables before finally topping the dish with the bechamel and a sprinkling of grated *mizithra* cheese. Setting the two *moussakas* aside to go in the oven later, I made the crumble topping and tackled the washing up.

With the cooking out of the way, I tore off my pinny and examined our video recorder. Since we had recently invested in a DVD player, I hoped that Marigold wouldn't notice if I sneaked the outdated video player down to my mother. I would never hear the end of it if Violet Burke was deprived of her evening dose of Corrie and she was sure to hold me responsible for the mangled state of her own machine. Dot still religiously sent Vi out of date video cassettes; to the best of my knowledge, my mother had almost caught up to current events on the street.

Recalling how Violet Burke had introduced Panos to the Mancunian soap opera brought a smile to my face. The welly wearing farmer had been a good companion to my mother. Since his death, Vi had sworn off further dalliances with the opposite sex. Some of the local old-timers had tried out a few dubious chat up-lines but my mother had simply rebuffed them with a sharp retort, Panos' emerald proudly displayed on her ring finger if they needed a slap.

With the video recorder unplugged ready to be carted down to the *apothiki* on my mother's return, I decided to head into my office and pen a few lines of 'Bucket to Greece.' Although I had not an iota of interest in acquiring a sham accolade from dubious sources, Milton's boast about the five-star literary award he had paid for, had revitalised my interest in penning my own Bucket saga.

What with one thing and another this year, I had barely had time to dip my quill in the ink and commit any words to parchment. There had been the emergency dash to rural Albania to deposit Guzim in the bosom of his family, rather than have him recuperate from his moped accident in the Bucket spare bedroom. Then, there had been the fallout from all the drama at Haralambos' funeral; being the shoulder for Tina to cry on had eaten into my writing time.

Alas, my literary intentions were thwarted when Marigold phoned from the village shop, desperate urgency in her voice.

"Victor, there's an English couple here that are interested in the apartments. Cynthia put up a poster not ten minutes ago and it caught their eye."

"Keep them there. I'll be right over," I promised, almost falling over my own feet in my haste to get down to the Punto. Burning rubber, I raced through the village, determined not to let a possible pair of renters slip through my fingers. Pulling up outside the shop, I saw Marigold chatting to a very smartly dressed middle-aged couple, their brown leathery skin marking them out as a pair of ardent sun worshippers. The fake smile plastered across Marigold's face sent alarm bells ringing but I determined to focus on the task in hand: filling some empty dates on my rental calendar.

Introducing myself, the man responded with a curt, "Squire," offering a rather damp, limp handshake. His sweaty palm was understandable; despite the heat of a June afternoon, Mr Squire was dressed from head to toe in tweed. Mrs Squire, showily dressed in designer labels with her eyes hidden behind enormous dark sunglasses, didn't deign to speak, her immobile features hinting at plastic surgery.

Avoiding my eye, Mr Squire managed to look down his nose at me. "We've been led to believe that you have luxury apartments for rent."

"Indeed, the apartments are finished to a very high standard. Actually, I should have said almost finished. The local craftsmen are just putting the final touches…"

"So, they're not finished," Mr Squire snapped.

"Well, almost. You're welcome to see for yourself," I invited, suggesting the couple jump in their hire car and follow the Punto.

Joining me in the Punto, Marigold adopted an exaggerated whisper even though there was no chance of her being overheard. "They're dreadful snobs. He kept going on about the high standards they are used to in the Gulf."

"Dubai?"

"Saudi. They're English but live over there."

"Wads of tax-free cash can make even the most unenlightened countries appealing. He's probably used to a gold-plated toilet. How on earth did they end up in Meli?"

"Apparently they are driving around Greece to view the cultural sights."

"They're a bit off the beaten track up here." As

much as I loved my adopted village, I had to admit it could hardly be described as a cultural oasis. I had assumed the apartments would appeal to tourists who enjoyed walking and exploring nature. Mrs Squire was likely to come a cropper if she attempted to trot around the village on her precariously high designer heels.

"I hadn't expected any walk-ins just yet as potential guests. Still, let's see if I can sell them on the place," I said. I couldn't care less if they were the ghastliest snobs going as long as they had the wherewithal to pay for a stay.

Arriving at the apartments, I led the way into the downstairs unit since Barry and Blat were still working upstairs. "Let me show you around," I invited.

Neither of the Squires uttered a word as they looked around, their vinegarish expressions fairly oozing disdain. Although the apartment lacked a few finishing touches, it was well presented, the double bed set on a raised platform in the arched living room alcove, complemented with mood lighted.

"What time is breakfast served?" Mr Squire asked.

"Well, it isn't. It's not a hotel." Contemplating making a quick call to Violet Burke to see if she'd be willing to rustle up a full English and deliver it on her bicycle, I decided it was a non-starter. Considering the speed at which my mother pedalled, the food would likely be stone cold by the time it was delivered; moreover, it wouldn't do to set a breakfast in bed precedent.

Entering the bathroom, Mr Squire pointed at the toilet and demanded, "What's that?"

"It's a toilet," I replied, wondering what planet he lived on if he needed to be told what a toilet was.

"I'm perfectly aware it is a toilet," Mr Squire barked. "I was referring to the sign above the toilet roll dispenser."

"Well, it's a sign indicating that toilet paper must not be flushed down the toilet."

"What on earth is one supposed to do with it?"

"A convenient bin will be provided. It's on the list of things we still need to acquire…I'd be happy to lend you ours…"

"That won't do at all, it won't do at all. I've never heard anything so disgusting."

"I'm afraid it's common practise around these parts. The pipes are so narrow that paper would block them…"

"Toilet tissue in a bin. The very thought would turn my wife's stomach."

"You'd probably need to drive as far as Athens before you could find a toilet that allows you to flush paper," I pointed out, thinking anyone with even a cursory interest in visiting Greece would have surely read up on this. It was hardly a state secret and millions of tourists managed to cope without having a meltdown. "Even in Athens, you'd probably have to find a five-star establishment that has suitable pipes…"

"Come on, Mrs Squire, we're leaving. This has been a complete waste of our time," Mr Squire pontificated, pushing past me gracelessly with a definite sneer on his face. His wife followed hot on his heels. Since she was yet to utter a word, I was unable to conclude if the contemptuous look in her eyes was directed at my clearly lacking apartment or at her arrogant husband.

"Did you hear that? He called his wife Mrs Squire," Marigold hissed.

"I know, how bizarre. I just wish I could be a fly on the wall. I'd love to see if the pair of them can manage to keep their legs crossed all the way to Athens until they can find a lav that meets with their approval."

"You sound just like your mother," Marigold observed as the Squires drove off. "What dreadful people. They seem like the type who believe rules don't apply to them. No doubt they will defy the loo roll convention and go on their merry way wilfully blocking toilets across Greece."

"I expect you're right," I concurred. If they had stayed, no doubt the size of the plumbing bill would have dwarfed any rental revenue.

Taking my hand, Marigold said, "I'm sorry you

didn't manage to get a booking out of them, darling."

"Not to worry. We've got Violet Burke's Hooray Henrys arriving on Sunday and from what I recall, they're very easy going."

Chapter 8

One of a Kind

Whilst Marigold busied herself preening and primping for her evening out, trying on and discarding any number of perfectly adequate frocks, I took advantage of the peace and quiet. Settling into my favourite spot on the balcony, I relaxed, indulging in nothing more taxing than drinking in the view and watching the early evening comings and goings of my neighbours. With the repping season upon me and all the stress of the new apartment venture, I was painfully aware that such moments of downtime would soon be in short supply.

V.D. BUCKET

My moment of leisure was short-lived, disturbed by Violet Burke shrieking up at me from the pavement below. "Victor, get down here, lad. I need you."

Leaning over the balcony, I spotted my mother doing a passable imitation of a vulgar fishwife, arms folded across her tweed clad chest in veritable harridan mode. Cringing at Violet Burke's insistence on summoning me in such an indecorous manner, I supposed her common display might be slightly preferable to her banging on the ceiling with her broomstick to attract my attention.

Slipping the video recorder under one arm and grabbing one of the nectarine crumbles, I made my way down to the *apothiki*, almost tripping over a pair of wellington boots left on the downstairs doorstep. Feeling a pang of nostalgia for the days when Panos would park his wellies on Violet Burke's doorstep, I was greeted by my scowling mother.

"What is it this time?" I demanded.

"Keep your voice down, lad. I've got company," Vi hissed, seemingly oblivious to her own strident cries that I get down there pronto.

Presuming company would account for the wellies, I slapped a suitably welcoming smile on my face as I entered. Indoors, I discovered Yiota comfortably ensconced on my mother's sofa, her skin emitting a peachy glow. Considering she had been up before dawn, Panos' granddaughter looked remarkably fresh; she must have had a busy day flogging *vlita*, along with other perishables, on the market.

"The crumble just needs popping in the oven. The video recorder is only on loan until I can find you a new one," I told my mother, neglecting to mention that if Marigold noticed the video machine was missing it was likely to be immediately yanked back upstairs. Fortunately, unless Marigold had a sudden yen to watch one of her 'Prisoner Cell Block H' videos, I was confident she would fail to notice the machine was gone. Now that the days were longer, my wife preferred to spend her evenings outside in the garden or on the roof terrace, rather than glued to the telly.

"That's right good of you, lad. You might as well hook it up to the telly now that you're here. Yiota loves a bit of Corrie with a nice cuppa." I was unable to glean from my mother's words if she was aware of the girls' night in over at Sherry's. I decided to keep mum on the subject in case the other women had deliberately excluded Violet Burke: it was no secret that, on occasion, they could find her company overbearing. "Yiota wants to know if you reckon it's worth her taking a chance on that Albanian of yours."

"Guzim?"

"Of course, Guzim. How many Albanians have you got?"

"Just the one in the shed," I quipped.

"Guzim has done the odd day's labouring for me and I'm considering making it a more permanent arrangement," Yiota confided in excellent English. Since she spent so much time with Vi, Yiota's English had improved no end, and, quite remarkably, she spoke without a trace of my mother's northern slang.

"Guzim did a good job in the fields today and he has quite a way with the sheep. He talks to them."

"Your sheep understand Albanian?" I joshed. "I'm sure that Guzim would be up for that. I know he prefers to work locally and he's more suited to working in the fields rather than mucking in as part of a building team. He has a way of riling up his compatriots."

"So, you would recommend him?" Yiota persisted.

"Well, in spite of all his grizzles, grumbles and gripes, he does get the job done satisfactorily." Recalling Vangelis' reservations about my initially hiring Guzim to do my garden, I felt it only fair to fill Yiota in on some of Guzim's shortcomings. "You should be aware he has a tendency to pull on the heart strings to open the purse strings. He will try and manipulate you into giving him extras on top of his wages; the contents of your wardrobe won't be safe."

"I'm sure that Yiota would be right happy to sling any old frocks Guzim's way," Vi declared with a deadpan expression.

"To be fair, he's more or less laid off the poverty gripes of late. Since our visit to Albania, he hasn't once complained that his wife eats all his money." Changing the subject, I addressed Yiota. "How are you enjoying the farming life?"

"I love it. It's very hard work and long hours but I have never been happier…"

"There's no denying that Giannis puts a smile on her face. He's right easy on the eye and no mistake," my mother interrupted. "I keep telling the lad he ought to make an honest woman of Yiota. I told him straight, 'Stop wasting time and marry the lass.'"

A deep blush reddened Yiota's cheeks. Coming to the young woman's defence, I told my mother, "You can't go around embarrassing Yiota like that."

"Luckily, Giannis doesn't understand a single word that Violet says," Yiota said, fine lines crinkling the corners of her eyes.

"Aye, I'm going to have to work on my Greek so I can talk some sense into the daft lummox."

"I'd be happy to lend you some of my textbooks, Mother," I offered.

"I'll stick with my way of picking up the lingo by chatting to Greek folk. I don't want to end up sounding like one of them dictionaries of yours," Vi said pragmatically. "Here, Yiota, have you heard how my Victor went round carping on about how the sheep ate his bagpipes? He picked that up from one of his phrasebooks."

"It wasn't bagpipes. The sheep ate my sandwiches," I corrected.

"I hadn't heard that one," Yiota said. Breaking into a wide smile, she added, "But I did hear how Victor was obsessed with the handsomeness of the prime minister."

"I'm never going to live that one down," I admitted, reflecting that Violet Burke perhaps had a point about picking up Greek from conversing with the locals rather than parroting obsolete phrases from an outdated phrase book.

The sudden sound of the toilet flushing took me by complete surprise since I had presumed the three of us were alone in the *apothiki*. A very familiar looking figure, short, stocky and unshaven with a prominent hole in the toe of his sock, emerged from the bathroom. My jaw dropped to the floor in shock and I could feel beads of sweat breaking out on my forehead.

"What the…? Panos?" I could feel the colour draining from my cheeks at this sudden apparition of the welly wearing farmer risen from the dead.

"Course it's not Panos, you daft 'apeth. This fella reckons he's Panos' brother, Petros." Making no attempt to hide her sceptical tone, my mother appeared to be under the impression that the familiar looking stranger was trying to pull a fast one.

"Petros is my great uncle," Yiota clarified with a warm smile.

"I never knew Panos had a brother…" I spluttered, completely taken aback by Petros' uncanny resemblance to Panos. Initially thinking it odd that Panos hadn't mentioned a sibling, it dawned on me that my many conversations with Panos had primarily centred on chickens, sheep and vegetables. Apart from unburdening his feelings to me about my mother, Panos had not been one for divulging the personal.

"I already told you, Violet, I go by Hal." Extending a calloused hand in greeting, Petros, or Hal, crushed my fingers in a vice-like grip.

"And I already told you that I go by Mrs Burke," Vi snapped, clearly not welcoming any familiarity from this stranger.

"Hal?"

"Aye, it kind of stuck after I caught the biggest halibut the boat ever landed. Here, take a look." As he spoke, Hal passed me a crumpled polaroid photograph of his much younger self holding the largest halibut I had ever clapped eyes on.

Hearing Hal speak in American-twanged English with barely a trace of a Greek accent, shattered the image that Panos was back in the land of the living. On closer inspection I realised that although the two brothers could easily be mistaken for twins, Hal's heavily lined face was in fact far more weatherbeaten than his brother's had been. Also, Hal appeared to be more solidly stocky than Panos as well as having a bit more hair. I thought for sure that Panos wouldn't have been caught dead flaunting a vibrant bandanna around his neck; he would have instantly dismissed it as a scarf only fit for sissies.

Slipping a protective arm around Yiota's shoulders, my mother said, "This Petros character, or whatever he calls himself, was just telling me that he's come back to Meli to claim his inheritance."

"His inheritance…" I repeated.

"The farmhouse and the land," Hal emphasised. "They belonged to me and Panos, fifty-fifty."

Openly glaring at Hal, Vi added, "The very same house that Yiota has made into her home."

"And her home it will remain," Hal said firmly. "I've no intention of making Yiota homeless."

Smiling broadly, Yiota said, "I've insisted my uncle must stay with me. My grandfather often spoke fondly of his brother and I'm so happy to meet him."

With an expression that could have curdled cream, Vi spat, "Well, Panos never mentioned him to me and we were practically engaged." A look of regret clouded Vi's eyes as she twisted the emerald gracing her ring finger, the ring she would have accepted if Panos hadn't gone and popped his clogs before he got the chance to propose.

"Communication between the two of you was a tad limited," I pointed out to Vi, recalling how Panos had very little understanding of the memorised English phrases he had regurgitated in his efforts to woo my mother. "So, Hal, how long are you planning to stay in Meli?"

"I'm planning on stopping in Greece for good now that I've retired."

Even though Yiota appeared delighted to have discovered her long-lost great uncle, I anticipated that if Hal had any plans to contest her inheritance, his unexpected arrival may well throw a spanner in Yiota's decision to stay in the farmhouse and farm the land.

"Retired. So, you don't have any plans to farm the land?"

"Nah." A nasal snort emphasised Hal's negative. "I always hated farming, got no time for it. That's why I up and left all them years ago. The sea was my calling."

"Ah, a navy man?"

"Nah, fishing was my thing. I've spent my life riding the oceans on commercial fishing boats. Been all over the place. I battled the three Atlantic graveyards..."

"Atlantic graveyards?" Even Violet Burke was curious.

"North Carolina, Cape Cod and Sable Island. Sable's Canadian. I spent the last decade in Alaska…not a day went by when I wasn't covered in salmon slime."

Watching as my mother's cat, Petey, slunk over to Hal and rubbed herself affectionately against his leg, I wondered if Hal's skin had permanently absorbed the fishy smell of salmon. My mother's frigidly icy glare melted slightly as Hal bent down to stroke her beloved pet.

"Who's up for a cuppa?"

"Not for me," I replied. Even though I was dying to hear more details about the sudden appearance of Panos' previously unmentioned brother, I remembered that Spiros was due for dinner at any moment and I'd left the *moussaka* in the oven.

Unburdening me of the video recorder that I was still clutching, Hal addressed my mother. "I'll get this set up for you, Violet."

"It's Mrs Burke to you," Vi snapped, heading into the kitchen to make a brew.

Although time was short, I followed her into the kitchen. Realising what a huge shock I had experienced on first setting eyes on Hal, I felt a twinge of concern for my mother who must have been doubly shocked.

"Are you okay, Mother, or did the bombshell rattle you?"

"What bombshell?"

"The shock of seeing Panos' double."

"You need to get your eyes tested, lad. That fella out there looks nothing like his brother. Panos was one of a kind."

"That he was," I agreed. Since there was no denying that the two brothers were as alike as two peas in a pod, I could only presume that my mother was choosing to deny reality for some reason. Perchance Hal's arrival had stirred up feelings that Violet Burke had buried with Panos.

Chapter 9

A Load of Old Codswallop

Setting the kitchen table for dinner for two, I was relieved that having Spiros round didn't require digging out Marigold's best bone china or carting the food up to the roof terrace. Spiros would be more than happy to dine informally in the kitchen. I had just finished throwing a Greek salad together to accompany the *moussaka* when Spiros pleasantly astonished me by ignoring Greek time and arriving bang on the appointed hour. He certainly surprised me though by announcing that Vangelis would be joining us momentarily.

Fortunately, I calculated that the *moussaka*, being on the generous side, should easily stretch to three. If my guests were particularly ravenous, I could chuck some extra tomatoes in the salad to bulk it out, or they could fill up on crumble. The extra guest meant that the cats could well be deprived of their usual leftovers. Luckily, the tick-ridden felines remained locked in the spare bedroom, well out of temptations reach of our meal.

Spiros' formal attire immediately put me to shame. I had failed to anticipate that he would turn up done up like the dog's dinner in a suit and tie, a decorative mauve silk pocket square adorning his breast pocket, his unruly eyebrows noticeably trimmed. When I had seen Spiros earlier, he had been sporting baggy jogging trousers paired with a grubby undershirt; presuming he wouldn't bother to change, I had made no effort to dress for dinner, even allowing my own high standards to slip by forgoing a tie.

"You're looking very smart, Spiro, though really there was no need to change into a suit," I said, just as Vangelis rolled in, his plaster specked builder's denim more suited to a building site than the Bucket residence.

"The suit is not for you, Victor," Spiros clarified. "I put the ceremonious dress for a *rantevou* to showing a house. There is a rich doctor who is to thinking he want to move to a small village. The house need much the work so I ask the Vangelis to come and meet the doctor too."

Spiros' words made me recall how he had summoned the local builder to offer his expert opinion on our very first viewing of the Meli house which we now called home. Now, the three of us were such good friends that Vangelis thought nothing of turning up for dinner uninvited, knowing he would always receive a warm welcome in the Bucket household.

"I come to escape the Athena. I am in the dog-house," Vangelis announced as I opened a couple of bottles of chilled *Mythos* for my guests and set an extra place at the table. Sinking into a chair and swigging a hearty glug from his bottle, Vangelis shed plaster dust all over my spotless table.

"What's landed you in Athena's bad books?" I questioned.

"She not to want me to do any work for a doctor. She refuse to have any doctor to live in the village. When I insist to take the look at the house with Spiros, the Athena was so angry that she threw the *pistolaki* at me."

It struck me as a tad extreme for Athena to lob a hair dryer at her husband.

"But it would be handy having a doctor living in the village," I pointed out. "Especially as so many of the residents are not exactly spring chickens."

"Victor, he is the human doctor, not the...I

cannot to think of the English word…the *ktiniatros*."

By referencing a veterinarian, it appeared my mention of spring chickens had gone clear over Vangelis' head, just as Athena's apparent objection to a doctor moving to the village left me completely baffled.

Donning my oven gloves to remove the *moussaka* from the oven, I asked why Athena had a problem with a medical professional living locally.

"It is the difficult, much the difficult. Myself, I am in the two mind about it. If the doctor to buy the house I to show him, I earn the good commission, and it would be much the work for the Vangelis and the Barry." Spiros' brow furrowed as he added, "The last time there was a doctor who live in the Meli, it not to work out the well."

Scooping large portions of steaming *moussaka* onto the plates, I waited for my guests to elaborate.

"The Spiros and I, we were the teenager when the doctor Loukas move to the village," Vangelis began. "He was the marry with the two young child. The people like the family, the doctor much the popular. Loukas was the good friend with my father."

Winking broadly, Spiros added, "Even though he was the marry, the Loukas spend the much time with the Uncle Leo, if you to get my float."

"Drift," I gently corrected, fully aware that my use of Greek included far worse malapropisms than

Spiros' blunder. "But you just said he was married."

"I think he was in the cupboard."

"I think it was the wardrobe," Vangelis argued. Running his fingers through his hair, he dislodged another spattering of plaster dust.

"It's the closet," I corrected. "So, let me see if I've got this right. Athena doesn't want a new doctor in the village in case homosexuality is rife among medics."

Even to my own ears, my guess that Athena objected on the grounds that being gay was contagious, sounded completely ludicrous. Vangelis' wife had been nothing but welcoming to my out and proud son, Benjamin, and his life partner, Adam.

"No, it was the Loukas' ideas, very much the strange ideas...how you say, eurythmics?"

"Eurythmics?" I parroted, wondering what sort of warped logic was heading my way.

"He mean eugenics. The Loukas not to like the old people," Vangelis volunteered. Tucking into his steaming food, he declared my cooking *poly nostimo*, very delicious.

"It was more than the dislike," Spiros added. "The doctor have many the theory that the natural order of life is to die at the seventy."

"Threescore years and ten," I mused, wondering quite where this theory was going.

"Ah, the English Shakespeare to make that." A

knowledgeable shake of his head accompanied Spiros' words.

"Although Shakespeare did indeed reference threescore and ten in 'Macbeth', I believe it actually originates from the Bible," I said.

"The doctor, he believe that anyone over the seventy year is steal the extra life from the younger person," Vangelis explained.

"How absolutely bizarre," I said.

"But the Loukas believe it. He insist anyone over the seventy must to should die," Spiros said. "He was the kindest doctor, he minister very good to all the villager less than seventy year, but he much resent the people who dare to live the one day longer. He was much the vocal with his opinion. My father like him very much but he put the scare on the old people. All the people want to live to be the one hundred year but the doctor think to live the long life is the sin."

"At the seventy-five year, Athena's *yia-yia* was the picture of the good health. One day she fall sick and the doctor was call. He shout and lecture that it was her time to go, she should die so that the younger person can live," Vangelis said, making me wonder if the doctor had been wishing death on his patients in order to perchance harvest their organs or for some other nefarious purpose. Surely a learned professional could not believe such a load of old codswallop. "The *yia-yia* drop dead the two day later. The Athena swear he scare her to death."

"I wonder now the more people are to live longer, the doctor Loukas may have change his cut-off date to eighty year," Spiros speculated.

"He cannot to change his opinion," Vangelis stated emphatically. "You not to hear? The Loukas make the suicide at seventy."

"Yes, I remember now," Spiros confirmed.

"It's all most peculiar," I noted.

"Whenever anyone old to die after seeing the doctor, the villagers become more and more angry with the Loukas," Vangelis continued. "My own *yia-yia* and *pappous* refuse to see him…they were the terrify they would to drop dead if he treat them."

"And by avoiding the doctor, they both went on to live the long lifes," Spiros added.

"Did the villagers suspect the doctor of committing geronticide?"

"The what?"

"Killing the elderly."

"The many think he frighten the old into the early grave," Vangelis said.

"But the many think it was just the, how to say…"

"A coincidence" I proffered.

"Yes, the coincidence," Spiros agreed.

"So, he wasn't another Harold Shipman?"

"The who?" my guests queried in unison.

"An English doctor who went round murdering

his elderly patients by giving them lethal injections. It was headline news when he was found guilty back in 2000. They reckon he'd been at it for close to three decades."

"The villagers not to think the Doctor Loukas murder the patients with the hand on," Vangelis clarified. "They think he petrify them into the early grave."

Stifling a chuckle at such superstitious twaddle, I couldn't resist a germane sally. "Death by an unpleasant bedside manner."

"Enough of the people so angry to drive the doctor from the village," Vangelis said. "In the end, he move to one of the city hospital. His reputation in the village was ruin."

"But even if this doctor really did scare some village folk into an early grave, it doesn't explain why Athena would tar every medic with the same brush."

Spearing a ring of green pepper from the salad, Vangelis admitted, "The Athena not want to take the risk."

"You must to talk the Athena round," Spiros urged Vangelis. "The house the doctor view has been the empty many year. I can to make the good commission if I can to sell it and the renovate is the good job for the you and the Barry."

"Yes, I think I must to defy the Athena and take the job if the doctor buy the house."

Changing the subject, I commented on Spiros' newly spruced eyebrows.

"The Athena do the Spiros' eyebrow before she throw me in the dog house," Vangelis said. I made a mental note that if my eyebrows ever became unruly, I would let Athena loose with her tweezers.

"Another beer or some wine?" I offered my guests.

"No, I try to drink less the alcohol." Spiros declined my offer whilst Vangelis accepted another Amstel. I felt grateful for the change of subject. Sometimes, the superstitious leanings of some of my neighbours went far beyond the rational. Helping himself to another generous portion of *moussaka*, Spiros failed to spot the irony of serving himself seconds when he proclaimed, "I want to look the less fat when the Sampaguita return."

To be fair, Spiros had indeed trimmed down over the last year, reversing the course of what had been a burgeoning belly. He rarely missed his daily three-kilometre walk, striding along in all weathers.

"An admirable goal," I encouraged.

"I try to find the new drink for the evening when I watch the movie, but it is the difficult. The Fanta and Sprite have much the sugar."

"Have you considered switching to tea?"

"I not much to enjoy the *tsai*…"

"But you've probably only tried *tsai tou vounou*," I said, referencing the local mountain tea, the twiggy brew so despised by Violet Burke. "I have different types of tea you could try, Spiro. I'm quite partial to Early Grey myself or you could try orange and ginger."

"It is too much the work to cook the water," Spiros declared.

"Boil. You boil water, you don't cook it."

"I not want to cook the water," Spiros insisted.

"It's easy if you invest in a kettle," I assured him, adding the Greek word for kettle to avoid any confusion. "*Ena vrastira.*"

Despite electric kettles being readily available in Greece, they had failed to catch on with much of the Greek population of Meli, boiling a pan of water on a slow heating hob remaining the preferred method of heating water.

"I to get the shock of my life this the afternoon in the graveyard. I look over at the grave of Panos and think the Panos had to risen from the dead," Spiros confided.

I was grateful that Spiros had broached the topic as the arrival of Hal had been playing on my mind ever since I had encountered him in the *apothiki*. Hopefully the undertaker would be able to spill more light on the subject.

"I ran into him earlier," I revealed. "I don't mind admitting that his resemblance to Panos rather shook me. Quite uncanny. Did you know Hal before he left the village."

"No, he leave the Greece more than the fifty-year ago. This is the first time he has make the return."

"And now he's reappeared to claim his inheritance," I said. "His return could make things quite awkward for Yiota if he's got his sights set on the farm. She's been working so hard to make a go of it."

"You know this is often the way in Greece, Victor. The farm and the house belong to the Panos and this Hal both. The Yiota think she inherit the all because she not even know the brother was still the alive. Now he still live, the Hal have the right to half."

"Like the Manolis and Christos," Vangelis said. The three of us needed no reminder about the animosity that had simmered between that pair of brothers until they buried their differences to open the *kafenion*.

"I speak with the Yiota earlier," Spiros said. "She is much the happy to have the uncle come home. I advise to her to be the cautious. Right now, the Hal is the new and shiny relative to Yiota, but no one to know his character. He could to try and sell his half of the farm…"

"Leaving Yiota high and dry," I mused.

"The Giannis is not the happy," Spiros added. "I speak to him and he is not the happy. He was to thinking to ask the Yiota to move in together with him…"

"At his mother's place?"

"No, at Yiota's. But now he would be stuck living with this unknown uncle who has moved in. Giannis thinks the Yiota must to look after the Hal. If she use all the spare time to cook and clean for the uncle, she will have no time for the Giannis."

"She'll wear herself out if that's the case," I observed, wondering if Giannis would do a disappearing act in the circumstances or if he would stick around. Almost certainly he hadn't imagined a third wheel would be part of the arrangement if he and Yiota moved in together or tied the knot in marriage. "What do you know about this Hal?"

"I know he to break the parent heart when he to leave the Meli. They never know if he dead or live. When I to speak with the Hal in the graveyard, he tell me he had the wander passion…"

"Wanderlust."

"The wanderlust to travel the seas. He tell me he never to marry…"

"Did he say why he came back to Meli now?"

"He say it was the dream to retire to Meli and spend the days fishing. He know he can to live for the free with his brother in the house they inherit…"

"So, he didn't know that Panos was dead…"

"No, it was much the blow for him…"

Spiros left his sentence unfinished as his mobile trilled.

Answering the call, Spiros listened intently, a sombre look clouding his face. Leaving the table, Spiros strode over to the balcony, his words hushed as he responded to the caller. Ending the call, Spiros announced that he must leave. "That was the daughter of the Kyria Kompogiannopoulou. She find the Sophia dead in the house."

Vangelis and I immediately offered our condolences, expressing our shock at Kyria Kompogiannopoulou's unexpected demise.

"I always to think her bladder would be the death of her but the daughter say she just collapse…I must to go. I will let you know about the funeral."

With the sad news of Kyria Kompogiannopoulou's death and Spiros' early departure, the mood was melancholy as Vangelis and I tucked into our nectarine crumble. After scraping his bowl, Vangelis announced he must get back to Athena, saying his wife would need comforting if she had heard the sad news about Sophia.

Feeling pretty disconsolate myself, I decided to treat myself to a leisurely soak in the outdoor spa. I would fill the bath with bubbles and raise a glass to Sophia.

Chapter 10

A Right Sweet Tooth

As I loaded the dishwasher and cleaned up the kitchen, I reflected that the dinner had been a resounding success. Both of my guests had tucked heartily into the *moussaka*, assuring me that if they didn't know better, they would have sworn it was made by a bona fide Greek. Vangelis had been particularly delighted that for once the traditional Hellenic dish was free of hair and that the salad didn't have the distinctive taste of hair spray that routinely contaminated most of the dishes which Athena prepared in her kitchen.

Adding a generous measure of bubble bath to

the outdoor tub, I filled it with hot water by attaching the hosepipe to the bathroom tap and feeding it out of the window. Changing into my swim shorts, I hoped that my wife wouldn't use the death of Kyria Kompogiannopoulou as an excuse to splash out on a new black outfit in town the next day. I considered rifling through her wardrobe and placing a few suitable dark frocks in easy reach. Realising that Marigold would have a fit if I took such a liberty, I resisted the urge to meddle, instead pouring a glass of red wine to enjoy in the spa and grabbing the telephone in case my wife needed to contact me.

After taking the precaution of lighting both a citronella coil and a citronella candle to keep the pesky mosquitoes at bay, I emitted a sigh of pleasure as I lowered my body into the luxurious bubble bath. By now the garden was dark, and, for once, it appeared that the Albanian shed dweller wasn't lurking in the vicinity, ready to spring out at any moment and put a damper on my enjoyment. Perchance Guzim was getting an early night in before our trip to town the next morning.

Mulling over the sad death of Sophia, I smiled at the memories of the time we had served together in the village shop, recalling how we had both been carted off in a police car for opening the store on a Sunday, the occasion revealing her passion for *galaktoboureko*. She had been a kind-hearted soul who would be sorely missed in the village.

The ringing of the telephone disturbed my musings. Tempted though I was to let it ring without answering, I knew I would be in for an earful later if it was Marigold that I risked ignoring.

I was delighted that I had decided to answer when Benjamin announced down the phone, "I've got some news, Dad. Adam and I have definitely decided to go ahead with a civil partnership."

"*Bravo*," I congratulated. Ever since the UK Civil Partnership Act had come into force the previous December, my son and his life partner had been considering taking the legal plunge. The pair of them alternated between wanting to go for it or holding out in the hope that one day in the not-too-distant future, gay marriage would be legalised. "It makes sense to dot all your I's and cross all your T's."

"We were hoping that you and mum would come over for the occasion…"

"Have you set a date?"

"We were thinking September, but the month is only tentative as yet."

"We wouldn't miss it," I assured my son whilst hoping the date didn't clash with greeting new arrivals at the apartments or with my repping job: if it did, we would muddle through somehow.

"I expect that mum will be excited when you tell her about our plans," Benjamin said.

"Excited will be an understatement but I think you should call your mum now on her mobile to break the news yourself," I advised. "She really won't appreciate hearing it second-hand from me."

"Fair point," Benjamin conceded, promising to call his mum directly."

"I will look suitably surprised when she breaks the news to me," I promised, bidding my son goodbye.

Relaxing in the sea of bubbles, the darkness of the night surrounded me like a warm blanket as I ruminated that if Benjamin and Adam went ahead with their plans, it would be the second occasion of the year necessitating a trip back to England to celebrate nuptial rites. Cringing at the recollection of the first occasion, I felt certain that the boys' event would in no way resemble the brash display of vulgarity that I had been dragged along to by Violet Burke.

True to her word, my mother had shelled out for the flights back to England and for a night in a hotel to mark the occasion of Kevin's wedding. It was nothing more than a flying visit since we had a flight back to Athens booked directly after the wedding. Vi had been keen to stay a tad longer but the cost of the flights practically quadrupled in price from the next day and my mother wasn't one for frittering her cash on unnecessary expenses. Since I had no desire to linger in Warrington, a one-night stay suited me fine.

Although Dot had invited us to stay at hers, the place was already chock-a-block with Kevin and Chardonnay Billings bedding down in what had been Kevin's bedroom, and that little tyke, Tyrone, filling the tiny box room. As soon as we had landed and checked into our hotel on the evening before the wedding, Violet Burke insisted we drive straight over to Dot's place in the hire car since she was eager to catch up with her old friend.

"'Appen we can do a trolley dash round Tesco on our way to the wedding tomorrow," Vi suggested, desperate to replenish her dwindling supplies of tinned Spam, and Fray Bentos steak and kidney. By now, my own tastes had acclimatised to the healthier Greek diet and I could happily live without what had once been English essentials. Saying that, I still had a yen for a tasty Tesco silver skin pickle.

"As long as a trip to Tesco doesn't make us tardy," I agreed. It really wouldn't do to turn up late at the wedding and risk drawing unnecessary attention to ourselves. I mentally crossed my fingers that my mother wouldn't get too carried away in Tesco and go over the top. Even though she had paid for our jaunt to England, I just knew I would be the one responsible for forking out for any excess baggage fees.

Spotting a newsagent's shop en route to Dot's,

my mother told me to pull over. "I need to get some sweets for Kevin. The lad's got a right sweet tooth."

"What is he? Five-years old." My quip earned me a withering look, making me miss Marigold.

Returning to the car with her handbag bulging, my mother's annoyance was forgotten. "That place was just like Rita's Kabin on Corrie. You don't get sweet shops like that in Greece. I got Kevin some Caramac bars and a handful of sherbet dib dabs..."

"The ones with the liquorice?"

"That's the ones. Here, I got your Marigold some Parma violets." Thrusting a small paper bag under my nose, Vi announced, "I reckoned you're the mint imperial sort."

"How well you know me." Mint imperials were most definitely right up my street.

The warm welcome we received from Dot was almost drowned out by the over excited antics of Chardonnay's now four-year-old, chocolate-smeared son, Tyrone. I surmised that the combination of too many sweeties and too many E numbers might be responsible for the boy's out-of-control behaviour as he bounced up and down on the sofa before launching himself across the room, landing on and almost flattening Dot's ancient looking sausage dog.

"Tyrone, put a sock in it and get off Chips before you do him some damage." Shrugging by way of apology, Dot said, "I'm stuck with the little bugger. I promised Chardonnay that I'd babysit while she's off on her hen-night."

"Oh, have we missed her?" I didn't bother to hide my evident relief.

"The little madam's only gone and stuffed Tyrone full of lollies and chocolate before she left. I reckon she's done it out of spite because I refused to let her put Chips in a red tutu tomorrow. She had a fancy to dress the dog up as a ring bearer but now she's roped Tyrone into doing it instead. Chardonnay's only gone and kitted him out like some posh-boy Little Lord Fauntleroy in some poxy, red velvet, page boy outfit."

"He won't look posh with that snotty nose," Vi remarked. "I suppose it was too much to expect that Chardonnay to teach the nipper how to use a hankie."

"Well, I reckon he's going to look a right little ponce," Dot said with a heavy sigh. "Them lads on the estate will make his life a misery if they spot him all done up like a toff."

"At least with Chardonnay off on her hen night, we're spared putting up with the little scrubber this evening," Vi said. "No doubt she'll be right full of herself tomorrow when she gets your Kevin's ring on her finger."

"She's not all bad, Vi, considering that rubbish family she came from."

"'Appen you're right, Dot. It must take a lot of

living down, being a Billings. We shouldn't blame the lass for the horrible stock she comes from."

Although Dot's home was exceedingly clean and as neat as a pin, I couldn't help but notice some nasty orange smears on the pink cushions and the gold dralon sofa. Thinking perchance Chardonnay had been stuffing Tyrone full of Terry's chocolate oranges, I realised Dot would have her work cut out vanquishing the nasty stains. Noticing that I was distracted, Dot followed my eye.

"How many times do I have to tell that Chardonnay not to sit on the sofa in her fake tan?" Removing the covers from the cushions, Dot chuntered, "I can't fathom why the lass felt the need to add another layer of the stuff. She spent all afternoon down the tanning salon. 'Appen she'll look like the orange man off the Tango ad by tomorrow."

Dot's reference to Tango man reminded me of how I had been forced into a gruesome orange uniform when I first started repping.

"I'd better give our Kevin a shout or he'll be late for his stag do," Dot said before yelling up the stairs, "Here, Kevin, get your backside down here sharpish, lad. Your Aunty Vi's here for a visit. She's come all the way from that Greece."

"All right, keep your hair on, Mam. I'll be down in a tick."

"Is the wedding going to be a big do?" I asked Dot.

"There's a nice church ceremony planned. It's the same vicar what christened my Kevin…"

"That vicar with the problem?" Vi gave Dot a meaningful look.

"Aye. I just hope he can manage to stay sober for long enough to pronounce them husband and wife. Then, after the church bit is out of the way, that nightmare Edna Billings has gone and hired a room at the local working men's club. She reckoned they'd save some money if she put on the spread herself. She's catering what she's calling a Buff-Et."

"Pretentious cow," Vi scoffed.

"A Buff-Et," I chortled, the ridiculous pronunciation inspiring fond memories of when Nikos had mixed up his canapés with a canopy at Barry and Cynthia's wedding reception. "No doubt washed down with cans of lager."

"I can't say that I'm surprised that Edna Billings has never heard of a buffet, she's more of the hoovering up from a trough kind," Vi mocked just as Kevin bounded downstairs.

Dot's son was a lanky beanpole with a mop of greasy brown hair falling over his eyes and a rash of rather nasty looking pimples garnishing his chin. The loud Hawaiian shirt Kevin had paired with jeans featured garish tropical fruits, a walking testimony to his apparent lack of clothes sense.

"Aunty Vi," Kevin cried in a high-pitched voice as Violet Burke swept the young man into a bear hug. "Ooh, you've got me my favourites," he squawked, immediately cramming a Caramac bar into his mouth.

"You're not going out in public in that horrible shirt." Vi's disapproval echoed my thoughts.

"The lads are all wearing them," Kevin protested.

"'Appen you'll just blend into the crowd then," Vi suggested. "How many of you are off on this stag do, then?"

"Me, Todd and Wayne."

"What, just the three of you? Is that the best you could manage? 'Appen my Victor could tag along to make up the numbers?"

"That would be great." There was no doubting Kevin's genuine enthusiasm for the idea. "I've got a spare Hawaiian."

"I think I'll sit this one out, but thanks for the invitation."

"Don't be such a misery guts, Victor. The lad's getting wed tomorrow and he deserves a proper send off."

"He won't want me cramping his style," I argued. "Anyway, I'm dead on my feet after all that travelling."

"'Appen you're right. They're young lads, after all, and you're a bit of a prude."

"Guilty as charged," I agreed, happy to be labelled a killjoy if it meant avoiding a tacky evening full of strippers, an evening that perchance may culminate in a naked Kevin being tied to a lamp post. To be honest, I was pretty clueless as to what the youngsters got up to these days.

"You'd be right welcome, Mr Bucket," Kevin reiterated. Looking like an overgrown schoolboy about to blub, he shoved another Caramac bar in his gob. At the rate he was devouring chocolate bars, his pimples would likely have bred another batch by the morning. There could be a lethal explosion of gunk if Chardonnay's piercing hit an engorged spot as they kissed at the altar.

"Now, don't go getting too plastered tonight or staying out till all hours," Vi advised, ruffling Kevin's hair.

"Your Aunty Vi is right. You'll be needing your wits about you in the church tomorrow."

"It's all right, Mam. I've been practising my 'I do.'"

Spotting Kevin's nerves, I decided to offer him some advice.

"I wasn't much older than you when I tied the knot with Marigold and we've been wed for almost forty years now…"

"Talk like that will have the lad doing a runner," Vi interrupted. "Who in their right mind wants to spend the next forty years saddled with Chardonnay Billings?"

Drawing himself up to his full height and squaring his shoulders, Kevin announced in a firm tone, "I do." I have to say I had nothing but admiration for the way in which Kevin stood up for his bride-to-be; there's not many folk brave enough to stand up to Violet Burke. "I still can't believe a right pretty lass like Chardonnay said yes to me."

"Well, you did put her in the pudding club." There was no end to my mother's lack of tact.

"What's the pudding club?" Tyrone yelled.

"Never you mind," Vi snapped.

"Are we having jelly?"

"How about we have a nice chippy tea?" Dot offered.

"With jelly," Tyrone persisted, wiping his runny nose on his hand and then smearing said hand along the length of the sausage dog.

"Here, Mam, I forgot to tell you. Chardonnay's getting the keys to that council flat next Friday so we'll be moving out."

Dot immediately burst into tears at the news that her only son would be leaving home, proclaiming between sobs, "I'm going to miss you that much, our Kevin."

"It's all right, Mam. I'll be back every time that I have a row with Chardonnay or whenever anyone from the council is on the snoop. The lease is only in her name and she's not telling the council that we're getting wed."

"Is she ashamed of you, lad? And her as common as muck," Vi said.

"No, she just doesn't want them knowing or it will bugger up the benefits she gets as a single mum," Kevin explained.

"You might be losing your Kevin, Dot, but at least you'll be shot of that noisy little bugger," Vi crowed, pointing at young Tyrone who was taunting Chips by dangling a Caramac bar in front of the sausage dog and then yanking it out of reach. It was clear that Vi was just itching to clip young Tyrone round the head. "And don't forget that Chardonnay could pop out that sprog any minute. You won't want to be stuck with a screaming baby, Dot. It'd drive you nuts."

Violet Burke appeared oblivious that her remark was in very poor taste considering that she had chosen to dump me in a bucket at the railway station: perchance I had driven her nuts by bawling as babies do.

"I just hope that the baby doesn't come tomorrow and mess up the wedding," Dot said, sniffing mightily into her hanky. "It's already nearly a month overdue and Chardonnay is right adamant that she won't be induced. She'd expected to have dropped the sprog and got her figure back by now. Instead, she's going to be waddling to the altar like an inflatable duck."

"I'd best be off, Mam," Kevin said, giving Dot a kiss on the cheek.

"Don't get up to anything too daft," Dot advised

as he left for his stag do. "Right, who's in the mood for a nice bit of battered cod with some mushy peas?"

"With jelly." It appeared that Tyrone was another one that was keen on always having the last word.

Chapter 11

Living it up in Spain

The sound of something singeing combined with the slight smell of burning momentarily distracted me from the memories of Dot's son's wedding flooding my mind. Pulling myself into an upright position, I watched as a moth flitted too close to the citronella candle, its wings brushing against the lighted wick. Feeling too comfortably content to shift my position and damper the wick, I continued to soak in the outside spa, running more details of the trip back to Warrington through my mind.

On the day of the wedding, Violet Burke had

been up at the crack of dawn; demanding we get an early start, she reminded me that we needed to dash to Tesco before arriving at church. The church had been booked for ten in the morning, apparently a necessary precaution; any later in the day and there was a good chance that the vicar would be too blathered to perform in an upright position. Reduced to downing a nasty cup of instant coffee in the hotel bedroom since the dining room hadn't yet opened for breakfast, I was slowly losing patience with my mother's incessant wittering.

"You look like you're heading to a funeral rather than a wedding, lad. That black suit's a bit doom and gloom. I suppose it's a hangover from your public inspection days."

Rather than confirm that my suit was indeed one that I had worn during my illustrious career, I attempted to look enigmatic. In contrast, my mother was once again done up in the overly tight, vibrant lemon frock that she insisted on calling her Jackie O, last flaunted at our vow renewal service. The dress was once again paired with the matching pillbox hat featuring dangling plastic grapes. Violet Burke's outfit was so bright that it dazzled, making me reach for my sunglasses.

"Pairing those glasses with that suit makes you look like a mafia don," Vi opined.

"Well, with a bit of luck, a menacing look should keep that ghastly Billings' lot at a distance,"

I retorted, dragging the cases along to the hire car. Whatever her many faults, I was glad that my mother wasn't one of those women who insist on spending hours tarting themselves up for a wedding. Content to plonk the pillbox on her head, there hadn't been even a hint of Violet Burke demanding the services of a hairdresser.

"Ooh, it's a bit nippy out here," Vi complained, rubbing her goosepimples as a gust of wind swept her hat across the car park. "Be a good lad..."

"I'm on it," I called, chasing after the pillbox and rescuing it just before it landed in a puddle.

"I'd clean forgot about how miserable the Warrington weather gets," Vi bemoaned. "'Appen we're a bit spoilt in Greece."

"That we are," I agreed, wiping her hat down as it began to rain. By the time I'd loaded the cases into the car, it was fairly bucketing it down, hardly an auspicious sign for a wedding day.

Heading to Tesco, I concentrated on driving on the left whilst my mother mithered on in my ear about wedding stuff.

"Dot reckons that Chardonnay is going for the glamorous look..."

"Does that mean the rusty tongue piercing will be coming out? I take it that Chardonnay won't be exchanging vows in her pyjamas," I quipped. Even though I had only met the bride-to-be once, she had made a lasting impression, pushing her trolley around Tesco in her nightwear. "Let's hope that young Kevin discards the Hawaiian theme for the wedding."

"He only had that on for the stag. He's more of an anorak type in general. Dot said Kevin's getting wed in red. Chardonnay picked out his suit. She fancied them matching."

"So, she's not wearing white?"

"I should hope not. She's hardly going to kid anyone she's a virgin bride with that bump on display. Dot showed me the dress last night; it's a bit on the brazen hussy side."

"How so?"

"She's getting wed in a skin tight red mini."

"Well, we can only hope that Chardonnay is so brazen-faced that she doesn't blush or she'll clash with her dress."

Pulling into Tesco's car park, my mother tied a plastic rain mate over the top of her pillbox. "I hear tell these are coming back in fashion."

"You don't happen to have a spare one?" After spending much of my glittering career wearing a hair net, I had no qualms about showcasing a plastic rain mate in the supermarket. Alas, despite rummaging through her ginormous handbag, Vi failed to come up with a spare.

Entering the store with my mother, I experienced a sense of deja-vu. Once again on a mission to fill the trolley with all the essentials that were lacking in Greek supermarkets, Violet Burke raced around as though the trolley was a Formula One racing car. My senses were overwhelmed by the sheer volume of choice, the battle of the brands evident. After the relative paucity of options filling Greek supermarket shelves, I felt the abundance on display in Tesco to be a tad over the top.

"Ooh look, Victor. Olives. Do you want to take some back home for your Marigold? You know how she loves them."

"There's no point in taking coals to Newcastle."

"But these olives aren't Greek," my mother argued.

"Which means they are inferior to our local ones which are renowned as the best in the world."

"You sound just like that Nikos. He's always banging on about Greek stuff being the best. Ooh, look, Victor. They've got that Greek yoghurt."

"It's not Greek yoghurt, Mother. It's Greek style. Hardly the same thing at all."

"Chuck me a few boxes of that PG Tips, Victor. I can't see any of that twig muck.

"Tsai tou vounou."

"Aye. I reckon it's got a fat chance of catching on over here."

"The twigs would probably pierce the bags," I joked.

Restricting my own selection to a couple of jars of silver skin onions left plenty of space in the trolley for Vi's many must-haves. I must confess though, as soon as her back was turned, I sneaked some of her heavier items back on the shelves, noting her tendency to prefer weighty tinned food to fresh. Fortunately, the dried marrowfat peas she bought to transform into mushy peas would be virtually weightless by the time I discarded their cardboard boxes and siphoned the peas off into a plastic bag to chuck in the suitcase. Boxes of peas were soon nestling side by side in the trolley with Vi's perennial favourites of Fray Bentos, salad cream, and malt vinegar. Watching my mother lob a couple of heavy tins of Tate & Lyle black treacle into the trolley made my mouth water in anticipation of her home-made parkin. Nobody makes a parkin as good as my mother. I would even venture that her parkin was worth any excess baggage fees.

Done up in her wedding finery, Violet Burke definitely stood out, attracting some strange looks from the other shoppers. However, she had honed her ability to ignore them down to a fine art. Anyone that gawped just a moment too long was painfully rewarded as she wheeled the full weight of the trolley over their toes.

"Here, if it isn't Violet Burke." A short, drab woman with a sour expression accosted my mother by placing a hand on her arm.

"Madge, two meat and potato pies with extra chips and a serving of curry sauce on the side," Violet

Burke responded to the woman, shaking the hand off her arm.

"I heard tell that you'd upped sticks to somewhere hot and exotic."

"That's right. I'm living it up in Spain now."

I interpreted the warning look that my mother shot in my direction as a clear instruction: *don't dare contradict me.*

Violet Burke obviously had her own reasons for not choosing to share her private business with this Madge person.

"So, what are you doing back here?"

"I'm just over for Dot's lad's wedding."

"Her Kevin?"

"That's the one."

"He must be all grown up now if he's getting wed. Who's the lad getting hitched to?"

"Chardonnay Billings."

"Ooh, dear. He's wedding trouble, then." Madge's sour expression morphed into one that was almost gleeful, her eyes lighting up at the prospect of some juicy gossip. "I wouldn't fancy my lad getting mixed up with that motley crew."

"It is what it is. With Kevin being a right sensible lad, I'm inclined to give the lass a chance."

"Not much else you can do," Madge reluctantly agreed.

"I'd best be getting on. This trolley won't fill itself."

"I don't half miss you and Dot down the chippy…"

"Mardy old cow," Vi muttered under her breath, wheeling the trolley away. "You know summat, Victor? I reckon moving to Greece has given me a whole new lease of life. If I'd stopped over here after the chippy shut down, I might have ended up as miserable as that Madge, with nowt better to do but tear other folk down."

"Well, you've had plenty to say about Chardonnay Billings yourself," I pointed out.

"Aye, but I have to trust that young Kevin knows what he's doing. Anyhow, even if he's making the biggest mistake of his life today, it's not the end of the world. I mean, I've got through four husbands and I've lived to tell the tale." Steering the trolley towards the checkout, Vi said, "Right, this lot will have to do or we'll be late for the wedding."

Winking at my mother, I kept a straight face as I teased, "And don't forget, we need to transfer this lot into the suitcases before we fly back to Spain."

Parking up at the church, I saw a young woman walking towards the vestibule in a poufy white, ball gown style dress.

"Hurry up, Mother," I urged. "It looks as though the bride is already here."

"I've no idea who that is but it's definitely not

Chardonnay Billings. 'Appen there's another wedding this morning. That Billings' lot will have the vicar if he's gone and cocked up the timings."

No sooner had I parked than Dot came running over to the car, calling out, "Vi, we need your help. We've got a right emergency on our hands."

"Has your Kevin not come home from his stag?"

"No, it's not that. Kevin's here. He's out back with his best man, Wayne. The emergency is Chardonnay's feet. She's back in the vestry and her feet are that swollen that she can't manage to shove them into her shoes. She's that desperate, like. She'd picked out these lovely red patent leather stilettos…"

"I thought she was ten months pregnant," I blurted, thinking Chardonnay's choice of shoes sounded most unsuitable for a woman in her condition.

"That's why her feet are all swelled up, you muppet." Vi rolled her eyes before turning to Dot and barking, "What do you expect me to do about it?"

"Well, I reckoned that with all your experience of suffering from swollen feet, you'd know how to handle it." Dot sounded increasingly desperate.

"Don't go getting your knickers in a twist, Dot. I've got an idea," Vi volunteered. "Victor, get my case open. I might have nicked a pair of them fluffy white backless slippers from the hotel."

"Might have?" I queried. "You either did or you didn't."

"'Appen I did," Vi confessed, rummaging through her case. "I suppose I could give Chardonnay a lend of these."

"They'll be better than nothing," Dot eagerly agreed, grabbing the slippers and sending a thumbs up in the direction of the bridesmaid waiting in the vestibule. "It's either these or her going barefoot. 'Appen they'll go all right with her dress; it looks like a baby doll nightie."

"There was nowt baby doll about that red frock you showed me last night." Vi frowned in confusion.

"Aye, well, that turned out to be a bit of a disaster. Chardonnay's bump got in the way of the zipper fastening. We tried sticking clothes pegs on the back but it gaped open so wide it was hopeless."

"So, what's she ended up wearing?" Vi asked.

"She'd got this sexy white nylon nightie thing for the wedding night, so she's wearing that. This lot of muppets are bound to think it's silk. It's a bit on the risqué side but what else could the lass do? Luckily, we managed to keep her dry getting her into the church. If she'd got drenched, the nightie would have ended up being see-through." Dot was nothing if not pragmatic, a trait she shared with Violet Burke. "It was wishful thinking, Chardonnay reckoning she could squeeze into the red. She thought for sure she'd have dropped the bump by today but she's well overdue."

"Well, let's just hope she doesn't drop it before she gets to say 'I do'. I can't be flying over again if you have to postpone," my mother insisted. "I've got people relying on me back in Meli."

"Ooh, I know. That lot of lazy expats that you clean for wouldn't know one end of a feather duster if it tickled them in the face," Dot sympathised.

As Dot disappeared with the hotel's purloined slippers, I watched as some of the other guests began to arrive. Not wishing to sound unduly snobbish, there was no denying they were a right old shower of chavs. A handful of men in shiny nylon tracksuits appeared to have modelled their fashion choices after Jimmy Savile: they seemed to be under the deluded notion that an ostentatious display of chunky gold chains elevated their casual attire into dressed for the occasion.

A bevy of young women trailed behind them in skin tight mini dresses that emphasised every bulge. Their orange complexions and matching bare legs made me think that fake tan must be all the rage in Warrington. It occurred to me that having a tan, even a patently fake one, was ironically seen as desirable in Warrington which lacked consistent sunshine, whereas in the Mani, the young Greek women who could take advantage of months of free sunshine, favoured the pale look and wouldn't be caught dead sun bathing.

I recognised Edna Billings from the time she had catcalled insults at me from the doorway of her council flat: surprisingly, she had ditched the pink shell suit for her granddaughter's wedding, instead pouring her flabby frame into a lurid puce frock so tight that it appeared as if her chest was in danger of escaping the bodice, the seams threatening to burst open at any moment. Moreover, the dreadful Billings' woman had trowelled on so much makeup that she looked like a clown.

"That Edna Billings looks like mutton dressed as lamb," I said to my mother. "Though, in truth, the phrase does any random muttons a disservice."

"You're more on the mark than you know, lad."

"How so?"

"Mutton's slang for a prossie. I know it's hard to credit that anyone would pay that Billings' woman for a feel but there's long been rumours of her being on the game."

Demonstrating a complete lack of respect for the church setting, Edna Billings was embroiled in a full-on slanging match with a much younger, skinny chap, done up like the Fonz in a leather jacket with greased back hair. Taking a break from the slew of expletives they were slinging at each other, the greaser pulled Edna Billings in for a smacker. I felt personally affronted by their crude display: not only was the churchyard setting a totally inappropriate venue for a coarse grab a granny public performance, I still felt the sting of Edna Billings referring to me as Violet Burke's toyboy. When the greaser finally unhanded her to light a cigarette, I noticed he appeared to be as toothless as Guzim.

I was still surveying the guests when Kevin came dashing over. My initial impression was that the groom looked surprisingly smart in his red wedding suit, his flopping fringe no longer greasy. Admittedly, the overall image was somewhat marred by the suppurating pimples on his chin and the profusion of Dachshund sausage dogs emblazoning his vibrant yellow tie.

"I've a favour to ask, Mr Bucket," Kevin hesitantly began.

"Say no more," I replied, already loosening my tie. As an unknown guest with no skin in the game, I was more than happy to go tie-less if it meant that Kevin could ditch his own joke of a cartoon tie in favour of something more formal. Naturally, my own grey silk tie was an impeccable choice for a church wedding.

"Really?" Kevin was so obviously grateful for my ready agreement that I expected him to do a Guzim and prostrate himself on the floor and grab my shin. "Mam reckoned you might be a bit reluctant to take over at short notice."

"Take over?" *What on earth was the lad talking*

about, I wondered. "I thought you wanted to borrow my tie."

"Course not. Me mam picked this doggie one out; it's brill. Me Mam reckons it looks the business. I need you to stand in as my best man, Mr Bucket." The plea of desperation in Kevin's tone was unmistakable. "Wayne's too hungover to do his best man duties. He's throwing up round the back."

"You want me to be your best man?" The notion was completely ludicrous. Traditionally, the role of best man should be served by a relative or a close friend, neither of which I could claim to be having never met Kevin until the day before. More to the point, I had no desire to thrust myself into a prominent role when the bride's side of the church would likely be filled with a bunch of tanked-up thugs. As Dot reappeared at Kevin's side, I tried to get out of it by pointing out that I didn't have a speech prepared.

"That's all right, lad," Dot assured me. "That Billings' lot won't want to hear someone droning on with a speech for too long. It'll only eat into their precious scoffing and drinking time. Summat short and off the cuff will do the job nicely."

"What about Todd? Surely, he'd be more suitable," I said, recalling the name of the third Hawaiian.

"He's not chucked up yet but he will if he has to speak in public," Kevin said.

"Todd's always been right timid, right from being a nipper," Dot chimed in. "I reckon there's no one else for the job but you, Victor. He'd have asked his aunty Violet but he can't go having his aunty as his best man."

"Why not?" It struck me as an eminently sensible solution.

"'Cos I'm not a man, you plonker." Vi rolled her eyes.

Finding it hard to resist Dot's wheedling, I reluctantly agreed to stand in as Kevin's best man, assured that my duties would entail nothing more onerous than standing by the young man's side at the altar, handing over the rings, and saying a few brief words at the reception. Looking on the bright side, I reasoned there was no guarantee that anything would actually go wrong.

Chapter 12

Flapping down the Aisle

"There's no need to be nervous," I reassured Kevin as he sweated beside me at the altar, a fine sheen of perspiration covering his by-now pulsating purple pimples. "You're about to marry the girl of your dreams."

"What if Chard changes her mind and does a runner?" Kevin rubbed his pimples vigorously as he spoke. I took a step backwards in case the rubbing motion prompted a suppurating explosion.

"I doubt she'll be able to run very far in her condition," I quipped as Kevin used the sausage dog tie to mop the sweat from his brow. "Ah, here come the bridesmaids now."

A couple of overweight young women in frumpy green dresses headed down the aisle, one of them sending a daggers drawn look at Dot when she loudly hissed to Vi, "Chardonnay made a point of asking her least attractive friends to be bridesmaids."

"She's not daft," Vi hissed back. "'Appen the lass didn't want anyone stealing the limelight on her wedding day."

Glancing around at the guests, I considered the bride's side of the church resembled a veritable clown show. Amazingly, Violet Burke could probably win the accolade of best dressed in her Jackie O and matching pillbox. As the mother-of-the-groom, Dot could have toned down the brash leopard skin look but then again, she was such a fan of Corrie that she may have been deliberately trying to emulate Bet Lynch's style. As the little rascal, Tyrone, tripped down the aisle behind the bridesmaids, I noticed Dot was moved to tears: it was hard to know if she was tearing up because she was about to lose a son or because she was about to gain a Billings.

As Dot had feared, Tyrone did indeed look like a right little ponce, done up in a red velvet number comprised of knickerbockers, a waistcoat, and a lopsided bow tie. Whilst the outfit may have looked cute on a cherubic child, it made Tyrone look like a little ruffian. It seemed a pity that no one had thought to rub a wet rag over his chocolate-smeared mouth. As he made his way down the aisle, he lobbed rather than scattered white daisies, presumably doubling up as a flower girl. Unashamedly using the bow tie to wipe his snotty nose, the resultant stain didn't quite match the one on the seat of his knickerbockers: I suspected he'd picked up the latter one from sitting in pigeon droppings.

"She's coming." Kevin gave me a sharp nudge in the ribs as Edna Billings started to walk Chardonnay down the aisle. I assumed that granny was standing in because all of Chardonnay's male relatives were banged up in prison. With her feet encumbered by the too-large backless fluffy slippers, the bride didn't so much float as flap down the aisle. If it wasn't for the veil flowing from the back of her head to the floor, giving her a decidedly bridal look, the combination of slippers and the baby-doll nightie might have made her look like she was off to bed.

The Fonz character lowered the tone by marking Chardonnay's entrance with a crude wolf-whistle, earning him a clip round the ear from Edna Billings as she passed his pew. The bride was halfway down the aisle when a couple of late arrivals sped past her, one of them almost yanking the veil from her head and clumsily leaving wet footprints on her lace train.

With Chardonnay and Kevin facing each other at the altar, I couldn't fail to notice that the bride looked very pretty: she'd clearly made more effort with her appearance for the wedding than she had for a casual trip to Tesco. Her long blonde hair had been brushed till it shone and there was no evidence of the gruesome piercing in her tongue that I had found so offensive. I thought Chardonnay's most attractive feature was the misty look in her eyes when Kevin took hold of her hands, a look that I interpreted as one of love even though Marigold has me down as an old cynic.

The vicar hiccupped his way through the service. Although the clergyman did a passable impression of being sober, his alcohol fuelled breath belied his actual sobriety. When he asked if anyone had any objections to the joining of the two people in front of him, there was a collective holding in of breath as though the gathered congregation expected someone to pipe up with a juicy objection at any moment. Thankfully, no one objected, giving the green light to the wedding progressing.

As the bride and groom exchanged their vows, I was grateful that my role of best man hadn't involved anything more taxing than calming Kevin's nerves, thus far at least. My self-congratulatory pat on the back proved to have been a tad pre-emptive when the time came to hand the rings over and I realised that Kevin had neglected to entrust them to me.

As Kevin scrambled through his pockets in search of the rings, Chardonnay hissed at him, "Who the heck is your best man, Kev. I've never seen him before. He looks like a taxman."

"Actually, we met in Tesco once…" I ventured.

"It's Mr Bucket. He's with my aunty Vi. I needed a replacement for Wayne right sharpish. He's still chucking up outside."

"Do you have the rings?" the vicar prompted, his patience visibly wearing thin.

"Our Tyrone's got the rings," Chardonnay suddenly remembered. "Where's he got to? Where are you, our Tyrone?"

"He was bored," Dot piped up. "'Appen he went outside to kick a football around or summat."

"I'm on it," I volunteered before dashing down the aisle in search of the little scallywag, lest anyone should accuse me of failing to take my best man duties seriously. Heading outside, I looked for the child, hoping he hadn't legged it to the nearest pawn shop to make a quick bob on the rings.

Spotting the child chucking stones at a loft of pigeons, I marched over to him and demanded he hand over the rings.

"Won't," Tyrone refused. "You can't make me."

I hadn't expected to have to deal with a bolshie four-year-old.

"But I need to give the rings to your mum and Kevin."

"'Appen I'll feed them to the birds," Tyrone retorted. Pulling the gold wedding bands from his pocket, the child taunted me by aiming them at the nearest pigeon.

"Just hand them over," I demanded.

"What's in it for me?" Tyrone had the cheek to ask. I could barely credit the nerve of this anything but innocent child holding me over a barrel.

"I'll swap them for these sweets," I bargained. Handing over the paper bag of mint imperials that Vi had given me the day before, I hoped that the extortive little rascal would choke on them.

"And a fiver. I want cash."

"You drive a hard bargain," I grumbled.

Handing over a five euro note, I smirked, having finally bested the little extortionist. Tyrone would be in for a shock when he discovered the money would be less than useless in the local sweet shop: I was pretty certain it would only accept pounds sterling rather than foreign notes.

Dashing back into the church with the rings, I cursed Dot for nixing Chardonnay's idea that the sausage dog, Chips, should act as the ring bearer. At least the dog wouldn't have shaken me down for a bribe.

It seemed to take an age for Kevin to shove the ring on Chardonnay's swollen finger; I could have sworn the bride was visibly ballooning in front of me, a ballooning I put down to her pregnant energy. When the vicar announced that Kevin could kiss his bride, the pair of them engaged in what could only be described as a prolonged snog more suited to the back-row of the cinema than to a church. With the show over, there was a practical stampede as the guests legged it to the working men's club for a booze up.

Even though it was still well before noon when we arrived at the reception venue, the drink was already flowing freely. I must confess that being amidst such an uncouth bunch, I felt a bit on guard, all too aware that I stood out like a sore thumb with no chance of fitting in. Indeed, I felt more of a foreigner than I ever had in Greece.

Moreover, I had the added responsibility of coming up with a best man's speech on short notice. The wicked idea of doing the speech in Greek crossed my mind but it didn't seem fair to young Kevin who had already made a point of seeking me out to thank me for retrieving the rings. Gauging that Kevin seemed to be an all-round good egg, I could only hope that his alliance with the Billings' clan didn't turn him into a scrambled mess.

Approaching the crowded bar to secure a couple of glasses of what appeared to be knock-off

Asti spumante for my mother and Dot, I spotted the girl done up in the poufy white ballgown. "Dot, why's that girl dressed up like that? She looks more bridal than the bride."

"That's Danielle. She's got a right nerve turning up here. Chardonnay will be that livid if she spots her. That Danielle's got a thing for our Kevin. He used to knock around with her but he dumped her when he took up with Chardonnay. He reckoned Danielle was as mad as a hatter."

"She must be looney tunes all right," Vi agreed. "Fancy turning up at someone else's wedding in a dress like that. Look at her making cow eyes at your Kev."

It was hard to imagine that Kevin was such a babe magnet. He was hardly a looker and he didn't have a muscle to his name. He struck me as shy and unassuming, and he certainly had nice manners.

Accepting their fizzy wine, Dot and Violet Burke disappeared together in search of a toilet. Mindful that I would need to drive to the airport later, I sipped a glass of sparkling water, attempting to make myself as inconspicuous as possible by blending into the wall to one side of the buffet table, the guests more interested in booze than food. Call me a snob, but I really didn't fancy engaging with any of the Billings' clan: I found them too vulgar for words and the pews had hardly been overflowing on Kevin's side of the church. Apart from Wayne,

Todd, and the possibly deranged ex-girlfriend, it appeared that Kevin was a bit of a Billy no-mates.

My hope to go unnoticed was thwarted when I spotted Kevin pointing me out to a young man who immediately made a point of seeking me out. As the sallow, pimply youth joined me, I noticed his Hawaiian shirt was marked by a visible trail of dried vomit, indicating my new companion was the original best man, Wayne, his loud and fruity shirt hinting he perchance hadn't made it home the previous night. Shaking his clammy hand, I instantly assured him that I would have no problem if he wished to resume his role of best man.

"I can't, I'm going to chuck up again any minute. I reckon I must have had a dodgy kebab last night." I took the precaution of taking a couple of steps back from Wayne, just in case he hurled: there was no way I was going to risk being the target of projectile vomit. Handing over a scrumpled piece of paper, Wayne added, "Kev reckoned you might need a lend of my speech…"

Wayne's face turned visibly green as he spoke and he scarpered at speed before he could complete his sentence. Scanning the paper which he'd passed me, I found it difficult to make head or tail of his almost illegible scrawl, though the gist of his speech appeared to comprise some rather lame jokes about Chardonnay being up the duff and this being a shotgun wedding. The rather pathetic joke was followed by a comment that Wayne could see how surprised all the guests looked by the news that the bride was no longer a virgin. It was hardly original stuff and there was certainly nothing down on paper that I felt comfortable borrowing for my own speech. I could only hope that Kevin would forget about it.

Casting my eyes over the buffet table, I noticed it positively groaned under the weight of an unappetising brown spread featuring some rather pallid sausage rolls and greasy looking Warrington eggs in the starring role. Potted meat, Spam, and corn beef sandwiches with stale looking crusts rubbed shoulders; bowls of salt and vinegar crisps vying for attention with curly cheese Wotsits and pork scratchings, the chunks of cheese on the cheese and pineapple sticks a bit green around the edges, a clear sign of mould.

The tangy aroma of vinegar drew my attention to the pickled gherkins. Attracted as I am to a sharp pickle, the large pickled onions on offer were suspiciously discoloured, indicating they were on the turn and a likely carrier of botulism. Alas, there wasn't a single Tesco silver skin to tempt me. The piece de resistance was the wedding cake composed of three Battenberg cakes sloppily piled on top of one another and held together with an uneven layer of jam, topped with wedding toppers in the form of a plastic bride and groom.

Still attempting to be as inconspicuous as I could, I watched as the little squirt, Tyrone, made a beeline for the cheesy Wotsits. Unaware that I was clocking his every move, he crammed a fistful of the corn puffs into his mouth before grabbing a handful of crisps. His tongue lingered as he licked the salt and vinegar flavouring from the crisps before chucking them back in the bowl, turning it into a veritable Petri dish of bacteria. Suddenly realising that he was being observed, the boy snatched the plastic bride and groom from atop the wedding cake. Sticking his tongue out at me, he ran off with his illicit bounty.

My low-profile cover was blown when Edna Billings sidled up to me carrying a large platter of individual pork pies.

"I can tell that you're that impressed with my spread, lad. Can you credit that I fixed all the grub myself? The price them caterers wanted was right shocking. Shocking as in daylight robbery, I tell you. Our Chardonnay had her heart set on something right posh like a sit-down chicken Kiev, but I told her straight, 'I'll do you a Buff-Et that will do you proud, lass, and there'll be none of that garlic muck.'"

Looking at the manky looking platter of pork pies rather grandly topped with a few sprigs of parsley that Edna Billings was adding to the table, I thought that I would rather chow down on Nikos' canopy than take a bite of anything that had come out of the Billings' woman's kitchen.

"Imagine the bride stinking of garlic." Edna Billings was off on another rant. "I told Chardonnay straight, 'Chardonnay,' I said, 'you won't be getting any tongue action with Kevin on your wedding night if he gets a whiff of your garlic breath.'"

"Hmm," I muttered, appalled at the crassness of this dreadful woman voicing her thoughts on the newly married couple's bedroom activities.

Stabbing one of the pork pies with her finger, Edna volunteered some rather worrying information. "I've just heated these up in the microwave. I nearly forgot all about them if I'm honest. I left them out in the kitchen overnight…"

"You mean you didn't refrigerate them?"

Edna immediately took umbrage. "I might have known you'd be one of them pernickety food snobs. There's nowt wrong with them pies, lad. They were only a few days past their best-before- date and a quick blast in the microwave will have zapped any nasties."

"I think you'll find that the heat resistant toxins, so prevalent in meat pies left out at room temperature, won't have been killed off. I would hazard that those pork pies are likely riddled with the bacteria Staphylococcus aureus…"

"I'd have put money on you using big words. You look the sort…how you got mixed up with the likes of Violet Burke is a mystery to me. She's that common. Mind you, she's always had an eye for a toy boy, but they don't normally go around spouting the dictionary." Pausing for breath, Edna thrust the bowl of salt and vinegar crisps under my nose. Adopting her version of a posh accent, she cackled, "Have a morsel of finger food."

"I'll give the crisps a miss, thanks all the same. I couldn't help but notice that young Tyrone gave them a thoroughly good licking."

"Eh, don't you go casting asparaguses on my great-grandson…"

"Aspersions," I corrected.

"Them an all…'Appen I'd better make the boy a cheesy Wotsit butty. He'll be half-starved after hanging about in that church."

Although retired from my illustrious career as a public health inspector, I couldn't in all conscience allow the wedding guests to tuck into contaminated pork pies. In my professional opinion, I was pretty certain that imbibing the spread would result in them coming down with a nasty dose of vomiting and diarrhoea, if nothing worse. However, since retiring from my illustrious career, I had no official remit, lacking the authority to officially declare the buffet a health hazard. At the very least though, I had a duty of care to advise the pregnant bride to steer well clear; in her condition, a bout of Salmonella could result in her unborn child contracting a nasty dose of

Salmonellosis.

As I mulled the most tactful way to advise the bride that consuming her granny's buffet could well mean she'd end up spending her wedding night up close and personal with the porcelain, I was distracted by Edna Billings crying out, "Help. Our Tyrone's choking. Somebody do summat. The little scamp's choking."

Chapter 13

Pilfered from the Pillbox

Racked with guilt, I felt the colour immediately drain from my face. Convinced that poor little Tyrone was choking on one of my mint imperials, I inwardly questioned how I could have been so callous as to wish the child would indeed choke on them. My blood ran cold: if Tyrone croaked it, the authorities may well charge me with wilful manslaughter for providing the offending mint. As the crowd of wedding guests stood around gawping helplessly, Chardonnay becoming increasingly hysterical. When Tyrone turned the same nasty shade of puce as Edna Billings' outfit, I leapt into action. Grabbing the child, I performed the Heimlich Manoeuvre, my timely intervention saving Tyrone's life as something shot clear out of his mouth. Following the offending mints trajectory with my eye, I watched as it landed down the cleavage of Violet Burke's frock.

The crowd of wedding guests clapped and cheered, several of them offering to stand me drinks for the rest of the day. Considering that I was responsible for almost killing the child, I took no pleasure in my sudden elevation to hero status.

"How did you know how to do that to save him, like?" Dot asked.

Having no wish to bask in false modesty, I replied in a subdued tone, "It's just something I managed to pick up."

After the terrible debacle of Violet Burke injuring the ribs of both Guzim and myself when she tried the Heimlich Manoeuvre out, I had taken the precaution of learning how to do it correctly: one could never predict when a choking emergency may occur.

Meanwhile, across the room, Violet Burke was having a good rootle around in her cleavage. I waited with bated breath, expecting her to produce one of my mint imperials and show me up as the guilty party responsible for causing Tyrone's blockage.

"Bloody hell. The little bugger was only choking on a plastic grape from my hat," Violet Burke cried out. Retrieving her pillbox from the table where she'd left it, she added, "The thieving little toerag has only gone and guzzled half of my decorative grapes."

My relief was palpable as I realised that I'd had nothing to do with Tyrone's choking emergency. Moreover, Violet Burke was blameless too since the revolting child had helped himself to the dangling grapes with wanton abandon, defacing her pillbox. The young lout in the making was already displaying criminal tendencies, not only by extorting money with menaces but by stealing Violet Burke's grapes, thoughtlessly ruining her best hat. I could predict with near certainty that the local borstal would feature heavily in young Tyrone's future.

Joining Violet Burke, I commiserated on the desecration of her pillbox. Watching as she piled a plate high with Warrington eggs and Spam sandwiches, I advised, "I'd steer well clear of the buffet if I was you, Mother."

"Why? I suppose that little tyke Tyrone has been sticking his grubby fingers in the food."

"I have it on good authority that the pork pies are decidedly questionable and the pickles are so rancid they could probably walk off on their own…"

"You're such a fuss pot, lad. You know me, I've got the constitution of an ox. Don't forget we missed breakfast," Vi said, dismissing my concerns out of hand and tucking into one of the dodgy pork pies with relish.

"Well, on your own head be it. Don't come telling me you weren't warned when you start to turn a bit green round the gills."

About to take a bite from one of Edna Billing's sausage rolls, Dot hesitated. "I reckon you ought to know what you're talking about, lad, what with you having been one of them public health inspectors. 'Appen I'll play it safe and just stick with a few pineapple chunks."

"There's no guarantee that Tyrone hasn't given the pineapple a good licking," I warned.

"'Appen I'll give the buffet a miss. What's got the most disinfecting qualities, Victor? Gin or vodka?"

"Well, gin does have anti-fungal properties…"

Before I could complete my sentence, Chardonnay Billings launched herself into my arms. "I thought our Tyrone was a goner there. You were that brilliant, Mr Bucket. You saved our Tyrone's life."

"It was nothing," I assured the bride, fairly confident that I would still have rushed to Tyrone's aid even if I'd known that one of my mint imperials wasn't the cause of his choking.

"You were just like one of them doctors off 'Casualty'."

"Well, I used to wear a white coat in my professional capacity."

Chardonnay pulled away from me, screeching at the top of her voice in a very un-bridal like way. "Ere, Nan, what's that scrubber Danielle doing here in a wedding dress? I never invited her."

"The best man invited me as his date," Danielle argued defiantly. Crossing her arms in front of her chest, she had all the signs of a future harridan in the making.

"You're here with Mr Bucket?" Chardonnay looked at me in disbelief.

"Chardonnay, I can assure you that I never saw that girl in my life before today," I protested before belatedly remembering that I was only a last-minute stand in for the real best man. "She must mean Wayne."

"Wayne. Wayne, get that useless lump out of here before I give her a thump," Chardonnay yelled.

Called to action, Wayne dashed over to Danielle, promptly throwing up all over her wedding dress. Mortified, Danielle fled the room.

"Serves the fat cow right," Chardonnay pronounced with a self-satisfied smirk.

With Chardonnay's good mood restored, I considered it would now be a good opportunity to warn the bride to keep well clear of the buffet food.

"There's no danger of me scoffing any pies today, Mr Bucket. My heartburn's that bad, I can hardly breathe. The only thing I'll be knocking back is the Gaviscon."

As a fellow sufferer of heartburn, I sympathised with Chardonnay's predicament. Considering she had just declared she could hardly breathe, I was surprised when the bride insisted we take a twirl together on the dance floor. Despite being encumbered by two left feet, I could hardly say no to the bride on her wedding day. As we gyrated together on the dance floor, I steered a clear course, avoiding the puddle of Wayne's vomit that Dot was busy mopping up. With Chardonnay twittering away in my ear, I realised she was in no way as bad as I had painted her in my mind and she was clearly very keen on young Kevin.

As a sudden rush of water soaked my trouser leg, I was surprised to see I was nowhere near Dot's mop bucket. Realisation belatedly dawned: Chardonnay's waters had broken.

By the time we checked in at Manchester airport for our flight back to Greece, Violet Burke was looking decidedly green. I had never seen her swollen feet move at such speed as she made a sudden dash for the toilets. When she returned, she was ashen-faced.

"I only just made it to the lav. 'Appen you might have been right about those pork pies…"

Unable to complete her sentence, she made a second run to the toilets. When she next returned, I couldn't hide my concern.

"Perhaps we should change our flight, Mother," I suggested. "You don't want to be having the runs on the plane."

"It's hardly a picnic having the runs at the airport," she pointed out. "It'll cost us a small fortune if we have to re-book our flights. 'Appen I'll take my chances on the plane. If I can squeeze into the onboard lav right sharpish when we board, I could stop in there until we land in Greece."

"You can't go hogging the toilet for the duration of a four-hour flight."

"I reckon I can," she argued.

Needless to say, Violet Burke got her way, monopolising the facilities from Manchester to Athens. Her absence allowed me to enjoy a peaceful flight, blissfully free of any of Violet Burke's typically embarrassing moments.

Back on firm ground in Athens, I dragged the suitcases through the airport, remarking, "Well, the wedding certainly proved to be eventful."

"When it comes to dodgy looking food, I'll never doubt you again, lad. I reckon I should have listened to you."

"Well, I am something of an expert in the field,"

I reminded her.

"And smug with it too. Hang on a tick, lad. My handbag's ringing." Retrieving her mobile from her bag, Vi hissed, "It's Dot."

Moving away to give her some privacy, I gave Marigold a quick call to let her know that I was on my way home.

My mother had a bit more colour in her cheeks when she rejoined me.

"Well, you'll never guess what, Son?"

"Tyrone has had to have the rest of your plastic grapes pumped from his stomach," I guessed.

"Chardonnay's only gone and had the baby. It's a boy and a big one at that. Eight pounds and four ounces. Dot reckons that Chardonnay was right keen to name the bub after you since you saved her Tyrone's life. She got a bit hesitant like when she found out your name was Victor…"

"I suppose that Victor isn't chav enough…"

"If you'd let me finish…she found out your name was Victor Donald and she didn't want to lumber the baby with VD for its initials. She reckoned it reminded her of them sexually transmitted infections."

"A pity that didn't occur to you before you saddled me with the shorthand for venereal disease," I snapped.

"Get away with you, lad. No one talks about VD anymore, it's right out of fashion…"

"But they were all the rage back when I was a teenager…"

"You're too sensitive, lad. Anyhow, Dot said that Chardonnay decided to go with Keiran…Keiran Victor. 'Appen she reckoned she'd put chav and posh together. I hope you're not too disappointed that she didn't put your name first."

"I'm happy she went with Keiran. Don't forget that I've already had one Victor named in my honour…Victor Mabel."

"Dot said they've been at the hospital all night waiting for Chardonnay to push out the baby. All the wedding guests were there too, down in A&E. Turns out that Edna Billings gave them all a right nasty dose of food poisoning."

Chapter 14

Braying and Sobbing

Rousing Guzim from his shed, I could barely conceal my mirth at the sight of the Albanian's latest attire. Despite the weather forecast predicting another sweltering June day, Guzim was bundled up in some grotesque plastic looking garb masquerading as leather, more suited for winter. Adjusting his woollen scarf, he caught my eye and started chuntering something about out how navigating the mountain road on a moped later was likely to get chilly.

Piling into the Punto for our trip to town with Sherry and Guzim, along with the two sedated, caged cats, Marigold alternated between two widely disparate moods: full of the joys of spring and mightily miffed with me. When she'd returned home from her girls' night out the previous evening, a tad worse for wear, she hadn't been able to find me, despite searching everywhere. Desperate to impart the news about Benjamin's impending civil partnership with Adam as though she'd personally matchmade their union, my unexplained absence annoyed her immensely. Even though Marigold had been a holdout, hoping the boys would wait on the off-chance that one day they would be able to legally enjoy a proper wedding, she was still overjoyed by their news.

Beginning to get concerned by my elusive absence, Marigold had searched high and low. Failing to locate me, my apparent disappearance burst her bubble, leaving her thinking the worse and fretting about me. It was well after midnight and her temper was up when she finally discovered me fast asleep in the outdoor spa.

Even now, Marigold was in no mood to forget that I had selfishly caused her unnecessary anxiety and distress by failing to apprise her of my whereabouts: she could barely bring herself to be civil to me that morning.

My wife wasn't the only one wearing her moods on her sleeve. I could barely get two words out of Guzim, a most unusual state of affairs. I had expected to find him brimming with excitement at the prospect of going to town and getting his hands on new wheels, but instead he was snuffling loudly into what I at first assumed was a filthy handkerchief. On closer inspection, I recognised it as one of my tea towels which he must have pilfered from the washing line. I would need to watch out that he didn't try to peg it back on the line. I had no wish to reintroduce the now contaminated cloth back into my pristine kitchen, even after a good boil wash.

Sherry was her usual braying self, blithely chuntering on about jolly nothings of any consequence, without pausing for breath. As I drove out of Meli for our visit to town, I wished that I'd had the foresight to invest in a pair of earplugs to drown out the sound of braying and sniffing emanating from the back seat.

Edging in close to Guzim, Sherry breathed in deeply, proclaiming, "You smell all man. I do so appreciate the smell of male testosterone."

"*Ti?*"

"I think you're confusing testosterone with manure," I enlightened Sherry. The whiff of chicken droppings clung to my gardener, prompting me to conclude *rather him than me*. By agreeing to give Guzim a lift to town, I had at least been spared the smelly toil of mucking out my own chickens.

"Victor, do ask Guzim why he's sobbing like a

faucet," Marigold demanded. "It's going to wake the cats from their stupor if he starts dripping his tears on them."

"Why can't you ask him yourself?" I muttered under my breath before leaping to do Marigold's bidding by asking the Albanian, *"Giati klais?"*

"Echo chasei tin Doruntina," Guzim snuffled between sobs, telling me that he had lost Doruntina. I could only hope that his blasted rabbit wasn't running amok in my salad patch: the creature was a complete nuisance when it came to taking nibbles out of my rocket. Guzim went on to say that he had spent all night looking all over Meli for his adored rabbit. *"Oli nychta epsachna pantou sto Meli gia to kouneli mou."*

"What's he saying?" Sherry asked.

"He's lost his pet rabbit," I reluctantly told her, fed up of always being expected to translate. Was it really too much to ask that my English neighbours made a bit of effort on the learning a foreign language front?

"Oh, how jolly sad," Sherry trilled. Looking in my rearview mirror, I watched as Sherry attempted to offer comfort to my Albanian gardener. Leaning in even closer and slapping a hand on his knee, she over accentuated her words by speaking very loudly and slowly. "It's very sad that you've lost your rabbit."

Rearing back as far as the confines of the back

seat would allow, Guzim managed a fearful *"Ti?"* Was it really too much to expect my English neighbours to understand that speaking to the locals as though they were dim-witted and hard-of-hearing wouldn't suddenly give them the ability to understand English?

"Victor, what's the Greek word for rabbit?" Sherry asked.

"Kouneli."

"Oh. Are you sure? I think you're pulling my leg again, Victor. You can be such a tease." Catching a glimpse of horsey dentures in the rear-view mirror as Sherry brayed at full volume, I failed to see what could possibly be construed as hysterically funny. "I know for a fact that Cynthia's cat is called Kouneli and it isn't a rabbit."

"There's no slipping one by you, Sherry. Cynthia's vile mutant cat is most definitely not a rabbit," I agreed.

Bringing the braying down a notch, Sherry pronounced, "You are a one, Victor. I don't know why some people say that you don't have a sense of humour."

By now, Guzim looked terrified, squashed up close to a practically manic English woman mauling his knee and blathering on about a Kouneli that wasn't remotely related to Doruntina.

"It's very sad," Sherry told Guzim. Even when she repeated her words at a higher decibel, Guzim was none the wiser.

"*Ti? Ti?*"

"I think your Albanian is trying to say he wants to stop off for a cuppa," Sherry trilled.

"We can't stop on the way or we'll be late for the vet," Marigold said, not bothering to enlighten her friend that *ti* was Greek for what.

"And he isn't my Albanian," I snapped in exasperation.

Blowing his nose loudly into my purloined tea towel, Guzim lamented, "*Doruntina mou, mou leipei poly.*"

"What's he saying now?" Sherry persisted.

Although Guzim had actually said 'My Doruntina, I miss her so', I told Sherry, "Guzim said he wants you to un-hand his knee. He says you're way too familiar and he's a married man."

Snatching her hand back as though Guzim's knee was on fire, Sherry cried, "Oh, dear. Excusez me, excusez me, Guzim."

"He doesn't understand French any more than he understands English," I pointed out.

"I thought excuse me would be more or less the same in any language…"

"Give me strength," I blurted, amazed by Sherry's ignorance.

"Victor, really. There's no excuse for being rude to Sherry." Marigold swivelled around in her seat to address her friend directly. "Take no notice of

Victor, he's got a grump on. *Me synchoreis* is Greek for excuse me. It crops up a lot at the monthly meetings to beautify the cemetery. You really should come along next time, Sherry. We don't just weed, you know. We always have a good natter over coffee and cake"

"But I can't jolly well natter in Greek like you, Marigold," Sherry protested.

"Then it's about time you jolly well learned." Sherry visibly recoiled from my sharp words. The blissful silence that descended was only broken by Guzim's continual sniffles.

Free from Sherry's constant demands that I act as her personal translator, I was able to appreciate the magnificent views. The olive groves lining the road stretched up into the rolling hills, dotted with goats and sheep grazing, the sea shimmering and sparkling down below. The sheer beauty of the vista softened Marigold's mood and she proffered a tentative apology for losing her temper with me the previous night.

"You do know that I was only cross because you worried me so much, Victor. You could have drowned, falling asleep outside in that old bath," Marigold tutted. "I had no idea where you were."

"I know," I acknowledged.

"You were rambling on about Chardonnay Billings in your sleep. It's a good job I know you think she's a complete slob, otherwise I'd have been jealous that you were dreaming about another woman."

"Having a nightmare would be a more apt description." Reaching across for Marigold's hand, I held it to my lips, relieved to be out of the doghouse. "You're the only woman I dream about, darling."

As we headed to town, Marigold filled me in on her girls' night out and I filled Marigold in on my dinner with Spiros and Vangelis. I also broke the sad news about Kyria Kompogiannopoulou's death, telling my wife that Spiros would call to advise me about the funeral. We agreed that we would both attend, even if it meant cutting our trip to town short. In addition to working under me during my stint as the manager of the village shop, Kyria Kompogiannopoulou had been part of Marigold's group that met to beautify the cemetery once a month.

"I've been thinking that we should add welcome baskets to the apartments," Marigold suggested. "People really appreciate that sort of thing…in fact, little touches like that could go a long way towards ensuring repeat business."

Marigold's mention of repeat business struck a chord. "What sort of things would you suggest we put in a basket?"

"Something to give them a taste of the real Greece…"

"Some nectarines from our trees," I suggested.

"And we've probably still got a few jars of my home-made courgette chutney lurking in the back of the cupboard."

"I was thinking of something more along the lines of traditional Greek items: a bottle of *retsina* or miniature bottles of *ouzo* or *raki*, a small bottle of olive oil, a jar of olives…maybe some Greek honey, olive oil soap…and *halva* of course…"

"*Halva's* a bit of an acquired taste." It was certainly a taste I had failed to acquire; the way the blasted stuff always stuck my tongue to the roof of my mouth gave me the sensation that I was chewing on out-of-date chalk mixed with superglue.

Marigold was certainly getting carried away with her list of Greek essentials. Perchance the notion of making a profit was alien to her spendthrift nature.

"I'm not opposed to the idea of welcome baskets per se but can't you come up with some items that aren't quite so pricey? Honey and olive oil aren't exactly cheap. *Tsai tou vounou* won't break the bank and nectarines from our garden are free."

"You're such a cheapskate, Victor."

"I'm just thinking about the bottom line. This is a business venture, after all."

"Well, if you insist on the *tsai tou vounou*, I'll need to buy some teapots for the apartments. It doesn't come in bags, you know."

"Forget the *tsai*. I don't want you wasting good

money on teapots."

"I think you should get some nuts to go with the *ouzo*," Sherry piped up. "You can't go wrong with booze and nibbles."

For once, something sensible had come out of Sherry's mouth.

"Let's compromise with a couple of miniature bottles of the cheapest *ouzo* we can source, a packet of salted peanuts, and some fresh fruit from our garden. I'll stop at Giannis' place later and see if he's up for bartering some miniature jars of honey in exchange for some fresh eggs from our chickens or aubergines from the garden."

"I'll pick up a couple of wicker baskets in town," Marigold said, delighted that I hadn't vetoed her idea to add welcome baskets to the rental accommodation.

Parking up in town, it proved useful having Guzim along. The Albanian willingly relieved the burden of my carrying Clawsome in her cage from the Punto to the veterinarian's office, leaving me with only Catastrophe to deal with. Even though the practice had only just opened for the day, the waiting room was already more than half-full with a motley collection of pets and their human companions. Looking around, I hoped that each pet had several humans attached to them since it would reduce the waiting time. After all, Marigold's two pampered imported domestics were outnumbered by the four of us.

Marigold was visibly disappointed that Lefteris, the tattooed, leather-clad young man with the pampered pet poodle, Fufu, wasn't at the veterinarians. It must have been a first.

"Lefteris is practically a fixture here. Such a nice young man and he thinks the world of his pet poodle," Marigold told Sherry.

"Look on the bright side," I consoled my wife. "If he's not here with Fufu then the poodle is likely enjoying good health."

Marigold rolled her eyes: clearly, she had no interest in Fufu's actual well-being. She just enjoyed being flattered by the poodle's owner and basking in the attention of a handsome, younger man.

"You'll probably run into Lefteris at the garden centre later," I reassured my wife. My remark instantly cheered Marigold up, which was more than could be said for Guzim. The Albanian shed dweller appeared to be deep in the throes of melancholy, his wretched mood exacerbated by the presence of a sickly-looking pet rabbit in the waiting room. Still carrying the caged Clawsome, Guzim tentatively approached the little girl holding the rabbit inside a cage on her lap, her mother warily eyeing the wistful looking Albanian with undisguised suspicion.

"Echo kai ena kouneli." As Guzim told the child that he had a rabbit too, he displayed his practically toothless gums. It really wasn't a good look.

Staring at Guzim in disbelief, the little girl pointed out that Clawsome was a cat, not a rabbit. *"Afto einai gata, ochi kouneli."*

"Afti den einai i gata mou," Guzim said, explaining it wasn't his cat. The child's mother put a protective arm around her daughter's shoulder, her expression indicating she thought that Guzim had made off with someone else's cat. It was only natural that she wouldn't want a practically toothless, dodgy looking cat thief done up in pleather, approaching her little girl.

"Einai i gata mas, eimaste oloi mazi," I reassured the woman, telling her it was our cat and that we were all together. I was even tempted to reveal that Guzim was my Albanian if it would help to allay the woman's unease. The woman visibly relaxed: clearly Marigold and I at least looked respectable enough to not be running around in the company of catnappers.

I was saved from becoming further involved when Barry phoned my mobile.

"Victor, Spiros asked me to let you know that the funeral is today at three-thirty."

"The funeral?"

"For Kyria Kompogiannopoulou."

I found it ironic that the first time Barry managed

to pronounce her name correctly was when she was dead.

"Tell Spiros that we'll be there."

"So, I had some more thoughts about naming the apartments."

"Do tell," I encouraged my brother-in-law.

"We could call them the Sofia apartments after Sofia Kompogiannopoulou. It's a Greek name and neither of our wives can object if we say it's in honour of the recently departed."

"That's brilliant, Barry, a solution that won't initiate a cat fight. Let's definitely go with Sofia."

No sooner had the call ended than Marigold started to interrogate me, demanding to know where I was going with some random woman called Sofia.

"Nowhere, darling. Barry suggested that we name the apartments Sofia in honour of Kyria Kompogiannopoulou." As Barry had predicted, Marigold could hardly object: it would make her look churlish. "We need to be back in Meli by three-thirty for her funeral."

"Look, Marigold. How peculiar. I could swear that handbag just moved," Sherry hissed, staring pointedly at a large leather handbag taking up the seat next to an elegantly dressed young woman.

"Oh, yes. I saw it move too," Marigold said just as a cute dog's head emerged from the bag. "It's one of those handbag dogs, a little shih tzu."

"It could do with a haircut," I observed, noticing

it could barely see due to the long fringe covering its eyes. As the little shih tzu began to yap uncontrollably, it no longer appeared quite so cute.

Just then, a man grappling with some type of exotic bird stepped out of the veterinarian's inner sanctum. The white coated vet followed him out, nodding our way in recognition; scanning the waiting room, he selected our cats as next up. Apologising to the gathered humans who had been there before us, the vet said he would hate for any of their pets to catch our cats' ticks so he was pushing us to the front of the queue. Leaving Guzim and Sherry in the waiting room, Marigold and I went inside with Catastrophe and Clawsome, trying to ignore the pinched and sullen faces of the people we had leapfrogged over. Not waiting around for ages was another first.

Releasing the still doped up felines from their cages, the vet gave them both a thorough examination by running his gloved hands all over their bodies. Just as we thought he was about to pronounce the pair of them to be tick free, the vet exclaimed that he had found one. Utilising a pair of tweezers that he deployed with laser-like precision, the vet extracted an engorged tick from the top of one of Catastrophe's back legs. "You must to feel them up and brush them the daily," he advised Marigold before saying he would administer an anti-tick serum to both of the cats.

Demonstrating how to do it, he used a comb to make a parting in the fur at the back of Clawsome's neck before targeting the spot with a few drops of serum squeezed from a tube. Repeating the procedure on Catastrophe, the vet advised we should administer the serum once a month during the tick season. Conveniently, he had ample supplies of the stuff to sell to us and what I presumed were vastly inflated prices.

With the cats duly de-ticked and, mercifully, still dopey, we were just exiting the veterinarian's clinic when I received a call on my mobile.

"*Ela, Victor, o filos mou. O Sami eipe oti se eide stin poli.*"

The thunderous voice almost deafening me needed no introduction; the distinctive boom could only belong to *Kapetanios* Vasos. Still, I was at a loss as to how the mute Sami had managed to tell Vasos that he had seen me in town.

"Beautiful towel. *Elate sti marina. Thelo na gnoriseis ton gio mou,*" Vasos yelled at full volume, telling me to come to the marina as he wanted me to meet his son.

"*O gios sas,*" I repeated incredulously, trying to recall if I had ever heard Captain Vasos mentioning a son before.

"*Ne, yie mou, Andrea.*" Vasos confirmed yes, his

son, Andreas. Continuing in the same vein, Vasos refused to take no for an answer, insisting I join them for coffee. I must admit that my curiosity was more than a little piqued. Certainly, if I complied with Vasos' summons, I would be able to get out of traipsing around the shops with Marigold and Sherry; the prospect of being a third wheel, only useful for carting their bags of shopping, was hardly inviting.

Telling Vasos that I would see him shortly, I exaggerated the truth somewhat by telling Marigold that the good captain had an emergency and needed my help. Since Marigold had Sherry for company, she was more than happy to see the back of me, having pointed out more than once that she found my presence rather cramped her style.

"Just don't go mad with my credit card. Remember we've set a tight budget for finishing the apartments," I reminded Marigold.

"As if you'd ever let me forget. You do go on, darling."

"You can have Guzim to help with your bags."

"Oh, no. Absolutely not. Guzim can go with you," Marigold insisted.

"I don't want to be saddled with Guzim," I argued.

"*Ti?*" Guzim piped up at the sound of his name, his head swivelling between the two of us.

"As you'll have to take the cats with you, Guzim can give you a hand with the cages," Marigold persisted, her tone brooking no argument.

"But the coffee bar at the marina is quite posh…"

"Ah, so you're off for an emergency coffee," Marigold crowed triumphantly, having clearly won that round. "Don't go leaving the cats in the car whilst you sit around drinking coffee. I don't want them overheating. Now, off you go with Guzim and I'll give you a call when we've got everything that we need for the apartments so you can pick us up and drive us to the garden centre." In one fell swoop I had been reduced to nothing more than Marigold's errand boy.

Linking arms, Marigold and Sherry disappeared amidst the throng of shoppers, leaving me to explain to Guzim that we would be driving to the marina to meet up with Captain Vasos. Consulting my watch, I pointed out that Guzim still had several hours to kill until his rendezvous at the bus station.

"*Mou aresei poly o kapetan Vasos*," Guzim gushed, his tone full of admiration as he declared that he liked Captain Vasos very much.

Chapter 15

An Unexpected Encounter with an Ex

P arking up at the marina, I headed towards the coffee bar frequented by Vasos. Whilst I strolled along, admiring the opulent yachts and luxury boats berthed on the clear blue reflective water, Guzim trailed behind me with downcast eyes. Considering his upbringing in a Communist country, I had expected he would at least have a grunt filled gripe about the flagrant extravaganza of wealth on display. Weighed down with the cats, Guzim appeared lost in his thoughts, seemingly oblivious to his surroundings.

Skipping up the steps leading to the swanky

coffee bar, I called out to Guzim, *"Min skontafteis sta podia sou,"* advising him, 'Don't trip over your feet.' Alas, my warning was delivered too late, Guzim indeed falling over his feet and sending the cage containing Clawsome flying. Watching as Guzim scurried to right the cage, I supposed it would be a toss-up as to which of my two companions, Vasos or Guzim, would embarrass me the most.

The always elegantly attired owner, Marinos, rushed forward to greet me warmly and guide me across to Vasos' table. It is a mark of Marinos' consummate professionalism that he didn't bat an eyelid at the sight of the pleather-clad and woollen-wrapped, toothless Albanian, carrying two cages containing the still doped-up cats.

Spotting Vasos sitting close to a very chic looking woman made me once again question my competence in the Greek language. I could have sworn that Vasos had told me he was with a son that I was pretty sure I'd never heard of, yet here he was looking most at ease in the company of a stylish and attractive woman. Presuming that Vasos was in the process of attempting to chat the woman up, I hesitated to join him. It wouldn't do at all if my arrival put a spoke in his pick-up plans, particularly as the woman's warm smile indicated his attention was anything but unwelcome.

As I reluctantly approached the table, the woman stood up to greet me. Tall and willowy, dressed in a floral halter neck sundress, brunette hair coiffed in a sleek shoulder-length bob, she extended a dainty hand with perfectly manicured nails.

"You must be Victor. It is such a pleasure to meet you. Vasos has told me so much about you." Her English was nothing less than impeccable. Noting my surprise, lilting laughter escaped from her lips. "I'm Eleanor, Vasos' ex-wife."

"Delighted to meet you, Eleanor," I replied, attempting to disguise my utter shock. Quite how Vasos had managed to persuade this graceful and fragrant creature to marry him was beyond me. I could only assume it must have been an arranged marriage.

"*Victor*, mucky fat, *o filos mou*," Vasos bellowed, jumping out of his seat to embrace me, the unmistakable scent of old sweat intermingled with Old Spice assailing me as he tacked a superfluous "Fray Bentos" onto his greeting. Violet Burke's influence had clearly left its mark on the good *Kapetanios*. It didn't escape my notice that Eleanor towered over her ex-husband.

"Do join us," Eleanor invited, gracefully including Guzim in her invitation. Addressing the Albanian in Greek, Eleanor noted the cats were beautiful. "*Ti omorfes gates*."

"*Einai oi gates tis Kyrias Bucket. Echo ena kouneli*," Guzim replied, saying the cats belonged to Mrs

Bucket and he had a rabbit. Remembering that Doruntina was on the missing list, Guzim started snivelling again; the Albanian shed dweller really could be most trying.

The four of us took our seats, Guzim plonking the cats at his feet. As Marinos took our order for coffee, a thousand questions buzzed through my mind. Watching as Eleanor and Vasos interacted politely and warmly, clearly at ease with one another, I reflected that Doreen and Norman could take some pointers from this divorced Greek couple on how to handle their separation amicably. The warring English couple seemed to be constantly adrift in a sea of hostility.

Addressing Eleanor, I remarked, "Your English is excellent."

"My second husband is English. Since he struggles to get to grips with Greek, we tend to converse in English," Eleanor explained.

"Beautiful towel," Vasos boomed, receiving an indulgent smile from his ex.

"My Greek must be worse than I thought," I told Eleanor. "I could have sworn Vasos said he wanted me to come along to meet his son."

"Yes, our son, Andreas. He's just in the toilet," Eleanor said.

"So, I'm not losing my marbles after all?"

"It's a miracle if you can hold onto your marbles when talking to Vasos."

"*Ti?*"

Addressing Vasos, I asked if he wasn't working today. "*Den douleveis simera?*"

"*Apopse tha kano tin krouaziera sto fos tou fengariou,*" Vasos replied, telling me he was doing the moonlight cruise that night, before adding that he was taking Eleanor along. "*Pairno tin Eleanor.*"

"Together with fifty tourists," Eleanor quipped. Smiling proudly as a strapping, handsome young man made his way to our table, Eleanor added, "Ah, here is Andreas now."

Leaping to his feet, Vasos reached up to throw an arm around his son's shoulder: it crossed my mind that if Vasos felt inclined to ruffle his son's hair, he would need to stand on a chair since Andreas, taking after his mother, towered above him. As Eleanor made the introductions, deep dimples creased Andreas' smile, accentuating his striking features; he was certainly fortunate in inheriting his looks from Eleanor rather than Vasos.

"Andreas is spending the month with his father," Eleanor said. "I will miss him terribly."

"Are you in the same line of work as your father?" I asked Andreas.

"No, I'm still at school…"

"At school…" I spluttered in disbelief, having pegged Andreas as being in his mid-twenties.

"Don't worry, Victor, everyone always assumes Andreas is older than his years," Eleanor assured me. "It's his height."

And his beard, I thought to myself, pretty sure that facial hair hadn't been a thing back in my own school days.

"It will be Andreas' last year at the *lykeio* and then he must decide if he wants to pursue his education at university or sign up for the navy…"

"Ah, following in his father's footsteps."

"The Hellenic Naval Academy for officers," Eleanor clarified.

Noticing that Guzim looked extremely uncomfortable, Eleanor instructed Vasos to put him at ease. Whilst my gardener and the captain made small talk in Greek, Eleanor filled me in on her short-lived marriage to Vasos, explaining his continual absences at sea had taken a toll on their relationship, the pair of them divorcing amicably when Andreas was little older than a tot.

Now happily married, Eleanor made her home in Kolonaki, a very desirable neighbourhood in Athens, renowned for its sophisticated boutiques and must-see museums.

During our trips to Athens, I'd had a hard time keeping Marigold away from the expensive shops in Kolonaki. Although the museums in that area held little appeal for Marigold, she had indulged my whim to visit the Benaki Museum. In turn, I had found my wife's choice of the Museum of the History of Greek Costume surprisingly fascinating.

Our tour of the classical Greek mansion housing the costume collection had given me a new appreciation for the invention of slacks. I couldn't imagine navigating my life whilst clad in a skirt, no matter how manly the ancients Spartans considered them; and don't even get me started on togas.

Whilst conversing with Eleanor, I couldn't help but notice that Vasos appeared to be abstaining from alcohol, a most unusual turn of events. Clearly the presence of Eleanor served as a good influence on the usually half-inebriated captain. Nevertheless, even being stone cold sober didn't do anything to curb Vasos' typical loudness. Shamelessly flirting with the waitress delivering the coffee, Vasos made no attempt to turn his volume down. Said waitress was a marvel of professionalism; whilst not embarrassing the good *Kapetanios* by ostensibly snubbing him, she saved her exaggerated eye rolls until his back was turned.

It dawned on me that instead of bringing Guzim along, I should have brought Sherry since Vasos would happily chat up anyone in a skirt. Even though they wouldn't be able to communicate in any meaningful way, Vasos' continual declarations of love would likely give Sherry's confidence a much-needed boost. Although Sherry had initially cried off men after her unfortunate experience with Heinrich, the German hippie, Marigold had confided her friend was now back on the market, so to speak. According to Marigold, the desperation Sherry often displayed around the opposite sex was fuelled by loneliness for companionship rather than from an actual desire to snare herself a romantic partner.

I don't know what got into me, but with no consideration for the consequences, I impulsively decided to do something nice for Sherry and invite Captain Vasos to join us for the expat dinner party at my home on Saturday evening. After extending an invitation, I added, *"Mia elkystiki anypantri gynaika pou pistevo oti tha sou aresei tha einai ekei,"* telling Vasos that an attractive single woman who I thought he would like would be there. Considering Vasos was hardly a catch, I felt no qualms about bending the truth in describing Sherry as attractive. Vasos' eyes lit up and he eagerly accepted my invitation.

Belatedly realising that I had rather overstepped the mark by usurping Marigold's position as the matchmaker of the Bucket household, I decided not to mention anything to my wife. Since it was highly possible that Vasos would at some point get so blotto that he would forget all about my invitation, I decided to keep schtum unless Vasos actually turned up in person. There was no need for Marigold to reorganise her seating plan on the off-chance.

If Sherry and Vasos hit it off, Marigold would

likely be so over the moon that she would forgive my meddling in her territory. If nothing else, Vasos' presence would keep Violet Burke happy. Even though the pair of them struggled with what one would characterise as holding a normal conversation, I knew for a fact that my mother preferred Vasos' company to any of the other invited guests.

Over the course of a couple of rounds of coffee, Vasos declared his love for me, for Eleanor, for Andreas, the cats, and even Guzim. It was fortunate that Vasos used English for his repeated vocalisations of his love since Guzim had a seeming horror of homosexual overtures and would likely get sniffy if he actually had the merest clue what Vasos was saying. No one could ever accuse Guzim of having an actual sense of humour.

Much as I was keen to get all the gossip from Eleanor about a younger Vasos, it was impossible to get two words out without the good captain interrupting with a continual barrage of "*ti*?" By the time that Marigold telephoned to summon me to pick up her and Sherry, I was unfortunately none the wiser about the juiciest details of Vasos' glorious past. With my curiosity unquenched, I corralled Guzim and the cats together, very much hoping to run into the charming Eleanor again soon.

Chapter 16

Sour Cherries

Dropping Guzim off at the bus station, I must confess that I was mightily glad to see the back of him, his visible sullenness wearing on my nerves. Moreover, I was relieved that he would be making his own way home on his about to be acquired moped, sparing me another agonising journey with Sherry scaring the living daylights out of the Albanian shed dweller. Hopefully, the shiny new moped should cheer him up. Although both Eleanor and Vasos had made a valiant effort of trying to raise Guzim's spirits, he was still in the pits of despair over his missing rabbit.

Guzim's fear that an unsuspecting Meli villager may have popped Doruntina into the oven was not inconceivable: rabbit meat often appeared as a regular staple on rural tables, Giannis the honey man breeding them as food. Even though I personally baulk at the very notion of eating rabbit, I could not say with any confidence that the odd morsel of bunny hadn't passed my lips. Greek neighbours often insist that I sample a taste of whatever is simmering on their stoves, refusing to take no for an answer, no matter how much I resist.

Rid of Guzim, I drove through the centre of town towards the meeting place. The town was bustling, the shady outdoor seating areas outside the numerous coffee-bars a magnet for shoppers and office workers enjoying a leisurely break. Spotting one of the bank tellers from my branch sipping a coffee, I noticed he appeared in no rush to return to work; no doubt the queue at the branch would be out the door whilst he idled. Fortunately, since I had no business at the bank, I would be spared cooling my heels, ticket in hand.

Reaching our appointed meeting spot, I picked up Marigold and Sherry, together with their numerous bags of shopping, ready to head to the garden centre. Cramming their many carrier bags into the boot, I doubted that amidst the clutter of cats and women in the Punto, that there would be any room left for any plants that may take their fancy. Sherry's weight proved handy when she helpfully sat on the lid of the overstuffed boot to press it down in the same manner applied to forcing a suitcase closed.

My wife brushed off my concerns about the hit to my credit card by proclaiming that most of their haul belonged to Sherry. I was wise to her fibs; if nothing else, Marigold was always consistent in her little white lies concerning her myriad spending sprees. If I had a Euro for every time she had pulled the 'this old thing' card, I would be rich enough to jack in my repping job.

Despite there being an abundance of garden centres dotted around the edge of town, Marigold's first choice was always the one owned by Lefteris' family. I had long surmised that her preference was influenced more by the flattering attention Lefteris paid to her, rather than the discount he invariably offered.

Parking up at the nursery, I left all the windows down so the dozing cats would have plenty of air. Sherry headed purposefully off on her own, finally allowing me some alone time with my lovely wife. I was instantly mesmerised by the glorious flowers and fruiting trees drawing my eye to the stunning kaleidoscope of colour on display. Knowing how difficult Marigold would find it to resist, I whispered in her ear, "Please don't get carried away, darling."

"As if. Oh, look, Victor. I do believe that's a

Morello cherry tree." Marigold discreetly sneaked a cherry from the tree. Biting into the luscious dark red fruit, Marigold winced at its sourness, a droplet of the glossy juice staining her lips. Picking another cherry, Marigold's fingers traced my lips as she fed the glossy stone fruit to me.

Grimacing at the sharp sourness, I said, "I can understand why the Greeks traditionally turn Morello cherries into syrupy spoon sweets."

"You should make a batch, darling. Your walnut spoon sweets were a resounding success."

"We'll never be able to shove the cherry tree in the car…" I objected.

"Why on earth would we want to? Only an idiot would plant a cherry tree in June." I sighed in relief, grateful that nature, in this instance, was firmly on my side. "You just stick to your veggies, Victor, and leave the fruit and flowers to me."

"And the herbs. They're your department too."

Smiling in agreement, Marigold took my hand, the two of us wandering around together, appreciating the beauty surrounding us, the garden centre an oasis of relaxation. Whimsical butterflies flitted around the plants, the soft drone of bumblebees filling the air. The two of us welcomed the gentle breeze offering some respite from the midday heat, the leaves on the fruit trees dancing to its tune. Clouds fluttered across the blue sky, ominously dark over the distant mountain.

Peering into the distance, I observed, "It looks as though we could be driving back through rain."

"Well, the garden certainly needs it." Marigold's upbeat response delighted me, all trace of her early morning grump now a distant memory.

"The weather could do Guzim out of a job this evening. He'll be spared a session with the hosepipe if we get a summer shower," I said. "Have you seen anything you need for the garden at the apartments?"

"Just a couple of bougainvillea for today. The colour of those magenta ones is just magnificent. Now that those prickly pear plants have been eradicated, I want to train the bougainvillea to grow against the outdoor steps, but I'll start them off in pots."

"Let's find Lefteris and show him what we want," I suggested, most impressed at Marigold's restraint. I had certainly got off lightly if she was happy to settle for just a couple of plants.

"Cooee, Marigold." Sherry's shrill call shattered the peace. Looking around, I spotted Sherry standing next to Lefteris, the former engaged in a brazen display of full-on flirting, the latter staring at Marigold's friend with a glazed expression as she trundled over polite boundaries by invading his personal space.

"It looks as though Lefteris needs rescuing."

"Talk about stating the obvious," Marigold snapped. It appeared that my wife wasn't too keen on Sherry hitting on her 'admirer'.

"As Violet Burke would say, Sherry ain't half got some brass neck…"

"You can say that again. She's bordering on the procacious. Poor Lefteris."

As we drew level with Sherry and Lefteris, Sherry immediately started gushing with all the exuberance of a burst water pipe. "I was just telling Lefteris that I already feel like I jolly well know him."

"That would account for her overfamiliarity," I hissed to Marigold.

"Marigold, I was just telling Lefteris how you never stop talking about him." As Marigold blushed, invisible steam coming out of her ears, Sherry placed a hand on Lefteris' arm, presumptuously stroking his tattooed flesh with an orange painted talon. "Marigold's always saying what a catch you are. She says you are the perfect gentleman; so handsome and always so attentive."

As Sherry continued to fawn over Lefteris, braying unprovoked laughter punctuated her pronouncements, exposing her horsey dentures. Marigold's eyes narrowed in annoyance. I could certainly sympathise with my wife: it was nothing but extremely bad form for Sherry to be making such a song and dance about Marigold's harmless flirtation when the object of said flirtation was standing in front of Marigold, not to mention in front of Marigold's husband. Knowing it was quite harmless and having long assumed that the tattooed motorcyclist was gay, I was quite prepared to indulge Marigold's enjoyment of Lefteris' flattery. However, the way that Sherry was banging on about it was clearly embarrassing my wife.

Prising Sherry's hand off his arm, Lefteris stepped forward to shake my hand and plant a couple of kisses on Marigold's cheeks. Appearing a tad shell shocked, the expression is his eyes screamed 'get me away from this mad harpy.'

"Marigold. As elegant as ever," Lefteris fussed.

"How's Fufu?" I asked, telling Lefteris that we were in town because we'd taken the cats to the vet.

Lefteris entertained us with tales of taking Fufu out on his motorbike. With the poodle comfortably ensconced in a basket, man and dog had recently enjoyed excursions to the historic seaside town of Kyparissia and to the Polylimnio waterfalls. I guessed that Marigold seemed to be taking a pertinent interest in the waterfalls to impress Lefteris since she had dismissed the idea of our visiting them out of hand due to the supposedly rigorous hike involved. She completely took me by surprise by suggesting the two of us take a trip to the Polylimnio gorge in the near future and have a dip in the waterfalls.

Since Marigold suddenly seemed so keen, I made a mental note to arrange a surprise day out as a treat. Knowing Barry was eager to visit the falls, I could perhaps organise an overnight trip for the four of us and Anastasia; now that my niece had turned three, she would surely be in waterfall heaven. Recalling how Sherry had turned up during our romantic weekend away at Monemvasia, I thought it best to keep my thoughts about a future trip to the falls to myself for now in case she got some ridiculous idea about tagging along.

Lefteris appeared suddenly flustered as a young man with movie star looks, carrying Fufu the poodle, approached our little gathering. "Marigold, you must to meet my friend, the Marco. He is from the Italy."

Turning to greet his friend with enthusiasm, Lefteris demonstrated far more fervour dropping double kisses on Marco's chiselled cheekbones than he had when dutifully kissing Marigold. The lingering looks passing between the two men almost certainly confirmed I'd hit the nail on the head about Lefteris being gay. Unfortunately, I was unable to eavesdrop on their conversation since it appeared that Lefteris had a hidden talent for speaking fluent Italian.

As the two men moved aside for a moment to chat privately, Sherry hissed to Marigold, "I do like your friend, Lefteris. Perhaps you could invite him along to the expat dinner party so I could get to know him a bit better."

"He's way too young for you, Sherry," Marigold snapped. "And anyway, he's gay."

"No," Sherry squealed incredulously.

"He wears leathers and has a poodle called Fufu that wears a pink bow," Marigold said. "Don't you think that's a bit of a giveaway?"

"I always harboured a suspicion that Lefteris was gay but never liked to point it out as you always seem so happy when he lavishes you with attention," I said.

"Of course, women lap up the attention of gay men. It's a harmless flirtation. Do you really think I'd flirt so openly in front of you, if he was straight?"

"Well, you might have mentioned it before now, Marigold," Sherry grumbled. "I've just wasted the last half-hour chatting him up. Mind you, we did have a lovely chat about composting."

When the two men finally drew apart, I commended Lefteris on his skill as a polyglot.

"Oh, do speak English, Victor," Marigold chided. "What on earth is a polyglot?"

"A person who has mastered the skill of speaking in multiple languages."

"So, that means you're a polyglot, Victor," Sherry piped up.

"Hardly. I can't even claim the title of being bilingual. I just rather muddle along in Greek whilst Lefteris has Greek, English and Italian under his belt," I said modestly. "Now, young Tonibler is what you would term a natural polyglot. He's only just turned seven and already he's a natural in Greek, Albanian and English. Only last week, he told me he fancied taking up Spanish or Japanese. I suggested learning Filipino would be a more practical choice as he could practise speaking it with Sampaguita."

"I speak the Spanish," Lefteris declared proudly. "I try to teach Marco the Greek but he not take to it like the goose to water."

Ignoring Lefteris' confusion between geese and ducks, I asked Marco, "Are you in Greece for long?" only for my question to be met with a blank stare.

"Marco does not speak the English," Lefteris explained before bursting into another bout of Italian.

Lefteris announced that Marco was leaving to take Fufu home. Amidst a flurry of goodbyes which Marco struggled to understand, the Italian departed. In what I discerned was an attempt to assure Lefteris that the Buckets were perfectly comfortable if he wanted to out his gayness, Marigold told him about Benjamin's plans to form a civil partnership with his long-term boyfriend, Adam.

"I cannot to see that happening here in the Greece," Lefteris remarked.

"You'd think the Greeks would be the first to authorise gay marriage," I opined. "Considering that the Greeks invented homosexuality."

"Did they really?" Sherry brayed.

"Of course not, it isn't something that was invented." I didn't attempt to hide the exasperation in my tone. "It's just one of Spiros' little sayings."

"Even if the Greek government was so inclined, it is too late for the Greeks to be the first," Lefteris said. "The homosexual marriage was the legalise in the Netherlands in 2001. The Dutch were the first to approve it."

"Perhaps Greece will be next," Marigold suggested.

"Marigold, you forget about the influence of the Orthodox church," Lefteris pointed out. "They make much the stink if the subject come up. They will never to accept it."

"Never say never," I advised.

Checking the time, I said that we needed to be making tracks if we were to make good time for the funeral. After Marigold pointed out the two bougainvillea which had caught her eye, Lefteris carried them over to the car.

"Your friend already pay for the manure," Lefteris told me, pointing to several large plastic sacks stacked next to the boot. "For you, my friend, I give the discount."

"Most generous," I said, wondering how on earth I was meant to cram Sherry's purchases inside the already bursting at the seams Punto. Since the boot was filled to overflowing, I didn't bother to open it. With Lefteris' assistance, the bags of manure were stashed in the backseat floor wells whilst Marigold had no option but to plant the bougainvillea on her knee in the passenger seat. With the caged cats balanced atop several carrier bags of shopping next to Sherry, I made a mental note to take any hairpin bends extremely slowly. I would never hear the end of it if Catastrophe suffered a catastrophic episode as a result of a daring Brands Hatch move on my part.

Chapter 17

Waiting to be Rescued

Flooring the accelerator, the engine groaned and protested as I willed the Punto to at least clear the crest of the steep hill we were climbing. It crossed my mind that the additional weight of Sherry, asleep in the back seat next to the two caged cats, wasn't helping, not to mention the abundance of shopping that Marigold and Sherry had squeezed into every last crevice of the car.

"I don't believe it. This can't be happening." Banging the steering wheel in frustration, the horn blared, waking Sherry from her stupor.

The engine spluttered one final croak before

dying on me, leaving the Punto stranded, approximately a forty-five-minute drive from home. Naturally, there was no convenient lay-by on the narrow and winding mountain road; instead, the Punto took up most of the narrow right-hand lane, leaving our rear end a wide-open target for anyone hurtling around the bend behind us. Fortunately, since it was siesta time, the road couldn't exactly be described as busy.

"What's happening, Victor?" Marigold's tone was laced with anxiety.

"It appears that we've run into a spot of car trouble." There was nothing like stating the patently obvious.

"What's wrong with the car, Victor?" Marigold persisted.

"Do I look like a car mechanic?" I muttered under my breath, my fingers blindly groping for the switch that would release the bonnet; I knew it had to be there somewhere. With the switch eventually located, I alighted the car and secured the rod thingy to hold the bonnet open. I patted myself on the back for managing this basic step; I must confess to having doubts that I could pull it off. Admittedly, my gesture was beyond futile since I was completely clueless when it came to the workings of the internal combustion engine. Nevertheless, it seemed to be the accepted thing for even the most mechanically inept of men to stare blankly at whatever mechanical things sheltered beneath the bonnet; for some reason, societal pressure spares the more fragrant sex from such nonsense. In my case, all that was missing to make me look the part of a competent bloke was a pair of oily coveralls and a wooden tooth pick to gnaw on.

Peering at the engine, I willed it to miraculously spring back to life. Marigold joined me, a desperate edge to her voice as she asked, "Can you fix it?"

"What do you think?" My question was rhetorical, my wife knowing full well how incompetent I am when it comes to anything along the lines of DIY.

"You'll have to do something or we'll miss the funeral," Marigold pressed.

"I think missing the funeral is a given unless we can be on our way in the next ten minutes. We were already running late even before the car conked out. I suppose I'd better call Spiros…"

"Is he good at fixing cars?"

"To explain why we'll likely miss attending Kyria Kompogiannopoulou's funeral," I clarified. "Now, let me think…we have breakdown insurance so we can call the insurance company for help, but we've not exactly broken down on the beaten track. I expect it will take some time for the breakdown truck to reach us. Marigold, grab the insurance document out of the glovebox so I can put in a call."

"Telephone Spiros first," Marigold instructed.

"It really won't look good if people think we just couldn't be bothered to turn up for the funeral. All the other ladies from my beautifying the cemetery group will be there. It wouldn't do my reputation any good if they thought I was deliberately swerving Sofia's burial."

After apprising Spiros of our problem and asking him to light some candles on our behalf in the church, I perused my insurance document. It certainly didn't help that every last word was penned in tiny Greek print which I struggled to decipher.

Squinting at the document, I said, "I really need to arrange an appointment with an ophthalmologist to sort out some decent reading glasses."

"Reading glasses won't improve your Greek reading comprehension," Marigold unhelpfully pointed out.

"Well, it would certainly help if I could actually see what I'm attempting to read," I retorted as Sherry stepped out of the car to join us. Digging a pair of pink heart-shaped reading glasses out of the depths of her handbag, she offered them to me.

"For goodness' sake. I'm going to look like Elton John in these," I grumbled, reluctantly putting them on. "Ah, yes. I can see where the insurance broker highlighted the telephone number I need to call if I need roadside assistance. I'll give them a call."

Apprehension gripped me as I spoke. Even though I could communicate pretty well when it came to face-to-face Greek, my telephone Greek remained abysmal, my go-to conversation opener invariably being, '*Milas Anglika?*' meaning 'Do you speak English?'

Dialling the number, I braced myself, mentally running the Greek for please speak slower, *parakalo mil apio arga*, through my mind. Inevitably, whenever I attempted telephone Greek, even the simplest of Greek vocabulary flew out of the window, leaving my speech on a par with that of a verbally challenged toddler or a gibbering idiot.

"*Kalimera. Milas Anglika?*" I asked as my call connected.

"*Mia stigma. Tha se valo.*" Turning to Marigold, I said, "She said 'one moment.' I think she's putting me through to an English speaker."

"You do know that it's the afternoon?"

"What?" My wife's ability to go off on an unrelated tangent never failed to amaze me.

"You said good morning. It's the afternoon…"

Offering the phone to Marigold, I invited, "Do feel free to take over and deal with it yourself…"

"There's no need to get in a strop, Victor. I was simply saying…"

"Look out," I warned, pulling Marigold along with me as I jumped backwards to avoid a car that came careening round the corner at great speed, the driver blasting the horn as he passed us. The horn practically drowned out the words from the other end of my mobile, a male voice asking in Greek for my number.

"*Ti arithmo?*" I said, asking what number whilst wondering what happened to my request for an English speaker.

"*Ton arithmo tou asfalistiriou symvolaiou sas.*"

"*Ti?*" As it belatedly dawned on me that he was probably asking for the number on my insurance policy, I ventured "*arithmo asfalisis?*" meaning number insurance. Resting the insurance policy on the boot of the Punto, I slowly and painfully recited each of the numbers in Greek.

"*Kyrie Kouva?*"

"*Nai,*" I said, confirming I was indeed Mr Bucket.

"*To noumero tou kinitou sou.*" Slowly reciting the number of my mobile telephone as requested, I wondered what number he would dream up to demand of me next; my inside leg or my waist measurement, or perhaps the number of chickens in my coop or the number of ticks that had set up home on the cats.

"No. No. This can't be happening." As my mobile phone died in my hand, I was tempted to throw it across the road in frustration.

"What's the matter, Victor? It's not like you to lose your temper."

Looking at my wife, I contemplated fibbing. If I

told her the truth, she would likely rub my nose in *I told you so*, having indeed warned me to top up my mobile phone credit before we ventured to town.

"My mobile has run out of credit and died on me. I didn't even manage to tell the insurance company where we are."

"Use mine, darling," Marigold offered, passing me her phone. I felt more than a tad guilty that I had assumed my wife's first reaction would be to lord it over me by pointing out my shortcomings. No doubt, the stress of the situation was making me judgemental.

Hoping I would be reconnected with the same man that had already taken the number of my insurance policy rather than going through the whole rigmarole again, I was about to dial when I was practically deafened by the sound of a motorbike approaching. A menacing machine roared past us. I was taken by surprise when the rider slowed down before turning back in our direction. I could feel my hackles rise as I imagined an outlaw biker had marked us an easy target to rob, no doubt assuming we were easy pickings. As the biker brought the powerful motorbike to a halt in front of the Punto, I moved to stand protectively in front of Marigold and Sherry.

As the leather-clad rider whipped off his helmet to reveal his glossy dark curls, Marigold proclaimed, "It's Giannis the honey man."

Considering that I had never seen Giannis wear an actual helmet before, it was no wonder that I had failed to recognise him. My relief was palpable as I realised it was a friend from the village rather than a Mad Max extra with abominable intentions.

Slapping bright smiles on their faces, Marigold and Sherry immediately started patting their hair, Sherry even going so far as none-too discreetly attempting to re-do her lipstick. The pair of them probably couldn't believe their luck that our knight in shining armour was the local pin-up. Ignoring their preening, Giannis commiserated with my bad luck in breaking down. Focusing all his attention on the engine, he told me that he could easily fix it and it would only take him about an hour. My relief was short-lived however when Giannis went on to add that he couldn't actually stay and fix it or he would be late for his *nona's* funeral.

"*I Sofia Kompogiannopoulou itan i nona sou.*" I expressed my surprise that Sofia had been Giannis' godmother, the intricacies of village relationships reminding me of an onion with many layers. I went on to assure Giannis it was no problem as I had breakdown insurance. "*Kanena provlima. Echo asfaleia gia vlavi.*"

After ascertaining that I had not, as yet, managed to arrange for a tow truck to come out to the Punto, Giannis took charge, using his own mobile phone to telephone the insurance company who promised to have someone with us in one hour, or maybe two; three at the latest. I greatly appreciated Giannis' assistance as it spared me the horror of attempting to pinpoint our location in my dismal telephone Greek. Moreover, I was totally bowled over by Giannis' kind offer to fix the Punto the next morning if I could get the breakdown truck driver to drop the broken-down car off at Giannis' motorcycle repair yard in Meli.

With help on its way, Giannis apologised, saying he really had to go, adding, "*Boro na pao enan apo eses piso sto Meli me to michanaki.*" Remarkably, Marigold understood his offer to take one of us back to Meli on his motorbike, proving my suspicion that she engaged selective hearing when it came to her Greek language abilities.

Much as I was tempted to leap up on the motorbike behind Giannis and wrap my arms tightly around his waist and let him transport me back to Meli, I resisted the urge, knowing I would never live down such an unchivalrous act. It really wouldn't do to leave two helpless women stranded by the side of the broken-down Punto, with no male protection, whilst I gadded off to the funeral.

"Marigold, you should go with Giannis. At least that way, one of us will be able to attend Sofia's funeral," I urged.

I cannot emphasise enough how much of a noble act this was on my part since it would mean I would be stuck alone with the braying Sherry for the foreseeable. Considering the way that Sherry was acting in a coquettish manner, practically thrusting her chest in Giannis' face, I at least consoled myself that she would be unlikely to attempt to throw herself at my head as she had done when Marigold had been back in Manchester. I don't mind admitting that I was hardly a sex symbol next to the younger and handsomer Greek. Moreover, Sherry was sober; on the occasion she had made a play for me, she had most definitely been in her cups.

As Giannis passed his crash helmet to Marigold, she visibly hesitated, complaining, "It will muss up my hair."

"If you think for one minute that I'm going to allow you to ride on that monstrous machine without adequate cranial protection, you've got another think coming," I snapped.

"Oh, Victor, you sound quite masterful," Marigold simpered, meekly popping the helmet on her head. Climbing up behind Giannis, my wife wrapped her arms around his waist, mouthing an apology to Sherry for leaving her stuck with me. It appeared that Marigold had forgiven her friend for throwing herself at Lefteris like a brazen hussy.

The motorbike had barely gone a couple of yards when it stopped and Marigold called out, "Victor, there's a carrier bag in the boot that I need.

The Marks and Spencer one."

"Seriously," I called back. Clearly, despite Marigold's earlier protestation that she had a perfectly adequate dark dress for the funeral, she must have gone and splurged on a new frock after all.

As the motorbike took off for a second time, I said to Sherry, "We could be in for a long wait."

"The cats are getting jolly restless," Sherry informed me. "Do you think I should let them out of their cages?"

"They have been cooped up a long time," I admitted. "You could let them out of their cages for a minute but only inside the car with the windows up. And just one at a time; don't let them both out at once. Marigold would have a fit if we managed to lose her precious felines."

"We really ought to give them some water," Sherry suggested.

Luckily, Marigold had purchased some bowls for the apartments. Retrieving a couple from the boot and filling them with water for the cats, I made a mental note to give the bowls a thorough scouring before putting them in the apartments, knowing from experience that cat licked crockery was perfectly safe for humans after a thorough wash.

From my vantage point on the road, I watched as Sherry released Catastrophe from her cage. Despite the miserableness of my situation, forced to wait helplessly for the tow truck to put in an appearance, I couldn't resist a smile when Catastrophe jumped into the driver's seat, resting her front paws on the steering wheel as though she was planning to drive off.

I felt quite buoyed up when the driver of an enormous concrete mixer truck ground to a halt beside the Punto. Blocking the road, he called out to ask if he could help, "*Boro na voithiso?*" After assuring him that help was on its way, he gave a friendly wave before driving off. I couldn't help but reflect that if I'd been stuck behind him and his *betoniera* in normal circumstances, I would have been inwardly cursing him for holding me up and forcing me to trail behind him like a snail in second gear. When the same offer of assistance was offered by another passing driver, my faith in humanity was restored. The Greeks really were a helpful lot.

My upbeat mood was short-lived when a sudden summer downpour threatened to soak me. Attracting Sherry's attention, I indicated she should pop Catastrophe back in her cage so I could safely open the door to escape the bucketing rain. Even though I was thoroughly drenched by the time the cat was once again caged, I didn't blame Sherry for taking an age, the scratches on the back of her hands a testament to what a struggle it was to control the cats. I knew from bitter experience how much the cats loathed their travel receptacles, never failing to fight tooth and claw to avoid being boxed up. Earlier today, I had cleverly avoided their scratches by slipping a sedative into their breakfast slop.

Settling in the passenger seat, a dreadful smell assailed me. If I had to hazard a guess, I would say it came from something as unsavoury as Manolis' dog vomit slime mould. Turning to Sherry, I asked, "What is that awful smell?"

"That darling cat ripped a hole in one of my bags of goat manure," Sherry confessed. "Sorry about that. It is a bit ripe."

"I really don't understand why you felt it necessary to buy manure in town when Meli is knee-deep in the stuff. There's goat muck everywhere, not to mention chicken droppings. Guzim even bags it up and sells the stuff."

"Well, this bagged variety has matured. Fresh manure takes time…" I tuned out as Sherry prattled on as though she was some kind of an expert in manure. "Victor, are you even listening? I was just saying that I'm getting into composting in a big way. Nothing goes to waste anymore. I bought a jolly big composting bin and chuck all sorts in. You wouldn't credit the sort of things one can compost; egg shells, coffee grinds, toe nail clippings and even hair."

"I don't think I'd fancy eating veggies that had been grown in that revolting mix," I said.

"Ah, well, my compost is strictly for flowers. I

don't grow veg but I do enjoy a jolly good forage. If nothing else, my relationship with Heinrich introduced me to the joy of gathering the marvellous greenery we have all around us. I got some fabulous weeds over the winter, just fabulous."

"Don't tell me you were liquidising weeds into that dreadful green gunk that Heinrich used to cook up."

"Good gracious, no. I haven't touched a drop of that vile sludge since Heinrich went back to Germany. I pick weeds for *horta*. I was practically living off the stuff over the winter. I must say, Victor, I find it very odd that you didn't include cooking *horta* during your cookery classes."

"I really didn't think that forage, clean and boil required an actual demonstration."

As a fresh whiff of the pungent aroma of goat manure assaulted my nostrils, I willed the rain to let up so I could escape the confines of the Punto and breathe in fresh air. Both of the cats were getting restless and it could be goodness only knows how long until the breakdown truck turned up to rescue us.

Finally, the bucketing rain let up, turning into a fine drizzle, allowing me escape the car. Admitting the stench of manure was making her feel a tad queasy, Sherry was right on my tail. The lush green fields smelled absolutely magnificent after their impromptu watering, the delicious scent of sage and thyme so good that they ought to be bottled as perfume.

I watched with interest as a tatty old moped slowly approached, labouring to make it up the hill. As the moped drew level with the Punto and stopped, I prepared to greet the scooterist and decline the inevitable offer of help.

"Guzim?" Unbelievably, until he removed the helmet from his head and I caught sight of his practically toothless gums, I wasn't certain that it was indeed the Albanian shed dweller: despite living in close quarters, I had never seen Guzim with an actual helmet on his head before. It appeared that the moped accident that had landed him in the hospital had taught him the wisdom of helmeting up.

"*Echeis katarrefsei?*" Guzim asked if we'd broken down.

"*Nai,*" I confirmed. Much as I was tempted to say I had simply pulled over to enjoy the view, I knew that a sarcastic response would fly right over Guzim's head; he didn't really do nuance. Instead, I assured him that help was on the way. "*Erchetai voitheia.*"

"*Kalos.*"

Desperate as I was to be shot of Sherry, a brilliant idea occurred to me and I asked Guzim if he could take Sherry back to Meli on the back of the moped. *"Boreis na pas tin Kyria Sherry piso sto Meli sto piso meros tou motopodilatou sou?"*

"Ochi." Without even feigning consideration of my request, Guzim's refusal was instant.

"Giati?" I asked why.

"Einai poly varia." Guzim came up with the excuse that Sherry was too heavy before protesting that she'd be all over him and reminding me that he was a married man. *"Kai tha einai pantou pano mou. Eimai pantremenos antras."*

Much as I would have loved to send Sherry off with Guzim, I could tell the Albanian was not for turning. Additionally, his newly acquired moped was clearly a pile of old junk. With Sherry riding pillion, it would likely conk out just as the Punto had done. I could almost guarantee that Guzim wouldn't have squandered any of his hard-earned cash on breakdown insurance.

Having failed to understand a single word of my chat with Guzim, Sherry piped up, "I've got a jolly good idea. I could go back to Meli on the back of Guzim's motorbike."

I reflected that if she'd only put as much energy into learning Greek as she had to foraging, she'd already know that she'd been rebuffed, dismissed as too heavy and practically labelled a man-eater by an almost toothless Albanian modelling the latest fashion in pleather. Thinking to spare Sherry's feelings, I pointed out that the moped was practically on its last legs and not up to transporting two people. "Besides, Guzim has only got the one helmet."

"*Tha pao. Prepei na psaxo gia tin Doruntina,*" Guzim said, telling me he was going and he needed to look for Doruntina.

"*Prosochi, oi dromoi einai vregmenoi,*" I said, telling Guzim to be careful and reminding him the roads were wet. Admittedly self-interest prompted my advice: I had no desire to transport an injured Guzim to Albania for a second time.

Waving Guzim off, I clocked the time. Since I was now officially missing Kyria Kompogiannopoulou's funeral, I resigned myself to learning all about the intricacies of composting.

Chapter 18

Nothing if not Gullible

After being stuck with Sherry for three full hours whilst we waited for the tow truck, I felt decidedly frazzled. I wasn't alone in my sentiment. The second we reached Meli, the breakdown vehicle driver had pulled over to let Sherry out, less than flattered over the unnecessary attention she had paid to his knee. After assuring him that Sherry had nothing to do with me, he very helpfully stopped at the Bucket residence, allowing me to pass the two cats and numerous bags of shopping to Marigold, before delivering the Punto to Giannis' yard.

Strolling home through the village from Giannis' place, I kept a cautious eye out; it really wouldn't do if one of the villagers spotted me carrying a caged bunny and ratted me out to Guzim. I had taken the precaution of borrowing a blanket from Giannis to toss over the cage to hide my cargo. Unable to face the prospect of Guzim continually snuffling over the loss of his bunny, I had purchased what I hoped was a near-identical rabbit from Giannis, in the hope of passing it off as Doruntina. Guzim was, after all, nothing if not gullible.

Eyeing up the choice of rabbits available, I had opted for one with fawn fur, pretty certain that the missing Doruntina was a similar colour with no particular distinguishing features. Despite Guzim's rabbit being a somewhat permanent presence around my garden, I had never gazed into its eyes to ascertain its eye colour. Crossing my fingers, I had plumped for a brown-eyed bunny, hoping it was a good match. Admittedly, I had never studied Doruntina closely enough to claim pinpoint accuracy in my quest to palm off a look-alike, but nevertheless, I hoped to pull the wool over Guzim's eyes with this new female rabbit. At least I was confident I'd got the sex right.

Reaching the house, I let the replacement rabbit out of the cage. Keeping a tight grip on the squirming creature, I made my way through to the garden where Guzim was on his hands and knees weeding my vegetable patch. I was relieved to see that the Albanian shed dweller had made it safely back on the clapped-out moped. Despite the endless wait to be rescued from the roadside, the breakdown truck had still managed to overtake Guzim on the final stretch to Meli.

"*Guzim, koita. Vrika tin Doruntina,*" I called out, telling him to look, I had found Doruntina.

Dropping the trowel, Guzim rushed over, a look of devotion on his face as I handed him the replacement rabbit.

"*Doruntina. Doruntina mou. Gyrises konta mou, poso mou eleipses.*" Gushing over the rabbit, Guzim told it how much he had missed it. Oblivious to the risk of catching myxomatosis or some other zoonotic disease, he lifted the rabbit close to his face and smothered it in sloppy kisses. The Albanian shed dweller was even more susceptible than I thought, immediately accepting the interloper on face value even though he was staring it right in the face.

Plonking the rabbit on the ground so it could start nibbling away at my salad patch, Guzim grabbed hold of me. Desperate to be free from his clutches, I squirmed as much as the rabbit had when it had tried to escape my grip. Fortunately, Guzim's attempt to drop a smacker on me was foiled by my superior height. Nevertheless, he declared that he loved me. "*Kyrie Victor,* I love you."

To say I was taken aback was an understatement,

those three little words being the very first English words that I had ever heard Guzim utter. I reflected it had been a massive mistake to drag the Albanian along when I met Captain Vasos as it appeared that the good captain had negatively influenced my gardener's vocabulary. It was bad enough having Vasos continually declaring his love for me without Guzim getting in on the bandwagon.

Finally releasing his hold on me, Guzim bent down to grab the rabbit that had so readily fooled him. As he lavished yet more attention on the imposter rabbit, from the corner of my eye, I spotted something moving about in the undergrowth.

"No, this can't be happening," I blurted.

"*Ti?*"

Ignoring Guzim, my mind went into overdrive as the moving creature came into clear view, revealing itself as the missing Doruntina. Quite how I was going to explain it away to Guzim presented a quandary.

Following my eye, Guzim spotted his rabbit. However, it did nothing to dispel the illusion that the fake Doruntina that Guzim was holding was the real thing. Considering it had been his beloved pet and bed companion for years, Guzim could be amazingly dense. My immediate assumption was to think that Guzim would simply adopt both rabbits. Whilst such a scenario would undoubtedly spell double trouble for my vegetable patch, it would at least let me off the hook for my, admittedly well-intentioned, meddlesome interference.

"*Apo pou einai afto to kouneli?*" Pointing at the real Doruntina, Guzim asked where that rabbit had come from.

"*Den gnorizo.*" Saying 'I don't know' was entirely truthful on my behalf: I genuinely had no idea where the missing Doruntina had appeared from. Hoping that Guzim would remain blissfully ignorant about my interference, I asked him if he'd keep both rabbits. "*Tha kratiseis kai ta dyo kounelia?*"

"*Ochi.*" There was no hesitation in Guzim's refusal.

"*Giati?*" I asked why.

Guzim was resolute in his reply, telling me that Doruntina was his pet and the other rabbit was nothing to do with him. "*I Doruntina einai to katoikidio mou, afto to allo kouneli den echei kamia schesi me mena.*" It appeared that Guzim didn't have a particular affinity to rabbits in general, just to the one that he thought shared his living quarters.

The back door of the neighbouring house opened and Kyria Maria stepped into her garden, prompting a totally unimaginable response from Guzim. I could hardly believe my ears when Guzim declared that Kyria Maria liked to eat rabbit meat and we should pass her the spare rabbit to cook up a treat. Dropping the fake Doruntina back on the ground, Guzim made a grab for the real Doruntina, calling out to attract Kyria Maria's attention as he did so.

"*Ochi. Stamata,*" I cried out, instructing Guzim to stop. Realising that my conscience simply wouldn't allow Guzim to give his actual pet to Maria to cook, it hit me that I had no choice but to fess up and come clean, telling Guzim that the rabbit he was holding and about to pass a death sentence on, was the real Doruntina. "*To kouneli pou kratas einai i pragmatiki Doruntina.*"

Staring into Guzim's confused face, I confessed that I had purchased a look-alike bunny to cheer him up. Amazingly, instead of my words prompting a fit of temper, they moved Guzim to tears. Between sobs, he expressed his undying gratitude for my gesture before tucking the real Doruntina under his chin and handing the replacement rabbit over the wall for Kyria Maria to cook, giving me no chance to grab the rabbit and claim a refund from Giannis. Racked with guilt, I fled the garden. Attempting to justify Guzim's behaviour, I rationalised that it was no different from my keeping chickens whilst happily tucking into a bird that we'd purchased in Lidl.

Back in the house, Marigold was positively glowing, rapturously enthusing about her marvellous time riding pillion behind Giannis. Considering her previously vocal objections to dangerous and monstrous motorcycles blasting through the village, I attributed her exuberance to clinging on tight to the local pin-up.

"It was just so exhilarating to feel the wind in my hair," Marigold gushed, running her fingers through her visibly flattened Titian locks.

"Don't tell me you took the helmet off," I chided.

"It's just a figure of speech, Victor," Marigold countered, attempting to suppress the involuntary smile crinkling her mouth.

"Well, whilst you were having such fun with Giannis, I was stuck with your ghastly friend, Sherry, for hours on end. That woman lacks an off button. I know far more about composting than anyone could imagine."

"At least you got out of having to sit through Sofia Kompogiannopoulou's funeral. It wasn't exactly a barrel of laughs."

"Did it go off without incident?"

"Yes. No one danced on her grave," Marigold said, reminding me of how Despina had cavorted around at Haralambos' funeral. "Papas Andreas didn't half go on. Even though Spiros was there in his official capacity, he still popped outside the church for a cigarette break. I was quite tempted to take up smoking so that I'd have an excuse to escape Andreas' endless droning."

"Did you kiss the corpse?"

"I really couldn't get out of it but I aimed an air kiss at Sofia's forehead. You must be exhausted after waiting around with the Punto so I thought I'd cook for you this evening. There was one interesting thing that happened at the funeral."

"Oh, yes. Do tell."

"That old commie, what's his name?"

"Kyrios Stavropoulos…"

"That's the one," Marigold confirmed. "He was in absolute bits. From what I could gather, he'd been enjoying a secret liaison with Sofia."

"No. I think you must have got the wrong end of the stick, Marigold. There was no sign of anything between them when she worked in the shop. He used to take his morning coffee there daily. I'm sure I would have noticed if there was anything between them."

"You're not the most observant when it comes to affairs of the heart, Victor. Though to be fair, I don't think it was general knowledge until he broke down at the funeral."

Slipping a pinny on over the new frock she'd worn to the funeral, Marigold opened a tin of cat food. Catastrophe and Clawsome instantly appeared, rubbing themselves against my wife's legs.

"They seem to have recovered from their ordeal," I noted.

"It was hardly an ordeal," Marigold argued. "We've never been in and out of the vet's so quickly."

"I wasn't the only one who had to endure hours of composting trivia. Your cats were a captive audience too. Now, what are you planning to cook?"

"I thought I'd do some baked feta in a tomato sauce and serve it with some boiled *vlita* and *skordalia*." By this point, I was so hungry that I'd willingly tuck into Kyria Maria's bunny if she passed it off as chicken.

"That does sound good," I enthused over the sound of my rumbling stomach.

Although Marigold had banned me from boiling up *horta* in the house since it took hours and made the place reek, boiling up *vlita* was allowed as it only took about fifteen minutes and didn't smell too much. *Vlita*, the cultivated version of wild *horta*, required less time to prepare as it wasn't nearly as bitter as the wild greens.

"I'll just need to pop out and collect the *vlita* from Yiota's farmhouse," Marigold informed me. "She told your mother that she'd put some freshly picked leaves to one side for us. Oh, darn, I can't drive there without Punto."

"Don't worry, I'll go," I volunteered. Since I had an ulterior motive for stopping by at the farmhouse, collecting the *vlita* would allow me to kill two birds with one stone.

Chapter 19

A Man in a Pinny

C ollecting the fresh *vlita* was nothing more than a convenient excuse to drop by at the farmhouse. Having grown quite fond of Yiota since Violet Burke had adopted her as a surrogate granddaughter, I shared my mother's concern that Yiota's long-lost great-uncle, Hal, might be taking advantage of the young woman and adding an intolerable burden to her already heavy workload. Taking an almost fatherly interest, I wanted to stop by to see the lie of the land. It wouldn't do if Yiota felt forced into sharing her home with a relative who was effectively, a total stranger.

V.D. BUCKET

Entering the courtyard, I braced myself, always wary of the reception I might receive from Panos' ferocious guard dog, Apollo. I don't mind admitting that I found the slobbering creature nothing less than terrifying; always mindful of the delight Apollo had taken in ripping a chunk out of Guzim's posterior, one snap of its jaw could reduce me to a quivering wreck.

Cautiously skirting my way past the cut-throat canine, it appeared that my natural trepidation was in this instance misplaced. Wearily disinterested in my presence, Apollo barely lifted his head: the string of drool stretching from his jaws together with the glazed expression in his eyes, making him appear like a doggy pensioner with all the stuffing knocked out of him. I couldn't help but notice that Apollo's appearance was somewhat changed, his usual shaggy black and grey coat absent most of the black, now almost uniformly grey. Not being up on canine hair trends, I made a mental note to ask Athena if dogs followed the human pattern of turning grey as they aged. For all I knew, Apollo might just be filthy and in need of a good hosing down.

As I approached the kitchen door, it was flung wide open. Hal stepped outside, clutching a plastic laundry basket. Once again, I was immediately floored by Hal's uncanny resemblance to Panos. Having paired a pair of wellies with a pair of knee-length shorts and a floral pinny, with what appeared to be Yiota's straw sunbonnet decorated with plastic flowers perched on his head, he looked quite the sight as he offered me a decidedly bombastic greeting.

"Victor, my friend, good to see you. I won't ask you indoors as my kitchen floor's just drying. Don't want it getting streaky."

"That's fine. I was actually after Yiota. She put some *vlita* aside for me."

"Yiota's still out in the fields. She's a hard worker, that one, a smashing girl and no mistake. Panos must have been very proud."

"Indeed, he was extremely proud of her," I assured Hal, recalling the many times that Panos had told doting tales of his granddaughter.

"Not sure what time Yiota will be back. I've got a *kakavia* on a low simmer for when she gets home."

"Ah, the classic Greek fisherman's soup."

"I went down to the coast first thing for a fresh *barbouni*…"

"Red mullet. Did you catch it yourself?"

"No, I bought it from a fisherman down there. I need to sort myself out with a boat; I want to do my own fishing. I sounded out some of the local fishermen this morning. I thought if anyone was retiring, I could have first dibs on their boat. Word is, they'd rather take the cash on offer from the Germans to destroy their boats than try and find a buyer. It's a shocking business."

I was familiar with the practice whereby retiring fishermen were essentially bribed with a European Union offer of a generous wad of cash to burn or bulldoze the boats that had afforded them their living. Although the EU directive was supposedly introduced to cut down on overfishing, the Greek fishermen that I had spoken to about it seemed convinced it was a German ploy to kill off the Greek fishing industry. Even though they spoke of the policy with derision, they were not above taking the cash when they decided it was time to hang up their nets and lines, and cash in their pensions. As if to give weight to the local view about Germans deliberately attempting to decimate the Greek fishing industry, the cash bribes on offer were invariably much more than the boats were actually worth, hence the reluctance of the fishermen to sell their boats to up and coming fishermen for a significantly lesser sum than the official bung.

"I won't give up though. It's been my dream to retire in Greece and fish from my very own boat. There's good fishing to be had in the Mani. If I can't find anyone willing to sell me a second-hand boat, I'll have to buy new," Hal said. "Any idea if Yiota is up for trying foreign food? I was thinking of doing a zupa rybna tomorrow."

"What's that?"

"A Polish fish soup." As Hal spoke, he started to unpeg the washing from the line, folding each item neatly before depositing them in the plastic basket. "I don't want to serve up something Yiota wouldn't be keen on eating. You know how a lot of Greeks will only eat Greek…"

"I do indeed. So, I take it that your own culinary tastes lean to the exotic?"

"Working the boats with men from all over who all mucked in with the cooking, I've tried all sorts. My best mate, Wojtek, was a Pole and he made a mean rybna soup; gave me his recipe. Lost him to a bluefin tuna in the Alaskan Shelikof Strait a few years back."

Before I could ask if the tuna had attacked his mate, Hal continued his story.

"Wojtek harpooned this massive bluefin and it ended up leading us a right old dance. Next thing we knew, he was being dragged off the boat. Somehow, Wojtek got tangled in the line attached to the harpoon. It was a tragedy that he never learned to swim." Pegs in hand, Hal made the sign of the cross as he spoke. "So, I thought I'd better play safe and do something traditionally Greek for Yiota until I've sounded her out on eating anything foreign. I'm thinking she's sure to like an authentic *kakavia*. I expect the poor girl will be quite famished after working all day in the fields."

"I'm sure that Yiota will appreciate you cooking

a meal for her…"

"Aye, well, it's only right that I should pull my weight. Farming's not my gig but I know my way around a galley and I can keep the farmhouse in shipshape order." The precision with which he folded the washing, not even flinching as he handled Yiota's smalls, gave credence to his words; the willingness with which he donned a pinny hinting he was more than happy to play the role of housewife to Yiota's farmer.

I have to say that I was pleasantly surprised to hear that Hal wasn't expecting Yiota to run around after him. Yiota had often voiced to my mother that although she was besotted with Giannis, she had reservations about making their relationship permanent due to his inability to lift a finger to help around the house whenever he spent time there, quite content to be waited on hand and foot. It was no secret that Giannis' mother, Ioanna, spoilt her son rotten, cooking and cleaning for her grown son and insisting there was no need for him to raise a finger. If Giannis moved in with Yiota, he would certainly add to her workload unless he mended his ways.

"I think that Yiota is quite adventurous when it comes to foreign food. My mother often cooks for her." Admittedly, I was bending the truth just a tad by referring to Violet Burke's cooking as adventurous, but there was no denying that Spam,

Fray Bentos and mushy peas were foreign to the typical Greek palate.

"Violet's quite the woman, I must say. She's got plenty of sass about her. I like that in a woman." There was no mistaking the note of admiration in Hal's tone.

"That's one way of describing her," I acknowledged.

"I can see why my brother was taken with her."

"Despite their inability to communicate in any meaningful fashion, they got along like a house on fire. What about you, Hal? I hear you never married?"

"I never did. It's hard to settle down when you're away for weeks at a time on the boats. Not many women fancy that lifestyle and of course, the smell didn't help."

"The smell?"

"Of fish. It's all-pervasive on those massive boats. When we were away from land for days on end, we had to dress the fish onboard. Some days, we were up to our necks in fish heads and organs, covered in scales and guts from dawn to dusk. I don't half miss it though."

"The smell?"

"No, that I don't miss. I miss being out on the sea but there's no denying it's a hard life. I thought it would be harder than it is to find my land legs but Yiota has made it easier, what with her being so welcoming. The house is nice and homely too, though I've a few home improvements in mind. I hadn't expected Panos to have made the place so nice."

"That's rather down to my wife, Marigold, and her friend, Doreen. They added some home touches to the place after Panos' passing in an effort to make Yiota feel at home. It was certainly a lot more basic before they tackled the place."

"It warms my heart to hear that Yiota has good friends like that."

"She's very popular and her work ethic hasn't gone unnoticed."

"It's a relief to me that Yiota speaks such good English and that she has English speaking friends. After fifty years away, my Greek is so rusty that I'm wondering if I should start having Greek lessons. I've been speaking Canadian and American for as long as I can remember. I can barely understand a word that young fellow of Yiota's says."

The irony of Hal's words struck me. Earlier, Giannis had confided in me that he was wary of Hal's intentions in returning to Meli and was considering learning English to better communicate with Hal and give him a good grilling.

"What do you think of Giannis, Victor?"

"He strikes me as a fine young man..."

"But is he good enough for my great niece?"

"I think that's for Yiota to decide."

"I'd hate to think he's hooked up with her for her inheritance…"

"Giannis has an inheritance of his own. His grandfather, Haralambos, left his house in Nektar to Giannis."

"I heard it burned down…"

"No. Fortunately, the fire only damaged the downstairs room that Haralambos was confined to."

"So, Giannis has got a house of his own," Hal pondered aloud, seemingly mulling the notion that Yiota's suitor wasn't attracted to her because of Panos' farm.

"Indeed," I confirmed whilst keeping my own counsel about my conversation with Giannis whilst I'd been choosing a suitable rabbit to palm off on Guzim. Giannis had disclosed that his plan was to renovate Haralambos' neglected house, doing most of the work himself but engaging Vangelis and Barry for any work that was beyond his own capabilities. Giannis had hinted that once done up, his grandfather's house might make a suitable marital home. Personally, I thought it would make an ideal rental spot for tourists but I'd not been daft enough to suggest it to Giannis; there was no point in introducing unnecessary competition for my own venture.

"It worries me that Giannis may take after the old man." Looking me directly in the eye, Hal appeared genuine in his concern. "You'll have heard about the old man's reputation?"

"His reputation certainly wasn't good. Although I never met Haralambos, I heard some terrible things about him. I've never heard anything bad about Giannis. This very afternoon, he helped me out of a fix when my car broke down."

With the washing from the line all neatly folded in his basket, Hal announced he would get the *vlita* that Yiota had set aside for me. Removing his wellies, he stepped into the kitchen, reemerging with an enormous box of the green stuff.

"I can't accept all that," I said. There was enough cultivated *horta* in the box to feed a family of six for a month.

"Don't forget that it shrinks when you cook it," Hal reminded me, insisting I take it all. There was so much *vlita* that we'd be eating the stuff for breakfast, lunch and dinner unless I could persuade Violet Burke to boil some of it up for the expat dinner party. I would need to turn on my persuasive charm, my mother having a natural antipathy for green vegetables, excepting her beloved mushy peas and her recently acquired liking for green olives.

"You'll stop for a drink, Victor? Come on inside, the floor's dried nicely," Hal invited. "I've got plans to rig up some shade out here and introduce some outside furniture."

"Doreen's your woman if you need inspiration for decorating the courtyard space," I said.

"Not come across her yet."

"She's a good friend of my wife," I said, realising that Hal hadn't had the pleasure of meeting Marigold yet. I briefly considered inviting him along to the expat dinner party, but recalling that Violet Burke hadn't appeared particularly enamoured of the village's newest arrival, I bit my tongue. There would be plenty of other opportunities for Marigold and Hal to get acquainted.

"Take your shoes off," Hal ordered as I entered the kitchen.

Looking around the familiar kitchen, I noticed everything was indeed in ship-shape order, everything neat and tidy. Panos' wedding photograph remained in pride of place on the mantelpiece above the open fire; polished within an inch of its life, the glass fairly gleamed.

"I've big plans for this room. I think it's a bit tired as is. A new state-of-the-art kitchen could be in order as I plan to spend a lot of time cooking. I've got a hankering for a walk-in larder. Did you modernise your kitchen when you moved in, Victor?"

"Marigold had her heart set on a Shaker but budget constraints forced us to settle for one from IKEA."

"I definitely think a new look is in order. I heard

that Panos met his end in this very kitchen."

"Indeed, he did. I was the one who found his body," I confessed, choking up as I clocked the very spot where I had found Panos lying in his stockinged feet. Hal appeared equally moved, a morose expression momentarily crossing his face. Visibly shuddering, he pulled himself together.

"How does a virgin bloody Mary grab you?" Without waiting for a reply, Hal busied himself adding lemon wedges and ice cubes to a pitcher before filling it up with tomato juice; a more than generous measure of Worcestershire sauce was next in the mix. Filling two glasses, Hal washed a couple of celery sticks to use as edible cocktail stirrers. "Cheers."

Repeating his toast in Greek, I raised my glass. *"Stin ygeia sas."*

"I don't do alcohol. I used to have a problem with it," Hal confessed. Removing the lid from the steaming pan of *Kakavia*. Hal inhaled the rich aroma. "Once I get sorted with a fishing boat, you'll have to join me."

"I'd be delighted to. But will you be allowed to take passengers? I heard the fine is quite steep if the sea police catch you with an unauthorised person in a boat."

"I've no plans to take out a professional license at my age, the paperwork would be a nightmare. As an amateur fisherman…" Hal took a moment to snort with laughter at the ridiculous notion he was anything but a consummate professional when it came to fishing… "I'll be able to take people out without risking a fine. Course it means that certain fish will be off limits…but they'll have to catch me with my catch."

The idea that there was a whole layer of bureaucracy concerned with policing which fish unlicensed fishermen were allowed to catch, struck me as almost Kafkaesque. Nevertheless, if Hal made good on his invitation for me to join him on his yet-to-be-purchased boat, I would subtly police his catch myself: it wouldn't do to have my reputation besmirched as a fisherman's companion willing to land a banned fish.

Chapter 20

All-Hands-on-Deck

The imminent arrival of our first paying guests in just two days meant that it was all-hands-on-deck for an early start at the Sofia Apartments on Friday morning, with even Marigold forgoing her customary lie in without too much complaining. With a name for the apartments finally settled on, Cynthia, having taken the day off work, demonstrated a previously unknown talent for sign painting, busily inscribing the words 'Sofia Apartments' on a couple of wooden signs with a proficiency hinting she was more than a mere dabbler.

Throwing herself fully into the creative role, Cynthia looked most out of character, showcasing her artistic bent in denim dungarees and a jaunty French beret worn at a fetching angle; fortunately, she didn't accessorise with a necklace cobbled together from a string of onions. Litsa was babysitting Anastasia, the death of Sofia Kompogiannopoulou having sadly deprived Barry and Cynthia of one of their most reliable babysitters.

As Cynthia made free with an artist's brush, her choice of words provoked an argument, Marigold insisting that we should drop the word apartments and replace it with the Greek equivalent of *diamerismata*. Even as Cynthia began to paint over the word apartments, the flaw in Marigold's argument became apparent since *diamerismata* was the word in transliteration rather than in actual Greek letters. I felt compelled to put my foot down and insist that Cynthia carried on with the original plan, asserting that the use of Greek might possible be perceived as a tad pretentious and would likely confuse the English tourists we were primarily hoping to attract. Moreover, even though the Greeks had their own word for apartments, I felt confident that most of them would be familiar with the English translation.

Vangelis and Blat worked tirelessly, concentrating their efforts on finishing tiling the outside patio, finally rid of the eyesore housing the outdoor loo. Indoors, Marigold had prepared the welcome baskets, adding miniature bottles of *ouzo*, bags of salted peanuts, and tiny jars of local honey. I would drop some freshly picked nectarines into the baskets on Sunday. Marigold was now standing over Barry, bossing her brother around as he fixed the finishing touches, hanging lightshades and mirrors, in addition to securing toilet roll holders to the bathroom walls. Barry was so impressed with his wife's previously untapped artistic handiwork that he mooted the suggestion that she should add a Greek mural to the walls.

"Oh, do get a grip, Barry," Marigold barked. "Cynthia's hardly Michelangelo."

"I didn't suggest that she paint the ceiling," Barry shot back.

Doreen had telephoned to say she was on her way over to help Marigold out with the soft furnishings. Apparently, the placement of cushions, rugs and bedding, was a two-person job: my offer to help had been slapped back with the lame excuse that I just didn't have the eye for it. Violet Burke had promised to juggle her various jobs around to enable her to pop in first thing Sunday morning to give the place a final bottoming before the paying guests arrived.

Despite the rest of the hangers-on, namely Cynthia, Marigold and Doreen, all generously offering their expertise for free, my mother planned to extort her going rate for charring. The mere suggestion that she should offer her services for free resulted in Violet Burke accusing me of trying to take advantage of a feeble old pensioner. Neither my mother nor I thought for one moment that she could ever be described as feeble but she had me over a barrel; no one did a good bottoming as thoroughly as Vi.

"Victor, I need you." Barry's cry buoyed me up, proving that I wasn't surplus to requirements after all. If Barry needed me, it showed that I must be a not insignificant cog in the wheel.

"What can I do for you?" I asked my brother-in-law.

"The rubbish is piling up. Can you bag it up and take it over to the bins?"

"You want me to go to the bins?" Admittedly my tone was a tad peevish. "I'd rather hoped my talents could be utilised for something loftier than dealing with the rubbish."

"Face it, Victor. When it comes to being of any practical help, you're even lower down the pecking scale than Guzim."

Since I didn't really have any witty come back to that, I accepted the derisory comment with good grace.

The amount of discarded packaging lying around was an utter disgrace. The small circular hand towel holder alone had arrived wrapped in an unnecessary amount of plastic inside a ginormous box, whilst the amount of cardboard and plastic wrapping a set of teaspoons required was quite unbelievable. Gathering up the waste, I carted it out to the Punto and drove it to the bins.

The large municipal bins were in an even more terrible state than usual. Along with the stinking garbage choking the metal receptacles, some ignoramus had dumped an inordinate amount of what appeared to be builders' rubbish on the ground by the side of the bins. I inwardly cursed whatever moron had seen fit to dump old cement bags overflowing with rubble, broken tiles and piles of discarded plasterboard. Clearly, someone didn't give a toss about the local environment. Considering we were attempting to encourage visitors to spend their holidays in Meli, this hideous blot on the landscape may well sully any first impressions of the village.

Staring in disgust at the mess that had been unceremoniously dumped at the side of the bins, I racked my brain, trying to pinpoint if any villager was currently in the process of renovating a property. The only culprits I could come up with were Barry and Vangelis but they would never stoop to resorting to such brazen rubbish pollution: at least not on their own doorstep. I felt extremely confident that they disposed of any building dross in a manner that complied with all the necessary protocols relating to construction and demolition waste management. Perchance some random builder from another village had driven out in the dead of night to unload his rubbish in Meli.

My mood improved no end when I saw the refuse collection truck approaching. Standing to one side, I offered a cheery *kalimera* to the intrepid workers tasked with the gruesomely smelly job of loading the rancid rubbish into the truck. My initial good mood went out of the window when, after emptying the metal bins into the back of the garbage truck, the bin men prepared to depart without chucking any of the building rubbish into their truck.

"*Ti les gi afto?*" Pointing at the left-behind waste, I called out 'what about that,' before insisting that they couldn't just leave it. "*Den boreis apla na to afiseis.*"

"*Den echei na kanei me emas,*" one of the bin men retorted, saying it was nothing to do with them.

"*Alla einai skoupidia.*" As I asserted, 'but it's rubbish,' the same bin man simply shrugged before repeating his claim that it was nothing to do with them.

"*Giati ochi?*" I asked him 'why not?' before pointing out it was very unsightly.

"*Parte to me to Dimarcheio.*" Telling me to take it up with the *Dimarcheio*, the bin man jumped on the back of the moving truck. Despite his refusal to remove the building debris, he gave me a cheery wave as the truck trundled off. As I watched them depart, I could have kicked myself, belatedly realising that I hadn't yet emptied the Punto; it was still stuffed full with the bagged-up waste from the apartments.

Whilst I occupied myself with emptying the Punto, the sound of a tinny bell clanging attracted my attention. Turning around, I watched as Violet Burke wobbled up on her bicycle.

"Here, Victor, grab that bag of rubbish from my basket and sling it in the bins to save me dismounting. It's not easy getting my leg over at my age," my mother puffed.

"Are you quite well, Mother? You appear to be out of breath."

"It's hardly surprising with my workload." Noticing the pile of builders' rubbish, Violet Burke immediately climbed on her high horse. "What on earth is all that mess? It's a flaming disgrace, that's what it is. Next thing you know, we'll be having vermin."

"It seems some builder has illegally dumped his rubbish."

"Whoever did it, wants locking up." Such a sentiment was quite mild for Violet Burke: I would have expected nothing less than her opining that the culprits should be hung, drawn and quartered.

Distracted by an approaching vehicle, Vi changed the subject. "What's that Hal fella doing driving Panos' pickup?"

"I don't know but it's good to see it finally getting some use. Panos rarely drove it."

"Well, you know how he was about that tractor of his. I hope that Hal fella isn't suckering Yiota in. I know she's not daft but, in my opinion, she opened her doors to him a sight too early. He's nowt but a stranger when all's said and done."

"Yiota had no choice. Hal has a legal claim to half the property," I reminded my mother.

"Well, you have a legal claim to my *apothiki* but it doesn't mean I'd put up with you moving in with me."

"Believe me, the feeling is mutual. Anyway, you'll be pleased to hear that rather than taking advantage of Yiota, Hal has been womaning up and donning a pinny to tackle the domestic duties," I said.

"Womaning up. That's quite witty for you, lad."

I have to confess to feeling a surge of pride in my mother's compliment.

"Hal is keen to buy a boat and start fishing," I confided.

As the pickup drew level, Vi stated, "My Petey's got a hankering for some fresh fish."

"She told you that, did she?"

"You don't half come out with some fool talk. Forget what I said about you being witty," Vi shot back as Hal alighted the pickup.

"A very good morning to you Violet, Victor."

"It's Mrs Burke to you." Despite my mother's sharp retort, her face reddened. "Where are you off to in Panos' car?"

"I'm off to the coast. I got word of a fishing boat for sale up at the marina in town. The owner has agreed to motor it down to the local harbour so I can take a look-see."

"My mother was just saying how much her cat fancies some fresh fish."

"I'll be happy to pick some up for you while I'm down there," Hal offered.

"Aye, well, don't be doing me any favours," Vi said, curtly dismissive, her lower lip visibly curling as she spoke.

"It's not for you, it's for your cat," Hal fired back. It appeared that Hal too revelled in having the last word. As one of the bin cats scuttled out from beneath the bins and rubbed itself against Hal's leg, he added, "I reckon some of these strays might fancy a nice bit of fish too."

"We were just saying what a disgrace it is," I said, pointing at the unsightly pile of building rubbish.

"That it is," Hal agreed.

"The bin men just left it. They said to take it up with the *Dimarcheio*. I'm tempted to phone them…"

"Faceless bureaucrats that'll likely just give you

the run around," Vi interrupted. "Jobsworths, the lot of them. Well, I can't be standing around gabbing like you two. Some of us have got work to do."

As Violet Burke pedalled off on her bicycle, Hal followed her with his eyes. "I think it will be better if Violet hears it from Yiota that I've taken over the cleaning at the farmhouse and done her out of a job. She might not be happy to hear she's got the boot. Mind you, Violet works too hard; by rights, she ought to be retired."

"I doubt she'll ever hang up her mop. My mother likes to keep busy."

"Let me know how you get on with the *Dimarcheio*," Hal said, climbing back into the pickup. "If you don't get anywhere, we could always pile the rubbish into the pickup once it's gone dark and dump it on the *Dimos* doorstep."

"Tempting though that is, I've a feeling it would be illegal."

Returning to the apartments, I described the state of the dumped rubbish to Vangelis, venting my annoyance at the situation.

"The bin men flatly refused to take the building rubbish away," I grumbled.

"The plastic you take was not from the construction," Vangelis countered.

"Not the rubbish I took," I clarified. "The rubbish that had been dumped by a builder."

"What rubbish? I not to dump any," Vangelis argued, seeming determined to misunderstand me.

Switching to Greek to better emphasise my point, I told him a builder had left old concrete, bricks and tiles by the bins. "*Enas oikodomos afise palio beton, touvla kai plakakia dipla stous kadous.*"

"*Plakakia,*" Vangelis repeated, a predatory gleam in his eyes. "Any *plakakia* worth the salvaging?"

"I wouldn't think so. They appeared to be broken." Vangelis looked suitably disappointed that he couldn't save a few bob by claiming dibs on some chucked out tiles.

"The bin men told me to take it up with the *Dimarcheio*," I said. "What's that all about?"

"The bin is for the household waste only," Vangelis explained. "When we have the rubbish from the construction, we must to telephone the *Dimarcheio* to ask where to take it. They will to tell the site."

"Somewhere local?" I asked.

"The Municipality will decide the where."

"Is that what you do with your building waste?"

"*Vevaios.*" Looking very sheepish, Vangelis avoided my eye as he said 'of course.'

"So, you always check with the *Dimos* before dumping your rubbish?"

"Yes." Since Vangelis still looked furtive, I pressed the point.

"Always?"

"Sometimes it is much the easier to throw it in the bin, but never on the own doorstep."

"Don't you worry about being caught?"

"Yes."

"Do they fine you if they catch you at it?"

"Fine? I not understand. They make us to pay money for making the random dump."

"That's a fine."

"Ah."

"Can you phone the *Dimos* to complain about the rubbish left at the bins?"

"No." Vangelis' monosyllabic responses were not only most out of character, but very annoying.

"No. Is that all you have to say on the matter?"

"Victor, look around. All the hands are working to get your apartments ready for Sunday. You think I have time to make the nice chat with the *Dimos*?"

Since I supposed that Vangelis made a fair point, there was nothing for it but to take the bull by the horns and telephone the *Dimarcheio* myself. My abiding fear of speaking Greek on the telephone was overshadowed by my justified annoyance at the abandoned carbuncle of crap sullying the village. Alas, my intention was thwarted by Marigold calling me from the garden where she was huddled with Doreen.

"Victor, do you think you could manage to hang these wind chimes from a tree? Doreen has brought them along as a gift."

"I think I could manage that," I agreed, hoping I could find a tree that was well away from the apartments. If the wind was up, the chimes would likely disturb any visitors, possibly leading to complaints. I reflected that I should perhaps suggest to Marigold that we replace the miniature bottles of *ouzo* with half-litre bottles on the assumption that sozzled guests may feel more in tune with any nocturnal chimes disturbing their dreams.

Chapter 21

Heart and Soul

By early Saturday afternoon, the kitchen in the Bucket residence had been completely taken over by Violet Burke preparing food for that evening's expat dinner party. Rather than risk being roped in to play chef's helper and being bossed around by her mother-in-law, Marigold had disappeared to Athena's to have her hair done: in her defence, she had already gone above and beyond, creating a superlative sherry trifle before she left.

Marigold's absence meant that I was the one charged with being at my mother's beck and call, chopping up vegetables and following her around with a dishcloth.

"Have you got a bottle of red going spare, Vic?"

"It's a bit early in the day…"

"For the stew, you daft 'apeth. I'm not one of them daytime tipplers."

"And what nation's stew will you be cooking up?"

"I'm doing Hungarian."

"I'm not really familiar with Hungarian cuisine," I admitted.

"Well, every fool and his brother know what Hungarian goulash is, lad," Vi countered. "So, I'm going to knock up a goulash for the main…"

"And for the appetiser?"

"Hungarian beetroot and Hungarian eggs. I did the eggs downstairs earlier."

"Hungarian eggs." Unable to resist a flippant sally, I asked, "I'm guessing they were laid by Hungarian chicks?"

"You sure like to think of yourself as a wag, Victor. 'Appen you're not as clever as you think…"

"It's not my fault if you've got no sense of humour…"

"The eggs were laid by your clutch. I gave the inside of their house a right good bottoming when I collected the eggs."

"Much appreciated, Mother."

"You need to have a word with that Albanian of yours…"

"How many times? Guzim is not my Albanian…"

"Course he is; he's like one of them third-removed types…"

Violet Burke's logic defeated me.

"What prompted you to say I should have a word with Guzim?"

"To give him some pointers on handling a broom. I reckon grasping how to slop a mop around the hen house is a bit beyond the mucky beggar."

"I think we can both agree that hygiene isn't Guzim's strong suit."

"Aye, that we can, lad."

Gathering the ingredients for the goulash together; beef chuck, onions, carrots, spuds, paprika and a bottle of wine, Vi instructed, "Pass me the potato peeler, Victor. Now, where do you reckon them Hungarian shepherds stored their surplus goulash back in the days before refrigerators were invented?"

"In a cold running stream," I guessed, having read that was a popular way to keep food cold during hot Greek summers before fridges were around.

"They kept it in a sheep's stomach."

"Are you sure you're not mixing your goulash up with your haggis."

"Hardly. How many Hungarian bagpipers wearing kilts have you ever come across?"

Openly chuckling, I wandered over to my collection of cookbooks. Knowing my mother's aversion to what she described as foreign muck, I was convinced she was making the whole Hungarian eggs thing up: I didn't for one moment imagine they were an actual thing. Thumbing through a cookbook that included recipes from Central Europe, to my surprise, I found a recipe for actual Hungarian eggs, Toltott Tojas.

Although the name had an exotic ring, they appeared to be nothing more original than a Hungarian take on devilled eggs. It occurred to me that perchance devilled eggs were an original invention of the Austro-Hungarian empire and the British may have simply appropriated the recipe. Voicing this idea to my mother, she gave me short shrift, emphatically stating that devilled eggs were invented by the ancient Romans.

Perusing the recipe, I read that the preparation of Hungarian eggs involved the yolks of hard-boiled eggs being mixed with onions, chopped ham, paprika and lemon juice, the spiced-up mix then stuffed back into the hollow that had housed the yolk. At least if Vi was serving up Toltott Tojas, my guests would be spared an appetiser that had been deep fried in lard.

"I've outsourced the pudding," Vi called over as she got stuck into peeling a mound of potatoes. "I've got that lummox Norman doing summat traditionally Hungarian for the pudding. I reckon you'd be better off sticking to Marigold's trifle; you can't go wrong with that."

"Is Marigold's trifle Hungarian?"

"Don't be daft, lad. She's hardly going to abandon her signature dish for something foreign."

"So, what's Norman cooking up?"

"He said he'd do a walnut torte. I reckon he's getting pretensions above his station. Why he couldn't just call it a tart and have done…"

"Tarts and tortes aren't the same thing," I schooled my mother.

"Course they are."

"They really aren't," I argued. "A tart has a pie crust whilst a torte is a layered cake."

Miffed at having no comeback, Vi chucked the beef chuck down on the chopping board, telling me, "This meat needs cutting up."

"I'm on it."

"I had supper round at Yiota's last night," my mother volunteered. "That fella, Hal, cooked. I have to say, the food wasn't half-bad."

"Polish fish stew?" I ventured.

"What are you, psychic?" Narrowing her eyes, Violet Burke peered at me intently before shrugging. "He cooked up some Polish potato pancakes on the side; right tasty they were."

"Did Yiota enjoy Hal's cooking?"

"The lass was that starved after a hard day's

farming that I reckon she'd have happily polished off a scabby donkey. Yiota wanted to break it to me gentle, like, that my charring services are surplus to requirements now that her uncle has taken over the cooking and cleaning."

"I'm sorry to hear that you've been done out of a job…"

"Well, it wasn't a job as such because I never let Yiota pay me, what with her being nearly family."

"I'm family and you charge me."

"Aye, but your Marigold and all them cats of hers make way more mess than Yiota. Anyhow, considering it was a week since I'd last been in Yiota's place to give the place a good going over, you could have knocked me down with a feather when I saw how spick-and-span the place was. Credit where credit's due, that Hal fella knows how to wield a mop and there was no sign he'd been cutting corners. There wasn't a single smear on the bathroom mirror and he'd squirted plenty of bleach down the lav."

"I noticed he was a dab hand when it came to pegging the washing out."

"'Appen he'll make someone a nice traditional wife," Vi said with a wink of her eye. "There's summat to be said about a fella what's not afraid of knuckling down to do the housework."

Having made quick work of preparing the beef and potatoes, we moved on to the onions and carrots. Working side by side in companionable silence, Vi nudged me, "We're chopping in rhythm again, lad."

"That we are…"

"Dum dah, dum dah, dum dah…"

Vi gave me another nudge, prompting me to burst into the lyrics from 'Heart and Soul.'

Swaying to the beat, the pair of us chopped and sang in unison. There was nothing original about our duet; we had shamelessly ripped it off from the famous scene in 'Frasier' where Daphne and Niles chop and sing. Although I had assumed the popular American television show was unlikely to tickle Violet Burke's fancy, she loved it. She was particularly enamoured of Niles, saying he reminded her of me. I had argued I was nothing like the sophisticated fop, Niles; my mother countered by pointing out that like Niles, I kept my tie tightly knotted whilst I cooked. Although by this stage our routine was old hat, it never failed to bring a smile to our faces.

The routine was something we'd developed the previous winter when we'd worked together in Takis' taverna kitchen, helping him to get up to speed preparing traditional British Sunday lunches in the hope that he would attract a regular clientele of expats yearning for a proper roast dinner. Takis was beyond delighted when every last table was filled, a scenario that was repeated week after week; no one could resist Violet Burke's Yorkshire puddings or the mouthwatering way she made the crackling crackle on her superlative roast pork. It had proved so popular that Takis had to squeeze some extra tables into the taverna to accommodate the crush of diners eager to sample Vi's rotating menu of roast beef, lamb, chicken, and pork.

Fortunately for me, it only took Takis a Sunday or two to pick up the basics, freeing me from the extra work. However, Violet Burke proved herself to be so indispensable to the operation that she became a regular fixture every Sunday, Takis even sending one of his waiters up to Meli to collect her in his car. Doubling Vi's wages, Takis proclaimed she was worth every cent. On one particular Sunday, Marigold and I had reserved a table. Arriving early, I had popped into the kitchen to say hello, only to surprise Violet Burke and Takis singing 'Heart and Soul' whilst chopping in rhythm. The moment stood out in my memory as a particular heart-warming one.

Takis' Sunday lunches had been such a success that word soon spread, even some of the local Greeks venturing down to the coast to sample Vi's cooking. Takis was particularly pleased to welcome Meli taverna owners, Nikos and Dina, as honoured guests. Considering their mutual dismissal of any food that their grannies hadn't cooked up, it was a testament of their respect for my mother that they cleared their plates.

When *Pascha*, Greek Easter, rolled around, Takis reluctantly put a hold on the British Sunday lunches though he had every intention of resuming them at the end of the tourist season. I was grateful that my mother was once again free on Sundays. As the local airport only welcomed flights on a Sunday, I anticipated that Sundays would be a popular changeover day for our newly refurbished apartments. I would need Violet Burke on hand to put her charring skills into action.

With the vegetables chopped, I cringed as my mother pulled a block of lard from the fridge. Realising from experience that it would be futile to advise her to brown the meat in the local extra virgin olive oil rather than cholesterol laden mucky fat, I kept my own counsel. Even though I kept schtum, Violet Burke could read me like a book. "You needn't start harping on about my lard, lad. It's the lard that's going to make this goulash authentic. You can't beat it for flavour."

Returning to the recipe in my cookbook, I was floored by what I read: lard was indeed listed as a key component.

"It sounds like there's someone at the door, lad."

"I hope it isn't Milton wanting to pester me about his great literary masterpiece again."

"At least he doesn't go all giddy at the sight of your ankles."

Opening the door, I was delighted that it wasn't Milton hovering, but young Tonibler clutching a book.

"Good afternoon, Mr Bucket," Tonibler greeted me, his English pronunciation perfect, albeit with a hint of a Mancunian accent that I suspect he had picked up from Violet Burke. "I came to return 'The Borrowers.'"

"Did you enjoy it?"

"It was fabulicious." Having purchased an excellent English dictionary for my young friend, I couldn't help but wonder if he curled up with it for bedtime reading, so advanced was his vocabulary. Moira Strange had been quite marvellous, securing the books I had listed as essential reading for the child prodigy on her frequent trips back to England. In addition to 'The Borrowers', Tonibler was making remarkable progress whipping through Enid Blyton's 'Mystery Of' books. I reflected that at the rate Tonibler was going, it was not inconceivable that we could begin to tackle Shakespeare together by this time next year. "Hello, Catastrophe."

Marigold's imported feline purred contentedly, rubbing itself against Tonibler's leg before slipping outside. Of late, Catastrophe had become almost daring, tentatively exploring the great outdoors on occasion though never venturing more than a couple of metres from the outdoor stairs.

"Have you got rid of that pest, Milton?" my mother called out.

"False alarm. It's young Tonibler," I said, ushering the boy through to the kitchen and leaving the front door ajar so Catastrophe could get back in.

"Eck, you're a right sight for sore eyes, Tony," Violet Burke declared. Beaming in pleasure, she rushed over to cluck the child under his chin. "Now, you grab a seat, lad. I've got a right treat for you."

"Is it chips?" Tonibler asked hopefully.

"No such luck. You know how Mrs Bucket can't be doing with the smell of fried food stinking up her kitchen."

Ignoring my protests, Vi grabbed the trifle that Marigold had prepared for that evening's dinner party, digging in deep with a serving spoon. The trifle audibly squelched as Vi spooned a substantial portion of the custardy confection into a bowl.

"Marigold will have a fit when she sees what you've done to her trifle," I objected.

"Your Marigold won't mind. She's got a right soft spot for the boy."

As Tonibler tucked into the trifle, a look of ecstasy on his face, Catastrophe dragged a bright green praying mantis inside, dumping it in one of the cats' feeding bowls. Marigold had trained her pampered pets so thoroughly that they wouldn't dream of eating off the kitchen floor, despite Violet

Burke's ministrations making the floor clean enough to actually eat off.

Chapter 22

That Guilty Look

Whilst Catastrophe amused itself by teasing the insect from a respectable distance, Tonibler adopted an almost reverential tone, asking, "What is that green thing?"

"It's an insect known as a praying mantis," I told him. "Apparently it's supposed to be good luck to see one."

"Does it bite?" Neglecting his trifle, the child squatted down on the floor tiles next to the bowl, all the better to observe.

"Only if it feels threatened," I said, shooing the decidedly un-threatening Catastrophe out of the way, the cat lacking even a hint of the killer instinct.

"Its eyes look like two apples surrounding a gnarled cucumber," Tonibler noted.

"So they do," I agreed, filling up with pride at the way Tonibler unhesitatingly dropped the word gnarled. I recalled that the very first time I had met the boy and began to teach him to read English words, I had determined that the silent 'g' on gnat would be too complicated for the boy to get his head round, yet here he was dropping a silent 'g' as confidently as Vi dropped her 'h's.

Quietly fascinated with the creature, Tonibler asked, "What do they eat? Can we give it some trifle?"

"I think trifle may be a tad rich for its digestive system. They eat insects. I believe that they even tackle prey that is bigger than them, such as frogs and lizards."

"That's awesome."

"And grasshoppers," I added.

"Mr Spiros told me that his wife cooks grasshoppers and he has to eat them. It sounds yuck. Mr Bucket, can I please have the praying mantis to take home with me. 'Appen it will make a good pet?"

"You don't want to go round dropping your aitches like me, Tony." Vi fondly ruffled the boy's hair as she gently corrected him. "Happen you'd be better off emulating my Victor. He talks right nice."

"You'll make me blush, Mother." I was delighted that she had made the effort to stick an 'h' on the beginning of her latest 'Appen to set a good example. Turning to the child, I told him, "I don't see why you can't take the praying mantis home as a pet though I'd advise you to keep it well out of the way of your kitten. You'll have to remember to keep it well fed on a diet of insects and live worms."

"It will be fun digging up worms." Tonibler's eyes sparkled with mischief behind his spectacles. I felt happy that his tendency to be a studious bookworm was balanced by his enjoyment of simple childish pleasures.

"Let me dig out one of Mrs Bucket's Tupperware boxes for you to carry it home in," I volunteered. "We'll need to box it up before Mrs Bucket gets home…"

"That we will," Vi concurred. "Your Marigold is likely to have a fit of the screaming habdabs if she catches sight of that praying mantis creature."

"Really? How can a grown-up be frightened of that little thing?" Tonibler's tone was incredulous.

"It beats me, lad. Mrs Bucket can get all in a flap over nowt. She got right hysterical over a couple of ticks," Vi tittered as Clawsome moseyed over to the food bowl to see what tasty morsel Catastrophe had dragged in. As the cat cautiously edged closer, the praying mantis adopted a defensive pose, extending its arms and swiping its claws in Clawsome's direction. Rushing over to shoo the cat out of the way before the praying mantis could attack, I marvelled at the insect's bravery in being prepared to take on something that so outweighed it; after all, the mantis couldn't possibly know that Clawsome was the very definition of a scaredy cat.

"It's a good job that Pickles spends most of its time outdoors. It would make mincemeat of that praying mantis," I said.

"Same with my Petey. She's right good at keeping the place insect free. She's got the hunter instinct," Vi said before turning to Tonibler and instructing him, "Now, finish up your trifle, lad, before it gets cold."

Her words provoked a fit of giggles from the child.

"Trifle is meant to be cold."

"There's no getting one past you, lad."

Scraping his bowl clean, Tonibler asked if he could borrow one of my tomes on hygiene standards. I was beyond thrilled by his request as I had hoped he would continue to develop his interest in the subject without my foisting it under his nose. Nothing made me swell with pride more than Tonibler taking an active interest in my hygiene manuals. The little gems he had picked up and passed on to his mother ensured the *kafenion* kitchen where she prepared lunches was worthy of a five-star hygiene accolade.

When Tonibler had told his father that he might like to follow in my glittering footsteps by becoming a public health inspector when he was old enough, Blat had brushed off his own disappointment that Tonibler didn't share his lofty dreams for his son becoming the mayor of great London. Saying that, Blat had sought me out to ask if the great mayor of great London had a personal public health inspector following him around. In my opinion, Blat had appeared engrossed as I explained the distinction between a personal food taster and a hygiene inspector. Barry insisted that Blat had been bored rigid, only listening because I was technically his boss on the renovation project.

"What particular aspect of hygiene do you fancy exploring next?"

"Natural toxins, I think."

"Toxins," Violet Burke barked. "Just be sure you don't go round poisoning folk willy-nilly. We don't want half of Meli coming down with roiling guts."

Brushing off Vi's concern, I rifled through the relevant literature, telling Tonibler, "Toxins are a truly enthralling subject...let me just find you a suitable read. Now, you may struggle with some of the vocabulary in this one. You mustn't hesitate to pop round and ask me about any of the words you don't understand..."

"Quick. Chuck Tony's new pet in that box. I can hear your Marigold coming," Vi hissed, desperately using a corkscrew to skewer an air hole in the Tupperware box so that Tonibler's new pet would be able to breathe.

Noticing there was no way to disguise the tampered with trifle, I winked at Tonibler, advising him, "Follow my lead."

The second Marigold bustled into the kitchen, I proclaimed, "Your hair looks lovely, darling."

Catching on fast, Tonibler echoed my words. "Hello, Mrs Bucket. Your hair looks lovely."

Patting her Titian locks, Marigold simpered. Bending down to plant a kiss on Tonibler's cheek and give him a hug, she said, "You're such a little gentleman. You won't go wrong if you listen to how Mr Bucket addresses the ladies."

"Pah, I heard Victor saying my hair looked better out of sight under my bicycle helmet," Vi scoffed.

"You forget that it's rather debatable if you're actually a lady, Mother. I think at best the term could only be loosely applied."

"Athena's done a right good job of covering up that bit of grey you had with red dye, Marigold," Vi proclaimed. If looks could kill, Violet Burke would have fallen forward and drowned head first in the vat of goulash she was stirring.

Ignoring the dig from her mother-in-law, Marigold headed towards the kettle before stopping dead in her tracks. "Someone has desecrated my trifle…"

"That would be my mother." I felt no guilt dobbing Violet Burke in. For the sake of domestic harmony, I much preferred that my mother should be the target of Marigold's wrath, rather than I.

"Even though Victor reckoned you'd see red, I didn't think you'd make a fuss if I gave little Tonibler a taste," Vi said.

"Fancy thinking that a trifling thing like a trifled with trifle would make me see red." Even though Marigold remained remarkably composed in the circumstances, I detected the glimmer of annoyance in her eyes that she was trying to hide.

"That's a great tongue-twister, Mrs Bucket," Tonibler said, repeating the trifled line under his breath.

The irritation lifted from Marigold's face when Tonibler aimed another compliment in her direction. "The trifle was so delicious, Mrs Bucket. Sensationally scrumpox."

"The word is scrumptious," I hastily corrected Tonibler.

"Is scrumpox not a word?" Tonibler asked, ever inquisitive and eager to learn.

"Not a word you need to concern yourself with," I said, my voice brooking no argument. Tonibler was far too young to be introduced to the subject of herpes, even if it was accidental.

Tutting at the hollowed-out dessert she had prepared earlier, Marigold took a practical stance.

"I suppose we'll just have to make do with Norman's tart tonight."

"So, he is bringing his bit of fluff along then? I can't see that Doreen being happy having her husband's floozy thrown in her face," Vi said.

"Doreen will be with Manolis," Marigold pointed out.

"And Norman's bringing a torte, not a tart," I added.

"What's a tart?" Tonibler piped up.

"A fancy cake…" I improvised without telling the child the word could be used in another context. Firing a warning look at my mother, I hissed, "impressionable ears," as I guided Tonibler towards the door before he could demand to know the meaning of fluff and floozy.

"Don't forget the Tupperware box," Vi reminded Tonibler, handing it over and sending him on his way with a heartfelt cuddle.

"What was in my Tupperware?" Marigold enquired.

"Just some trifle," I fibbed. There was no need to unnecessarily upset my wife by revealing we'd given house room to a bright green praying mantis during her absence. She'd only get herself in a state by imagining them everywhere. Even though it had been yonks ago since the snails that Barry and I had collected had invaded the house in what we fondly referred to as the great bucket breakout, Marigold still insisted on checking the bed was snail free before retiring for the night.

Whilst Vi busied herself adding the potatoes to the goulash, Marigold told me, "That building rubbish that you were making such a song and dance about at the bins has gone."

"That's odd," Vi said. "The bin men don't usually do 'owt on a Saturday."

"That's right. How strange," Marigold mused. "Victor. You've gone as red as a beetroot. You *know* something about it."

"'Appen he does. Look at that guilty look on his face," Vi concurred in a taunting tone.

"Perhaps that jobsworth at the *Dimarcheio* decided to do something about it after all, following my phone call yesterday." I could feel my face reddening as I purposefully laid a false trail.

"Pull the other one, Victor," Marigold snorted. "You never even got past the jobsworth's secretary. Your Greek was all to pot."

"There's no need to rub it in. At least I tried…"

My attempt to be put through to the mayor to discuss the disgraceful bin situation had once again been thwarted. Fobbed off with an underling, my efforts to communicate in my abysmal telephone Greek could only be described as futile. *Kyria* Jobsworth had stated emphatically that the *Dimos* would not be removing the building rubbish: either the builder responsible must do it or I was more than welcome to knock myself out and do it myself.

I was beginning to suspect that every time someone at the *Dimos* heard the name Bucket, they deliberately gave me the run around. I determined that in future, I would resort to putting in a personal appearance rather than struggling over the phone; though considering what had gone down the previous night, I reflected that it might not actually be the brightest move to show my face for the foreseeable.

"I can read you like a book, Victor. You have guilt written all over your face," Marigold accused, apparently determined not to let the matter drop.

"Nonsense."

"'Appen I might have seen you sneaking about in the dark last night," my mother said. "'Appen your Marigold should ask you about the company you've been keeping."

"Victor?"

Ignoring Marigold, I inwardly cursed Violet Burke for being such a busybody. Although I had been under the impression that my nocturnal carryings on had been undetected, perchance the twitching curtain in the *apothiki* window hadn't been the work of my imagination after all.

The previous evening, Marigold had turned in early whilst I relaxed on the balcony overlooking the street, basking in the cool night air, the quietude of silence surrounding me like a comfort blanket.

Not a single ray of moonlight had penetrated the inky black night, the darkness all pervasive. The sound of a vehicle approaching at a creep had drawn my attention, my curiosity well and truly piqued when the vehicle stopped, its headlights flashing in what I presumed was an attempt to attract my attention. Not wishing to disturb Marigold, I had slipped quietly down to the street.

Peering at the pickup by torch light, I spotted Hal beckoning me through his open window, the engine running. "Hop in, Victor." His tone was so hushed, I could barely hear him.

"What for? It's late."

"You'll see. Jump in," Hal insistently whispered.

As Hal spoke, I couldn't be certain but I thought that I discerned the curtains twitch in the *apothiki*. Rather than risk Violet Burke venturing out on the street in her candlewick monstrosity and curlers, I made quick work of joining Hal in the pickup. In turn, he made quick work of getting us out of there, only bringing the pickup to a stop when we reached the bins.

"Since the people at the *Dimos* are happy for us lot in Meli to put up with this mess, I thought I'd turn the tables and see how they like having it on their own doorstep."

"You don't mean…"

"I do. We're going to pile this lot into the back

of the pickup and dump it on the *Dimarcheio* doorstep."

"I'm pretty sure there must be laws against fly tipping on the doorstep of the *Dimos*," I argued.

"I heard that trying to reason with them got you nowhere."

"That's true," I conceded, righteous anger stirring within me as I recalled how I had been fobbed off as though I was nothing more than a blithering nuisance. The desecration of the Meli landscape deserved to be taken seriously.

"Those rubber-stampers at the *Dimos* might treat complaints a sight more seriously if they were the ones having something to complain about," Hal opined. "I decided that if that lot at the *Dimos* can't be bothered to remove this mess, I'll personally take it to them."

"I dare say you're right. Even so, I'm not a fan of law-breaking." Although not one for finding satisfaction in acts of petty vengeance, a vision of the staff at the *Dimarcheio* being forced to step over mounds of solidified concrete and broken tiles, filled me with a warm and pleasant glow.

"And I'm not a fan of living somewhere blighted by rubbish that no one will take responsibility for." Hal thumped the dashboard for good measure. "How about you keep lookout and I'll chuck that lot in the back."

Weighing up the wisdom of helping Hal out

with his mission, I reasoned that there was nothing remotely illegal in his removing the rubbish from the area at the side of the bins. Quite what he chose to do with it afterwards, was entirely another matter.

Alighting the pickup, I stood guard whilst Hal slipped his hands into a pair of luminous yellow Marigolds and began to haul the rubbish into the pickup's cargo bed.

"Panos would turn in his grave at the thought of his pristine pickup being polluted with rubbish," I said to Hal. "He even kept the plastic wrap on the seats to keep them immaculate."

"I can hose the cargo bed down tomorrow."

As Hal laboured, his actions disturbed the myriad of stray cats that had already bedded down for the night in and under the bins. Their proximity to any edible waste made their chosen sleeping spots very handy if they were overcome with the urge to tuck into a midnight feast.

A particularly straggly one-eyed feral had made itself comfortable by dozing off in a half-filled sack of concrete, still in its plastic state. It occurred to me that we were doing the local cat population a huge favour by removing the building materials: it would only take a quick burst of summer rain to activate the concrete into a hardened mass as it got wet, potentially trapping the cat in situ. I could just imagine Violet Burke demanding to have a concreted cat to decorate her mantlepiece in the manner of a modern Greek frieze.

By the time all the building rubbish was loaded and we set off towards the coast, it was nearing midnight. The lateness of the hour had worked in our favour since no one had come along to disturb us or catch us in the act. As we drove past the taverna, I spotted Nikos holding court to the few remaining customers, no doubt impressing them with his spiel about everything except the water being home-made.

"How did you get on yesterday, Hal? I recall you were off to view a fishing boat."

"We did a deal there and then. It was in great shape…"

"Fibreglass or wood?"

"Fibreglass. It's much more practical. The engine is sound. We shook on it but there's still all the paperwork to be sorted. You know what Greek bureaucracy is like…"

"I do, indeed."

"Tomorrow, I'm seeing a man about a donkey," Hal revealed, prompting me to think, what with boats and donkeys, Hal was certainly throwing his money around. "The donkey will be a gift for Yiota. I don't know how she's managed the farm without one. I remember the days when you couldn't turn round without tripping over a donkey but these days you hardly see them."

"I've spotted a few during the olive harvest…"

"But they're not as ubiquitous as they were when I was a youngster."

"It must have been so different in Meli back then," I prompted.

"The beauty of the place remains unchanged, but back then, there was no electricity and the road was nothing more than a track."

"Are you happy to be back?"

"Of course. There's no place like Meli, but things would have been better if Panos was still around. I'm still shocked to think that he's passed. I'd long hoped that we would live out our retirement years together. We were always close."

"Even though you didn't see each other for over fifty years?"

"I had my reasons for staying away. I might have even stayed away for good if I hadn't got Panos' letter. He wrote to me about fifteen years back to tell me that Stella had passed."

"Stella?"

"Panos' wife. I would never have come back if she'd still been alive. It wouldn't have felt right. Course, with me being all over the place on the boats, the letter was passed around from pillar to post. It only caught up with me a couple of years ago."

Hal sighed deeply before clamming up. Seemingly lost in thought, he drove on in silence.

His words had intrigued me, making me wonder why he wouldn't have returned to Meli if Panos' wife had still been alive. Despite my burning curiosity, I didn't feel it was right to pry. We covered a couple of kilometres before Hal spoke again, his tone reflective.

"You asked me something the other day, about why I'd never been married. The truth is, I was in love with Stella. I never said a word to her about it, nor to my brother, but it cut me up inside when the two of them announced they were getting wed. I left before the wedding."

It struck me that Hal was baring his soul and this may well be the very first time he had uttered those words aloud. There was a deep gravitas to his words which made me think his unrequited love had far more substance than Milton's carrying a torch for Violet Burke for all those years.

"When Panos wrote to me that Stella was gone, he said his greatest hope was that one day I would return to Meli and the two of us could reunite. It hits me hard to think he never knew that I didn't get his letter until 2004. If I'd come back at once, he would still have been alive."

The loss of those wasted years struck me, the loss of the years when Panos could have been reunited with Hal and the loss of the future that Panos could have enjoyed with Violet Burke.

"I'm that happy though to have connected with

Yiota, Panos' flesh and blood."

Although Hal was technically Yiota's great-uncle, it seemed that Yiota was likely to have a surrogate grandfather in Hal, just as she had a surrogate grandmother in Violet Burke.

"Get ready, Victor. I can see the *Dimarcheio* up ahead." Hal slowed the pickup on the empty and silent street. The beam of the headlights cast a glow across the steps leading up to the *Dimarcheio*, reminding me of the celebration we had enjoyed for Barry and Cynthia's wedding. It didn't sit well with me to think that another couple could possibly have their wedding blighted by having to step through mounds of rubbish to say their 'I do's.'

"Do you really think we should go through with it, Hal? We don't want to end up in trouble with the police."

I don't mind admitting that as the time to do the deed dawned nigh, I got a terrible case of cold feet, the righteous indignation I felt earlier replaced with guilt ridden panic.

"No one will know who dumped it here. It's just an old heap of building rubbish," Hal argued.

"But I telephoned the *Dimos* to complain about it…they could easily join the dots and connect it to the name Bucket," I said, vacillating between trying to persuade Hal not to go through with it and convincing myself that the staff at the *Dimarcheio* deserved it for being such jobsworths. "We could end up having to pay a large fine or even get a criminal record. The police have already arrested me once…"

"Never. I'd never have you down as the type to have had a run-in with the police. What did you do?"

"I opened the village shop on a Sunday."

"A real master criminal move." Hal could barely disguise the laughter that accompanied his words.

"You may laugh, Hal, but I can still remember the fear that enveloped me as I waited around in that dismal police station cell to hear my fate, wondering if my crime would lead to my deportation from Greece. What if they deport me for littering?"

"I can't do this to you, Victor. You're never going to rest easy if we dump this rubbish here…"

"I'm really not," I concurred.

"There's a load of bins by the football field. Let's dump it there instead…"

"And you don't think they'll connect it to us?"

"How about you stay in the cab while I do the dumping?"

"I suppose we'll still have accomplished our goal. After all, this rubbish is no longer polluting Meli."

"Right, to the bins it is," Hal announced.

From the safe distance of the pickup cab, I watched Hal, still in his vibrant Marigolds, unload the transplanted rubbish into the bins about a kilometre distant from the *Dimarcheio*. I exhaled in relief. There was no real way to connect the dumping back to ourselves since Hal's hygienic precaution of wearing rubber gloves meant he'd left no fingerprints to connect him to the scene.

There was no point in kidding myself that I was in any way cut out for dabbling on the wrong side of the law. Still, I reflected, it hadn't been a wasted journey; Hal and I had formed a special bond during our nocturnal adventure.

"Victor. Victor you're miles away." Violet Burke's strident tone pulled me out of my reverie and back to the kitchen where the expat dinner party preparations were still under way. "You're guilty of summat and no mistake."

"Stuff and nonsense. I admit I may have contemplated dumping the rubbish at the *Dimarcheio*…"

"Are you out of your mind, Victor?" Marigold was decidedly not amused.

"If you'd let me finish my sentence. I was about to add that I couldn't go through with it."

"Too much of a bloody wuss," Violet Burke decreed.

Chapter 23

Norman's Secret Squeeze

Whilst Violet Burke busied herself putting the finishing touches to the food in our kitchen, Marigold put the finishing touches to her appearance. At the same time, she delegated to me the task of greeting our guests in the garden where we would shortly be dining.

"How many people are we expecting?" I asked.

"Well, there's the two of us and your mother." Marigold started counting the numbers off on her fingers. "Then there's Doreen and Manolis, Sherry, Edna and Milton. Norman said he'll definitely be here but he failed to confirm if he'll be bringing his new lady friend; it really is most ill-mannered of him to leave me hanging. If Norman comes alone, I'll be top heavy with men. You ought to have words with him, Victor."

"Hmmm," I muttered noncommittally, having not the slightest intention of schooling Norman in the niceties of dinner party etiquette.

"Barry, Gordon Strange and John Macey are all flying solo this evening." Having run out of fingers to count on, Marigold frowned. "It really is most thoughtless of them. It's played havoc with my seating plan. Still, what can we do? Cynthia is on an overnight guided tour in Athens, Moira Strange is back in England for an ear shoot, and I suppose that John Macey found it quite impossible to find himself a date…I can't imagine he'd be able to find anyone desperate enough to couple up with him."

Barely able to tolerate John Macey, Marigold, unusually for her, appeared to have no interest in dabbling in a spot of matchmaking where the newest expat resident of Meli was concerned.

Adjusting the knot on my tie, I moseyed outside, clocking Sherry, naturally the first to arrive, wafting across the garden in a billowing orange kaftan, Guzim's shed clearly in her sights. Catching sight of the Albanian shed dweller stripped down to his underpants and hosing himself off outside his shed, I could sense his utter mortification as he realised that Sherry was bearing down on him. Hurriedly grabbing a grubby looking towel, Guzim secured it around his middle. With his modesty somewhat intact, he pointed the hosepipe at Sherry to keep her at bay.

Blindly oblivious to Guzim's embarrassment, it appeared that Sherry was attempting to make small talk with, or more accurately, at, my dumbstruck gardener. Reflecting that Marigold would have a fit if Sherry was trying to persuade Guzim to join our dinner party, I sighed in relief when I realised that Guzim wouldn't be able to make head nor tail of whatever nonsense Sherry was spewing in his direction. Although I find it beyond pathetic that some of my English neighbours can barely string two words of Greek together, there are times when it undoubtedly works to my advantage.

Apparently amused by her own witty sallies, Sherry threw her head back. Braying with laughter, she exposed her horsey dentures, causing my confused gardener to clumsily trip over his own feet as he hastily took a step backwards, desperate to put more distance between them.

"Cooee, Victor." Looking around, I spotted Doreen arriving, her plump cheeks unnaturally red. "I'm in a bit of a pickle."

"How so?"

"My Manolis *mou* can't make it because Christos hasn't turned up for his shift at the *kafenion*."

"My and *mou* are the same thing, Doreen," I corrected her for the umpteenth time.

Completely ignoring my point, Doreen continued, "Poor Manolis *mou* has worked all day and now, because his brother is a no-show, he has to work all night too."

"I'm sure Manolis will survive it. One could hardly describe a shift at the *kafenion* as hard labour."

My words were an understatement to say the least. One afternoon I had ventured into the *kafenion*, only to discover it empty and unattended. Striding over to the kitchen area, I had nearly jumped out of my skin to discover Christos taking a siesta on a camp bed. I had roused him with sharp words, pointing out that bedding down in the kitchen violated numerous hygiene rules.

"Not to mention that Marigold isn't going to be happy," Doreen said. "Manolis' absence will mess up her seating plan."

"It's already messed up since Norman failed to confirm if he's bringing his new lady friend along," I disclosed.

Doreen's mouth gaped and her cheeks turned even redder as I dropped this little gem. Even whilst mentally acknowledging that my words might possibly be interpreted as a tad insensitive, I refused to feel any guilt for dropping this bombshell on Doreen. It appeared that my wife was the one who had neglected to mention to her friend that she had invited said friend's estranged husband to bring along a mysterious plus one.

Marigold, looking quite exquisite in a turquoise fitted frock paired with matching sandals, her Titian tresses shimmering in the early evening sunshine, joined the two of us, asking "What's that about my seating plan?"

As Doreen filled Marigold in on Manolis' absence, my wife took a deep breath, remaining remarkably stoic in the face of her seating plan potentially going to pot. Attempting to console Doreen before she could get hysterical, I said, "There's plenty of other people coming. You probably won't even notice that Manolis isn't here."

"Must you be so insensitive, Victor? Doreen needs Manolis at her side to cope with seeing Norman bring along another woman."

"Why?" I retorted. "It's not as though Doreen has had any qualms about rubbing Norman's nose in her relationship with Manolis."

"It's hardly the same. Norman lacks the emotional intelligence required for it to affect him. Without the rock of Manolis by her side, Doreen will undoubtedly feel humiliated if Norman turns up with a bit of fluff clinging to his arm."

"Well, that's down to you, Marigold," I said. "You're the one that extended an invitation to Norman's bit of fluff."

"I've never even spoken to the woman," Marigold protested. "But you can't deny that we're all curious to see who Norman has taken up with. I'm sure she won't be a patch on Doreen."

Marigold's words failed to reassure Doreen. Even to my ears, Marigold sounded less than sincere.

Descending the stairs with a platter of food, Violet Burke called out, "Here, Marigold, there's another plate of these need carrying down."

Marigold rushed to it, apparently keen to avoid an awkward conversation with Doreen.

"Why are you bringing the food out now, Mother? Most of our guests are yet to arrive."

"I reckoned some of them might fancy one of these Hungarian eggs to help soak up the booze. You're lucky there's any left. I had to wrest the tray out of Maria's grasp when she popped round to mine for a cuppa. She goes crazy for my Warring...I mean, my Hungarian eggs."

Eyeing the contents of Vi's tray, I realised that her so-called Hungarian eggs were not even closely related to actual Toltott Tojas, the Hungarian devilled eggs I had expected her to serve up. Suspecting Violet Burke of pulling a fast one, I gingerly picked up a single egg to examine it more closely. Not only did it bear more than a passing resemblance to Vi's Warrington delicacy of pickled Scotch eggs coated in black pudding, dipped in beer batter and then deep fried, it even smelt the same as a Warrington egg.

Having managed to slightly compose herself, Doreen asked, "Are we having a Hungarian evening, Mrs Burke? How adventurous."

"Aye, that's right, lass. I've done this appetiser of Hungarian eggs and I've knocked up some Hungarian beetroot to be followed with Hungarian goulash. That dopey husband of yours is bringing the pudding. He reckoned he'd have a bash at knocking up a Hungarian walnut torte. Course, you'd do best keeping well away from that..."

"Are you trying to suggest that Norman might try to poison Doreen?" I quipped.

"No, I'm suggesting Doreen ought to knock the puddings on the head...she's starting to get right chubby."

"I'm nowhere near as chubby as you..." Doreen dared to challenge my mother.

"Aye, but back when I was your age, I was still a right looker with an ample bosom and shapely legs. You're in danger of being nowt but stomach and chins."

Blinking back tears, Doreen's voice quivered. "Well, really. You can be very rude, Mrs Burke."

"There's no point in sugar-coating the truth," Vi retorted. "I'll save you the bother of flouncing off. I've got to get back to the kitchen."

As Violet Burke ascended the outdoor stairs with a surprising spring in the steps, I placed my hand in the small of Doreen's back, guiding her towards the nearest bottle of wine. Accepting a very large glass of white, Doreen remarked, "I know she's your mother, Victor, but she has a very cruel tongue."

"Take no notice," I advised. "I think that bit of extra weight suits you. Manolis can't take his eyes off your figure."

"She practically called me fat," Doreen lamented between generous gulps of wine. In truth there had been no practically about it; chubby could only be interpreted as fat.

"I'm sure she meant curvy. Ah, there's Gordon and Waffles." I couldn't help but notice that Gordon had a pair of binoculars slung around his neck. I hoped he wasn't planning to spy on my neighbours. Marigold would not be amused if Gordon had such antics in mind; my wife had barely recovered from the time that Jehovah's witness had done a passable imitation of a peeping Tom by showing up at our bedroom window

"Excuse me while I go and greet Gordon." Slipping away, it didn't escape my notice that Doreen was already topping up her glass. If she ended up sobbing in a drunken heap, it would all be down to my mother's failure to keep her tongue in check and her foot out of her mouth.

As I greeted Gordon, Waffles immediately bounded forward to lick my fingers, no doubt attracted by the lingering scent of Warrington egg.

"Been looking forward to this evening," Gordon gushed. "It's no fun eating alone when Moira's away."

"At least you have Waffles for company," I consoled Gordon. "What's with the binoculars?"

"I've got quite into bird watching…"

"I didn't have you down as a twitcher."

"It's a recent hobby but quite fascinating. My interest was piqued when I saw what I thought was a vulture. I was just leaving to come here when I spotted some bee-eaters, so I thought it best to bring the tools of the trade along. I'd hate to miss any bee-eaters now they're out and about this evening…"

Gordon's words tailed off as he raised the binoculars to his eyes, fixing his sights on a small flock of birds perched on an electrical line. "Oh, I say. Darn good show. Here, take a look-see, Victor." Divesting himself of the binoculars, Gordon handed them over to me.

It took a moment or two for the birds on the wire to show up clearly in my sights. After a couple of adjustments, I zoomed in on a gloriously attractive bird, its yellowy-orange head almost glowing, its plumage an opulent green with unusually long tail feathers.

"I suppose their name of bee-eaters is self-explanatory," I ventured.

"Indeed. They like to make a meal of bees and wasps…"

"Well, I hope they don't reduce the local bee population. Giannis relies on them to produce his delicious honey. Mind you, it would be very handy if they devoured those annoying builder-bees. They're a dratted nuisance."

"Not sure I'm familiar with builder-bees." Gordon frowned in concentration.

"Those vile things that look like giant wasps with long wings. They make nests out of the red mud…"

"Ah, you could be thinking of dauber wasps," Gordon posited. "I had to destroy one of their nests last summer. A hair-raising job, I can tell you."

"Where was it?"

"In the top drawer of our wooden vegetable rack."

"They like to transport the red mud and set up home in anything made of wood," I said, reflecting that I hadn't been as brave as Gordon when it came to tackling a nest in the eaves of the Bucket residence. Chickening out of the dangerous task, I'd called Barry over to get rid of the nest and exterminate any larvae.

"I've a spare pair of binoculars if you fancy joining me for a spot of twitching one morning," Gordon offered.

"Not sure it's really my thing," I prevaricated.

Spotting the Goldendoodle making a beeline for Vi's platter of Hungarian eggs, I warned

Gordon, "I think you need to keep Waffles away from the food. There'll be hell to pay if Violet Burke catches him at it."

The pair of us dashed after Waffles. Bringing the dog to heel, Gordon instructed him, "Drop that egg at once, Waffles."

Staring at Gordon dolefully, Waffles clung onto the egg half-protruding from his mouth.

"He may as well keep it now. I can't go offering food covered in dog drool to our guests."

Without the slightest trace of guilt on its face, the dog continued to chomp down on the Hungarian egg with obvious enjoyment.

Even though Marigold had rejoined Doreen, I noticed her friend was still looking glum. Resuming my role of host, I topped up Doreen's glass yet again and made sure Marigold had a glass in her hand.

"Oh, no. What's she doing here?" Marigold groaned as our next-door neighbour, Kyria Maria, wandered into our garden. Clad from head to toe in black, she cast a dark shadow. "Do get rid of her, Victor."

"He'll do no such thing," my mother barked. "I'm hosting this do…"

"We're hosting. It's our garden," Marigold argued. "You just did the cooking."

"That's just semantics," Vi shot back. "Maria's my friend and I invited her."

"Well, you might have let me know, Vi, so I could have arranged the seating plan to accommodate her." Casting her eyes over the table, Marigold frowned in concentration. "I'm going to have to stick Maria next to you, Victor. I can't think of anyone else able to communicate with her in Greek."

"Put her in the seat next to you," I fired back. "Your Greek is certainly up to chatting with Maria."

"Don't be ridiculous, Victor. I can't have Maria monopolising my attention when I'm playing hostess."

"Then stick her next to John Macey," I said. "He's always banging on about having lived in Greece for sixteen years and boasting that he's fluent in the language."

"Now that is an excellent idea, even if it is a bit hard on Maria," Marigold agreed.

"Put me on Maria's other side so we can have a bit of a chinwag," Vi demanded. "Have you got any of that horrible twig tea for her to drink?"

"I think Kyria Maria will be more than happy with wine," I said.

Pouring a glass of wine for my mother to take over to Maria, I was distracted by the sight of the latest arrivals.

"You're dribbling, lad," Vi admonished as the wine I was pouring dripped onto my slacks, my concentration shot.

"I don't believe it. I just don't believe it." My words were no understatement. Barely able to credit what my eyes were seeing, I seethed in annoyance at the sight of a woman I despised hanging onto Norman's arm. The traffic cone bore had some nerve showing up with the unspeakably awful Smug Bessie from the book club in tow. My mind went into overdrive; surely the ghastly woman couldn't be Norman's secret squeeze.

Having failed to notice the new arrivals, Doreen quipped, "Victor, you sound more and more like Victor Meldrew every day."

"Well, really." I spluttered in annoyance, most put out to have Doreen compare me to the curmudgeonly character from 'One Foot in the Grave' even though it suddenly occurred to me that Doreen had more than a touch of the Mrs Warboys about her. "Wasn't Victor Meldrew the one that fed his wife's annoying friend through the wood shredder…." I started to say.

My words were drowned out by Doreen loudly exclaiming, "I don't believe it!" It appeared that Doreen had finally caught sight of the short, plump, drably attired, grey-haired woman, clinging to her still-husband's arm. "Norman really has brought another woman along."

Chapter 24

Scraping the Barrel

Whilst I reeled in shock, Doreen appeared stupefied, her eyes fixed on the pair as though in danger of blowing a gasket at any moment, stunned to see her husband really had managed to lure another woman along. I wondered how it was possible that I had not known that Norman had crossed paths with Smug Bessie. It crossed my mind that when Norman had asked my advice about bringing his lady friend to our gathering, I had been utterly remiss in failing to show enough interest to elicit her name. Although Smug Bessie was the last person that I would ever dream of welcoming to the Bucket residence, I reasoned I could hardly throw her out after Marigold had extended an invitation.

Not sure if I could keep a civil tongue in my head, I pointedly ignored the new arrivals, instead joining Doreen in knocking back a ginormous glass of wine. Watching Marigold rush over to greet Norman and his lady friend, it occurred to me that my wife had never, to the best of my knowledge, crossed paths with Smug Bessie. She was surely in for a treat.

Keeping a watchful eye from a distance as Norman introduced Bessie to my wife, I noticed the usual look of smug superiority that I associated with the overbearing book club bore had been replaced with a fake facsimile of a smile. Bessie didn't fool me: unless she had undergone a personality transplant, she would no doubt expose her true character as the evening progressed. I assumed she was waiting for an opportune moment to engage in her favourite sport, a spot of one upmanship, though she would certainly have a hard time impressing my wife.

Standing to one side of the herb garden where the scent of rosemary and thyme was utterly captivating, I continued to discreetly observe the threesome. I could have kicked myself for not taking more of an interest when Norman had been wittering on about his lady friend. If I had been in the know as to the identity of his date for the evening, I would have put my foot down and attempted to forbid Marigold from including her in our little soiree. Of course, the likelihood of Marigold taking any notice of my putting my foot down, was minimal to say the least.

Blissfully unaware of Bessie's poisonous personality, Marigold was in for a rude awakening if Bessie unleashed her true nature. Cringing inwardly as Marigold guided Norman and his companion towards the little huddle comprising myself, Doreen and Violet Burke, I slapped a fake smile on my face, knowing full well that my wife would expect nothing less of me. Leaving Norman to make the introductions, Marigold hurried away to play hostess and greet the latest newcomers, Milton and Edna, John Macey following close in their wake.

I couldn't fail to notice that as Norman steered his date towards us, he didn't look particularly elated to have Bessie clinging to his arm in a decidedly proprietorial manner. If anything, Norman looked distinctly uncomfortable. For her part, I noticed that Bessie hadn't exactly dressed to impress, looking particularly frumpy in wide-legged trousers paired with trainers, the shade of said trousers presumably chosen to match the same drab grey as her dreadful helmet of Brillo pad hair.

Violet Burke hissed in my ear, "That woman

looks right familiar, but I can't just place her. It's going to niggle me like an itch I can't scratch until it comes to me…"

"Bessie, this is Victor and his mother, Mrs Burke…" Norman introduced. Avoiding Doreen's eye, Norman was overcome with a sudden fit of coughing before he could introduce his wife to his date.

Offering Bessie a glass of wine, she accepted the beverage with a saccharine smile, failing to acknowledge that we had met before. Unsure if Bessie really didn't recall our previous encounters, I opted to take the path of least resistance and follow her lead. I reflected that perhaps the people that she lorded it over really made so little of an impression on her that she wasn't simply feigning ignorance as to my identity. Taking a pragmatic approach, I reasoned there was no point in ruining the evening by creating a scene or being rude to our guest without provocation. It would be time enough to take off the gloves, should Bessie choose to provoke.

For now, I assumed that Bessie would be keen to make a good impression on Norman's friends and neighbours. Certainly, the iron grip she had on his arm conveyed possession. It amused me to think she wouldn't be so smug about having landed Norman if she knew that none of us considered him an actual catch; if Norman had been an actual fish, any self-respecting fisherman would have tossed him back in the sea. I couldn't help but wonder how Norman's tedious talk of his traffic cone collection would fit in with Bessie's highfalutin literary pretentions.

Passing me a tissue, Bessie adopted a superior tone, telling me, "You appear to have wet your trousers."

"It's wine." Dabbing furiously at my slacks, I thought it dreadfully ill-mannered of her to point it out in such a condescending manner.

"Norman, you forgot to introduce Doreen," Violet Burke blurted out.

Smug Bessie's demeanour changed completely as the implication of Vi's little snippet dawned on her. With narrowed eyes, she looked Doreen up and down, her mouth curling in derision as she practically spat, "Doreen." Repeating the name, Bessie drew out the 'reen' part as though it had sixteen syllables, making her sound strangely like an automaton unable to turn itself off. "Doreen. Doreen. Aren't you Norman's ex-wife?"

Bessie's question was superfluous. It was obvious that as soon as she'd heard the name, she knew exactly who Doreen was. As she spoke, her firm grip on Norman's arm tightened, causing him to wince in pain. I interpreted her gesture as having a dual purpose: punishing Norman for failing to warn her that his wife would be present at this evening's social gathering, whilst signalling to Doreen that Norman belonged to her.

"The pair of them are still married," Violet Burke butted in before Doreen could reply, a look of disdain on her face. "Not to mention, they're still living in the same house."

"But Norman is getting a divorce, aren't you, Norman?" Running his hands through his hair and mussing his combover, Norman shuffled uncomfortably, biting his lip when Bessie continued, "Norman said that you'd got a new man, Doreen."

Coming in for the kill with all the skill of a smiling assassin, Bessie's voice dripped smugness as she targeted Doreen. "So, where is he? Your new man? Is it not working out?"

"He's at work." Sorely feeling the loss of Manolis' reassuring presence, Doreen's reply was practically a whisper.

"He can't think that much about you if he couldn't be bothered to put you before his job."

Never one to tolerate any nonsense, Violet Burke piped up. "You cheeky cow. You shouldn't pass comment on stuff you know nowt about. Doreen's landed herself a right good one in Manolis."

My mother was very loyal to Manolis: not only did he pay over the odds for her to clean the *kafenion*, he allowed her to be flexible with her hours. After emitting what could only be described as a manic cackle, Vi didn't bother to mince her words. "Bloody hell, Norman, talk about scraping the barrel. I didn't reckon you could do much worse than that dippy Doreen but…"

Visibly puffing up with indignation, Doreen declared, "Mrs Burke, I am standing right here."

"Aye, lass, 'Appen that was right out of order. Sometimes I can let my gob run away with me and be a bit blunt," Vi admitted with surprisingly good grace. Patting Doreen's arm, she added, "Still, at least it should buoy you up, knowing you've got more about you than this nasty piece that useless husband of yours has dredged up."

Blushing furiously, Bessie's face conveyed the impression she had stood in something nasty, the company on offer at the Bucket residence beneath contempt. Patting Doreen's arm reassuringly, I decided to attempt to diffuse what was becoming an increasingly awkward situation. "So, Norman, remind me again where you met Bessie."

"We met at…" Bessie began to reply.

"Let the bonehead speak for himself. Victor asked Norman," my mother interrupted, earning a withering look from Bessie.

Watching Smug Bessie in action, I realised I'd been too quick to judge Norman as delusional when he'd claimed to have a woman running after him. Bessie was already answering in the 'we' and putting her hands on Norman despite Norman's obvious discomfort with her hands on approach.

"I met Bessie at that taverna down on the coast when they were doing British Sunday lunches," Norman said, fidgeting in embarrassment and slanting his body away from Bessie.

"The Sunday lunches cooked by my mother…"

"That's right. We got to chatting and found we had something in common. Doreen and I had separated, and Bessie's husband had gone off with another woman."

Bessie shot Norman a look of contempt. It was clear that she didn't want it bandying around as common knowledge that her husband had left her.

"I've got it," Violet Burke cried triumphantly, aiming an extended finger in the direction of Smug Bessie's ample chest. "I knew it would come to me who you were. Talk about the irony…" Vi paused for dramatic effect.

"The irony?" Norman prompted.

"Aye, it's right ironic considering that the first time I ran into that woman hanging off your arm, she was right disparaging about Brits moving over here and eating food from the homeland. Do you remember that, Victor?"

Bessie squirmed uneasily, her confidence evaporating in this hostile territory where Violet Burke clearly held some sway.

"Yes, I remember." It was hardly a moment I was likely to forget. Violet Burke had just arrived in

Greece to try out living abroad on a permanent basis. The two of us had met up with Captain Vasos at the marina when Smug Bessie and her friend had entered the establishment. Admittedly, after downing a cocktail, Vasos and Vi had been a tad rowdy, but not rowdy enough to justify Bessie's labelling them as riff-raff and attempting to get them thrown out.

"I'll tell you what she said, it's all coming back to me," Vi continued. "She said summat about not being able to abide the sort of common Brits that move to Greece and insist on eating the same unimaginative food they ate back in England.' Yet now she's admitting to tucking into my British Sunday lunches. There's a word for folk like that...it's hypocrite."

"Nobody turns out a Yorkshire pudding as good as you do, Mrs Burke," Doreen flattered.

"And your stuffing and gravy are just superb." Norman's enthusiasm for my mother's roast dinners didn't go down well with Bessie. He really hadn't mastered the art of keeping his date happy.

"And the way she looked down her nose at my mate, Vasos. Talk about a right snotty cow." My mother was off again.

Bessie's left eye began to twitch as she came over all defensive. "English food wouldn't have been my first choice but Norman needed something stodgy and substantial to eat. He was practically starved when we met; he found it quite impossible to eat Doreen's cooking. Poor Norman never had a decent meal in all the years he was married to Doreen. Her culinary skills were so bad that Norman was in danger of wasting away."

"I told you about Doreen's cooking in confidence." Norman's voice was icy as he reprimanded Bessie. Although he and Doreen were estranged, he had never gone out of his way to deliberately humiliate her in public whilst Bessie seemed to derive a particular enjoyment from it.

Folding her arms across her chest in formidable harridan style, Vi fired back at Bessie. "You need your eyes testing, lassie, if you reckon Norman was practically starved. Have you not noticed the size of his gut? You've got some brass neck turning up here with someone else's husband in tow when you couldn't keep your own fella faithful."

"I think we ought to mingle, Norman." Bessie's words were anything but a suggestion, her haughty tone demanding immediate compliance. As she dragged Norman away by the cuff, she deliberately spoke loudly enough for Violet Burke to overhear. "I think that awful old woman must have dementia."

"'Appen I'm demented enough to drop something nasty in her bowl of goulash," Vi scoffed. Unlike Bessie, she spoke quietly. If something did indeed end up in Bessie's goulash, she would find it a total surprise.

Recalling that I had extended an invitation for Captain Vasos to join our gathering that evening, it occurred to me that if Bessie came over all smug and obnoxious, the best course of action would be to simply buckle up and enjoy the fireworks. It looked as though this dinner party wasn't going to be nearly as boring as the usual expat soirees I was forced to endure.

"You were quite magnificent, Mrs Burke," Doreen said in obvious awe. "You really cut that horrible woman down to size."

"Aye, well, I shouldn't have said what I said about you being dippy, lass. You're not so bad and I've got to admit that you've got a right talent with that sewing machine of yours. I'd take you any day of the week over that stuck-up Bessie; she's a flipping nightmare and no mistake. Right from the first time I came across her, I could tell she was right up her own backside."

"Well, you really were tremendous in cutting her down to size, Mrs Burke," Doreen enthused, clearly touched to have gained Violet Burke's grudging approval. "To think that I thought you didn't like me very much and then you went and stuck up for me like that."

"I can't deny that you have an annoying way about you but it pales in comparison to that horrible Bessie. And 'Appen I shouldn't have said you were fat earlier. It's better to carry a bit of weight rather than have no padding. You don't want to end up looking like a stick insect, like Marigold."

I didn't bother leaping in to defend my wife. If by chance she had overheard her mother-in-law's insult, Marigold would undoubtedly consider it a compliment.

Catching sight of Milton chatting to Gordon, I made a mental note to warn Milton not to out himself as Scarlett Bottom in front of Bessie. He might never recover from the cutting rejoinder such information would provoke.

Excusing myself to circulate amongst our guests, I spotted Kyria Maria heading back from the direction of Guzim's shed. Catching up with my elderly neighbour, she told me that she had taken Guzim some of the rabbit she'd cooked, the rabbit he gave her. *"Pira ston Guzim ligo apo afto to kouneli pou mageirepsa, to kouneli pou mou edose."*

Turning around in horror, I spotted Guzim relaxing on his stoop tucking into a plate of food with obvious relish, Doruntina running round at his feet. The scene struck me as oddly obscene; but for a twist of fate, Guzim would have been devouring his darling pet bunny.

Taking Maria's arm, I guided her over towards John Macey, telling her I had someone I'd like her to meet. As we approached, I heard Macey telling Smug Bessie that having lived in Greece for seventeen years, he spoke fluent Greek. It didn't escape my notice that as Macey bent her ear, Bessie hung on his every word, nodding approvingly. It appeared that at least one of our guests matched up to her high standards. At Bessie's side, Norman looked decidedly ill at ease, making me recall that Norman found Macey a crashing bore, a sentiment no doubt reciprocated on Macey's part.

"John, I'd like you to meet our next-door neighbour, Kyria Maria. I do believe that Marigold has seated you next to one another for dinner."

"Excellent. Good evening, Kyria. I'm John Macey. I've lived in Greece for seventeen years."

"*Ti?*"

Throwing the gauntlet down, I told Macey, "You'll need to speak Greek, John. Maria doesn't understand any English."

As I could have predicted, John immediately told Maria, "*Zo stin Ellada dekaepta chronia.*" It appeared that even in Greek, his main point of conversation was simply a translation of his pathetically tiresome boast that he had lived in Greece for seventeen years. I noticed that somehow an extra year had been added to his count since the last time he bored me with his familiar talking point. At any moment I expected him to whip out another of his predictable catchphrases, saying with all due modesty, that he bought his little house in Meli because it spoke to him.

I couldn't help but chuckle under my breath when Kyria Maria bested John's boast, telling him that she had lived in Greece for eighty-four years. *"Zo stin Ellada ogdanta dyo chronia."*

It didn't escape my notice that Smug Bessie was firing daggers drawn looks at Maria for interrupting her tete-a-tete with John Macey, nor that she was oblivious to the fact that Norman had seized the opportunity to sneak away.

I decided to catch up with Norman and warn him that his date was poisonous. If he intended to keep seeing Bessie, it was likely that his social circle would shrink considerably since I couldn't see any of the Meli lot willingly including her in their invitations. Certainly, as far as I was concerned, this would be the one and only occasion when Smug Bessie would darken the Bucket doorway.

Catching up with Norman, I was surprised when he said, "I'm looking for Doreen. I think an apology is in order."

"I don't think that Doreen said anything that warrants her making an apology," I said, amazed that yet again I was standing up for Doreen.

"No, you've got the wrong end of the stick, Victor. There was no excuse for Bessie speaking to Doreen like that. Ah, there she is."

"Do try and prise that wine bottle out of Doreen's hand, Norman, or she'll be half-cut by the time my mother serves up the goulash."

Appearing at my side, Marigold said, "Victor, can you start herding everyone together to eat. I've been waiting for Barry to arrive but he's not going to be able to make it. Litsa took a dizzy turn and isn't up to babysitting."

"I'm on it," I said.

"Actually, just give me a minute to swap a few of the place cards around. I'd planned to sit next to Norman's date in order to get all the dirt for Doreen, but that Bessie is just unspeakably vile. Why you let Norman bring such a terrible snob along…"

"It's nothing to do with me…"

"Did you know that her reputation precedes her? I've never met her before but I've heard about her on the grapevine and the general consensus is that she's quite insufferable."

"She's the one that I've told you about, the one who organises that expat book club."

"The one who looks down her nose at all those wonderful moving abroad books." Marigold's nostrils flared in anger. She didn't appreciate anyone passing judgement on her favourite genre of literature.

"That's the one," I confirmed. "Bessie considers such tripe must be penned by literary amateurs."

"I expect she only holds that view because her own experience of moving to Greece isn't interesting enough to be written down. Just wait until you publish 'Bucket to Greece', darling, that will bring her down a peg or two."

"My use of a pseudonym will spare me her unwanted opinion."

"And spare my blushes," Marigold said. "I bet that she's only taken up with Norman because she's very much the sort that requires a man on her arm for social standing...I heard that her clout amongst the Brits is fast diminishing now that she's single. You know how coupled up that expat lot can be."

"Cynthia has mentioned it more than once," I agreed.

It was to Marigold's credit that although she loved nothing more than a spot of matchmaking, she always went out of her way to include her single friends in any gathering.

"I doubt that Norman can elevate her position in the expat circle she travels in..."

"I'll put her next to John Macey at the opposite end of the table to us. They can one-upmanship each other," Marigold decided.

"Save an empty seat between my mother and Sherry just in case Captain Vasos shows up," I said casually.

"Captain Vasos...you didn't mention you'd invited him. Now let me think...if he does turn up, your mother will only monopolise him..." I could practically see the cogs whirling around in Marigold's brain as she made the connection.

"Vasos and Sherry, yes. It has potential. I can't think why it never occurred to me before. Victor, I do believe you may have been accidentally brilliant."

I had no intention of bursting Marigold's bubble by confessing what she found accidental was down to a spot of deliberate meddling on my part.

Chapter 25

Suet Dumplings

The desperate scramble for seats at the dinner table sent Marigold's seating plan into complete disarray. My only contribution to said seating plan had been to insist that Marigold keep me as far away from Norman as possible, to spare me his inevitable monologue on traffic cones. Aware that I would be risking Marigold's ire by messing up her boy-girl arrangement, I opted for a seat between Doreen and Gordon Strange, the latter at least being reliably good company. I breathed a sigh of relief, realising it would have been physically impossible to select a seat any further away from the venomous Bessie.

Glancing over, I couldn't help but notice Smug Bessie was monopolising Macey's attention and ignoring Norman. In turn, Macey was rudely ignoring Kyria Maria whilst openly fawning over Bessie.

Norman, the picture of morose, seemed to be hitting the bottle pretty hard. If my eyes didn't deceive me, he appeared to be furtively topping up his glass of red with some clear liquid from a hip flask. Either he was watering his wine down or topping his glass up with vodka. Remarkably, Doreen, having glugged a couple of bottles of water, had managed to sober up.

Violet Burke had produced two appetisers, Hungarian eggs and Hungarian beetroot dip. Avoiding what were patently Warrington eggs that had never even been within spitting distance of Hungary, I tucked into the beetroot. Gordon Strange remarked that he needed to keep Waffles well away from the Hungarian eggs as they were playing havoc with the dog's flatulent tendencies. Since the Goldendoodle was at that moment curled up on my feet beneath the table, eagerly snatching the Warrington eggs I was in the process of clandestinely sneaking its way, I plastered a look of innocence on my face and nudged the dog away with my foot. It wouldn't do to be implicated if Waffles let rip from under the table.

Both the taste and texture of Violet Burke's Hungarian beetroot appetiser was very similar to my *pantzarosalata*, a creamy Greek beetroot dip; remarkably, Vi's version proved to be irrefutably superior to the beetroot dish I regularly turned out. As I savoured the mouth-watering ambrosial flavours, it occurred to me that I hadn't seen my mother go anywhere near a beetroot during her afternoon preparations in my kitchen. Gordon couldn't get enough of the stuff; raving over the excellence of the Hungarian beetroot dish, he asked Violet Burke for the recipe.

"There's nowt to it, lad," Vi said modestly. "I just threw some yoghurt in with some boiled and mashed beetroots."

"I'm definitely getting a taste of garlic," Gordon said. "And is that dill? Did you add dill to it, Mrs Burke?"

"That sounds suspiciously like my Greek recipe for *pantzarosalata*, Mother. Are you sure that it's Hungarian?"

"Don't let on, but it's as Hungarian as my eggs, lad." A sly wink accompanied her words.

"Your Hungarian eggs are undoubtedly from Warrington."

"Aye, well 'Appen that I didn't have time to do the beetroot myself. I had to knock the cooking on the head and get over to the *taverna* to peel the spuds and clean the lav. 'Appen Dina might have cobbled the beetroot stuff together."

"That's why it's so good. This is Dina's secret recipe."

"That's cheating, Mrs Burke," Sherry dared to complain.

"So, sue me. At least it's edible, which is more than can be said for 'owt coming out of your kitchen."

"But if it's Greek then it isn't foreign. That goes against the grain of the expat dinner party foreign food theme," Sherry persisted, petulantly pointing out, "We're supposed to have food from different countries at these expat events."

Sherry's words prompted me to stand up and tap my glass with the tines of my fork to garner the attention of the seated guests. It struck me that now would be an opportune moment to raise a matter that I had been seriously mulling over for some time. With everyone's attention focused on me, I announced, "I would like to formally table a proposition."

"Are you campaigning for something political?" Gordon asked.

"'Appen he's standing to be big in the bins. There's nobody got more rubbish on their mind than my Victor," Violet Burke pronounced, her face deadpan.

"No, it's nothing as illustrious as a foray into politics. I want us all to take a vote on renaming this group the 'Greek residents dinner party group' and lose the expat label. After all, we are all bona fide residents of Greece with legally stamped residence permits."

Having expected my motion to pass easily since it was hardly controversial, it appeared that I had instead opened a can of worms. As my mother slipped away from the table and headed inside to check on the goulash, I reflected that I couldn't even count on the support of my nearest and dearest.

"What's wrong with expats?" Edna asked, squinting beneath a thick layer of sloppily-applied vibrant blue eyeshadow. "Milton and I have been proud expats since we first went over to Kenya, haven't we Milton?"

"We have, old girl. We've been expats for longer than we've been British."

"Being an expat doesn't cancel your Britishness," Macey pointed out to Milton's confusion.

"The term expat is good enough for my book club and that's very high brow," Smug Bessie opined even though it was no business of hers. Whether our dining group retained the moniker of expats or became known as Greek residents, I would go out of my way to ensure that this would be the last invitation Bessie would ever receive. If that meant shunning Norman, so be it.

"I find the word expats has a very cliquey ring to it and only seems to be applied to the British abroad," I expounded. "No one ever refers to Guzim as an expat…"

"Isn't that's because he's an illegal immigrant?" Doreen interrupted.

"I do believe that he's more or less legal now," I said. "And as a legal immigrant, he is an expatriate from Albania…"

"But Albania isn't British, old chap…" Milton griped.

The interruptions continued apace, Gordon Strange complaining whilst he slapped away a mosquito, "The problem with renaming the group residents is that anyone who is resident in Meli might decide to turn up…"

"Or anyone resident in Greece…" Macey added.

"We've always operated a strict invitation only policy," Marigold assured Gordon and Macey.

"I'm all in favour of changing the name to residents. It's much more inclusive," Doreen argued. "I don't want my Manolis *mou* to be excluded because he isn't an expat…"

"You can rest assured that unlike some at this table," I said looking pointedly at Bessie, "Manolis will always be welcome at our culinary gatherings."

"But, I say, strictly speaking, Manolis is not an expat," Milton piped up. "He's one of the natives, what."

"Didn't he live in Texas for years? Surely that

would make him a retransplanted native," Macey posited.

"He's not a tree," Doreen snapped. "Manolis is a resident of Meli and Victor wants to rename us the residents."

"The Greek residents," I reiterated.

"But, I say, old chap. Wouldn't we have to be Greek to be Greek residents…"

"Oh, for goodness' sake, Milton, do try and keep up." The local purveyor of porn was sorely trying my patience.

Having anticipated my suggestion to change the name of the group would be met with unanimous approval, I found the level of petty bickering most perplexing. If I'd realised it would cause such a commotion, I would have left them to spend the evening twittering on about house prices.

"So, are you suggesting we need to show our residence permits to get a seat at the table? I don't like that idea, not at all," John Macey carped, the frown creasing his forehead serving to emphasise the slug-like appearance of his eyebrows. "Don't like it at all."

"Don't say you still haven't sorted your permit out yet, Macey," Gordon volleyed.

"You haven't got a permit?" Marigold made no effort to disguise the hint of sark in her question. Once again, I could see my wife's cogs turning as she tried to work out if Macey could possibly be banned under the new group name if he didn't have an up-to-date stamped permit.

"Of course he has a permit," I jumped in. "He's lived in Greece for seventeen years…"

"And don't we all know it," Norman added, rolling his eyes conspicuously.

"Of course I have a permit. It's just that it says I'm a resident of Crete. I haven't got round to swapping it yet. It's on my to-do-list."

"The law states that anyone resident in the area for more than ninety days must acquire a residence permit. The Mani is most definitely not in Crete," I reminded Macey.

Even as I acquainted him with the law, it occurred to me that Macey may not have the necessary four-thousand euros lying around in his bank account, the amount necessary to prove to the Greek authorities that one had sufficient funds to support oneself. With a recent divorce and a large cash outlay on his new home in Meli, Macey may well have cleaned out his bank account and be running on empty. Of course, that was mere speculation on my part. Macey might actually be loaded but have an antipathy for dealing with the unfathomable layers of Greek bureaucracy.

As the squabbling continued, I tuned out until Milton caught my attention. "I say, old chap, are you still with us, what? We ought to put your motion to the vote."

"I'll second that," I agreed, supremely confident that the group gathered around my table would ditch the expat tag and affirm my motion by voting in favour of renaming the group the Greek residents dining club.

"All those in favour of sticking with expats raise your hand, what," Milton said.

Everyone except myself, Marigold and Doreen, raised their hands, voting to remain expats. Despite my annoyance at the blatant contrariness of our guests, I felt a surge of pride, knowing that Marigold had my back. Moreover, I was touched that Doreen had decided to demonstrate her loyalty.

"I say, motion denied," Milton declared. "Sorry about that, old chap."

"Not sorry enough to vote in favour of my motion," I peevishly admonished.

Glancing around, I noticed that Violet Burke was still absent from the table.

"My mother hasn't cast a vote," I pointed out.

"Her vote wouldn't have made any difference, Victor. I say in all modesty, the odds just weren't in your favour," Macey crowed, clearly relieved that he wasn't about to be called upon to produce his non-existent Greek residence permit in order to gain admittance to the next expat soiree.

"I wonder what can be keeping my mother. I'll just pop up to the kitchen and check what she's up to," I said, gathering up the plates to make room on the table for the goulash. Noticing that Norman appeared to be having difficulty remaining upright in his seat, I had a discreet word in Doreen's ear.

"He's been hitting the bottle pretty hard of late, but he seems to be hitting it harder than usual this evening," Doreen enlightened me. "I'll have a word with him. Just because we're talking about divorce, doesn't mean I have to abandon him to the bottom of a vodka bottle."

I considered it quite commendable on Doreen's part to demonstrate such heart, particularly in light of the way Norman's date had gone out of her way to humiliate Doreen.

"His date appears to be ignoring him," I observed.

"I expect he was seeing her through beer-goggles when he hooked up with her." It was most out of character for Doreen to revel in cattiness: I attributed it to the Bessie effect.

Heading indoors, I realised that Norman, in his drunken state, was in no position to drive Bessie back down to the coast, and even if I felt so inclined, which I didn't, I'd had wine. Cursing the lack of a local taxi service, I realised Bessie presented a predicament. Doreen could hardly be expected to give Norman's date a bed for the night. I supposed if push came to shove, I could round up Guzim and bung him a tenner to sling Bessie on the back of his moped, or persuade Vasos to offer her a lift home, if he ever turned up.

Indoors, Violet Burke was stirring a huge pan of goulash on the hob. As I joined her, she broke into a grin. "Pass me those bowls, lad. I'm about ready to dish up."

"You've been an age. What kept you?"

"I decided to add a special something to the stew."

"A special something?"

"Aye, dumplings…"

"You decided to add dumplings. They're going to go down like a lead balloon on a sweltering June evening." Catching sight of a packet of suet on the table, I pointed out, "They won't be very authentic. Hungarians don't use suet in their dumplings."

"Don't they, lad? Well, not to worry, I didn't have enough suet to knock up enough dumplings for everyone." As my mother started to ladle the goulash into bowls, she made a point of saying, "Now, make sure you give this bowl to that stuck-up Bessie. Do you remember how she looked down on dumplings?" My mind flashed back to the coffee bar at the marina. I had a clear recollection of Bessie opining that it was a filthy practice to eat balls of rendered animal fat. "With a bit of luck, the mardy cow will choke on them. Now, like I said, there's not enough dumplings to go around. I'm going to save some for when my old mucker Vasos arrives. He's been dying to get his mouth round my dumplings. It'll be a right nice treat for him."

"If he shows up," I said. "As I recall, you taught Vasos that suet dumpling was English for a cushion."

"Well, let's hope he's got the nouse not to sit on my dumplings."

"I'll take this bowl out to Bessie. Give me another one for Norman. He needs something stodgy to sober him up. I'll ask Marigold to come up and give you a hand getting the goulash out."

"Aye, she's been right helpful tonight," my mother grudgingly admitted.

"And do drop one of those dumplings of yours in my bowl," I pleaded.

"What, and get on Marigold's bad side. She'd have my guts if my cooking played havoc with your cholesterol...what's all that rumpus?"

The sound of a car door slamming and rumbunctious cries of 'beautiful towel' drifted up to the kitchen from the street below. It appeared Vasos had arrived.

Heading back to the garden, I presented the goulash with suet dumplings to Bessie. Tempted as I was to dump it in her lap, only my innate good manners held me back. As I deposited the other bowl in front of Norman, he stirred enough to grab my arm. Leaning towards me and struggling to focus, he confided in an over-exaggerated whisper,

"This dating malarky is not for me. Bessie has a really nasty streak, darned unattractive."

"Well, with a bit of luck, she might dump you before the evening's out. She seems to be making a very overt play for John Macey."

"He's welcome to her. What's all that din?"

"It's just Captain Vasos," I said as my friend strode in. Clearly Vasos hadn't received Marigold's dinner party style guide, turning up in shorts, a stiff-with-sweat tee-shirt, and a pair of grimy and flimsy flip flops.

Even with his diminutive stature, Vasos managed to make a grand entrance, bestowing random 'hellos,' 'spotted dicks,' and 'mucky fats' on the captive audience. I was delighted that Vasos had managed to make it; his high-energy level was just what the desperately dull dinner party needed to shake things up.

Jumping up to receive Vasos' kisses, Marigold introduced him to the table at large before guiding him towards the empty seat next to Sherry and making sure he had an ample supply of beetroot dip and Warrington eggs. Even though she towered over the good captain, Sherry appeared quite captivated by Vasos' endless flow of compliments, blushing and simpering as he boomed 'beautiful' in her direction, his deafening declarations of love going down an absolute treat.

As the sun made its radiant descent, blending seamlessly into the sea on the horizon, I reflected that Vasos' arrival had certainly livened up an otherwise dull as dishwater dinner party. Violet Burke's Hungarian goulash had gone down a treat with everyone except Bessie; the sight of the dumplings swimming around in her stew, enough to make her proclaim she'd turned vegetarian. Vasos' noisy entreaties had persuaded Guzim to join the party, the Albanian shed dweller surprisingly reluctant until he realised that Sherry had firmly attached herself to the good captain. For the best part of an hour, Guzim had nursed a solitary bottle of Amstel whilst gawping like a simpleton, confused by the constant ebb and flow of the English language around him, before retiring to his shed with Doruntina.

With the wine flowing and most of my duties as host behind me, I was content to simply sit and observe. Plonking herself down beside me, Violet Burke pulled an envelope from her pocket. "Take a look at these, Victor. Dot had some pictures from the wedding developed and posted me some copies."

Straining to see in the fast-fading light, I duly admired a photograph of a woman in a poufy white wedding dress who wasn't the bride and a green looking fellow done up in a fruity Hawaiian.

"Here's a lovely one of me in my pillbox before

that little bugger Tyrone scoffed his way through my plastic grapes. And look, here's one of you giving Tyrone the Heinrich Manure…"

"Here's one of Tyrone licking the cheesy wotsits…"

"Oh, my days. It's no wonder everyone came down with a nasty dose of food poisoning. The little sod's only rubbing the pork pies up against his velvet backside…"

"And I seem to recall he'd been sitting around in pigeon droppings…"

Continuing to sift through the pictures, I observed, "Little Tyrone has managed to photobomb himself into every single picture."

"Aye, that he did, lad. He's too young to realise that all those pics of him in those red velvet knickerbockers will come back to bite him in the proverbial…"

The two of us shared a chuckle at the thought of Chardonnay Billings whipping out the photos to impress any of Tyrone's future girlfriends. Then again, that would only arise if the young tearaway was able to get a day release from the borstal he was most certainly heading to, once he was old enough to have his collar felt.

Marigold wandered over to join the two of us, her face glowing with happiness. Throwing her arms around my neck, she proclaimed, "Victor, you're a genius. Have you seen how well Sherry and Vasos are getting along? Considering the language barrier, it's quite remarkable."

Glancing over, I watched as Sherry threw her head back and brayed with laughter at something Vasos had said. Oftentimes, I considered Sherry's laugh to be forced and a tad unnatural, but there was no disputing the genuineness of the moment she was sharing with the stocky *Kapetanios*.

"I think it could be a good match," Marigold mused. "Sherry's not got a snobbish bone in her body and she's not one to be easily embarrassed…"

"And Vasos can definitely be a walking embarrassment…"

"I sometimes think Sherry's got the hide of a rhinoceros, but it got a bit dented after all that carry-on with the German hippie."

"So, darling, you'll forgive me for meddling in your matchmaking territory?"

"Of course, but don't go making a habit of it. Let's hope it's not a ten-second wonder. Sherry was becoming a liability. Did you see the way she threw herself at Lefteris the other day?"

"Looking on the bright side, she didn't make a single advance on me when we were stuck at the roadside together."

"Why would she? I think you may have a misguided sense of your own appeal to the opposite sex."

That was me firmly put in my place.

Marigold went off to mingle and Vasos left his seat, booming, *"toualeta."*

"Give me strength," Vi snapped. "That dozy mare Sherry can't even understand enough Greek to direct Vasos to the lav. I'd best go and give him the tour."

As Violet Burke disappeared to point Vasos in the direction of the bathroom, Sherry wandered over.

"Victor, your friend Vasos is such a jolly character, he's cheered up my evening no end. With his English being a bit limited, chatting to him has brought home that it's really time for me to do something about learning Greek."

"And not before time."

"What do you advise?"

"Let me think. The classes that Marigold and I attended when we first arrived aren't operating anymore. I relied quite a lot on books to widen my vocabulary and, of course, nothing beats trying the language out with actual Greeks."

"But where am I supposed to find a Greek person to help?"

"Well, we are in Greece. Without stating the blindingly obvious, the country is chock-full of Greek speaking Greeks."

"Oh, Victor, you know what I mean. I worry that if I manage to pick up some Greek from a book and then try it out in the shop, for instance, Tina may think I am fluent. I'd end up in a jolly pickle if she started speaking Greek back to me; I wouldn't be able to understand anything she said to me."

"I don't think there's any danger of Tina thinking you're suddenly fluent," I said. "The trick is, if you just try the language out, people will be so happy that you're making an effort that they'll go out of their way to help you out. I have conversational sessions with Dimitris; it helps my Greek and in turn it helps his English. You could buddy up with someone in the same way."

"I don't suppose you could give me some basic lessons?"

"You suppose right. I really couldn't." Not wanting to be dragged down that path, I was adamant in my refusal. "Why not start off learning some basics from a phrase book and then go along with Marigold and her group when they beautify the cemetery? Marigold threw herself right in at the deep end when we first arrived in Meli and she's made some good Greek friends. And look at my mother. You could take a leaf out of her book. She didn't let a little thing like a language barrier get in her way, she got stuck right in, never worrying if she was grammatically correct."

It went without saying that Violet Burke never gave a thought to whether her English was grammatically correct either.

"I'll do it," Sherry declared. "Meeting Vasos has persuaded me that it's time to take the leap."

"If you apply yourself, you'll soon be able to manage a conversation with Vasos. And then there's Guzim; he's really big on muck. The two of you would be able to have some fascinating chats about composting if you're serious about learning the lingo."

"What's muck in Greek?"

"*Vorvoros.*"

"Here, Sherry," Violet Burke called out, plodding back towards us on her by now visibly swollen feet. "I reckon you might have pulled, lass. And a right good 'un this time. Captain Vasos wants to take you out on his yacht…"

"Really?" For once, Sherry seemed lost for words but her expression spoke volumes. She was clearly up for it.

"It's not a yacht, it's a tourist boat…" I corrected before Sherry could get ideas above Vasos' station.

"He's one in a million is that Vasos. He's got a heart of gold." Fine praise indeed from my usual critical mother. "I tell you, Sherry, if I was ten years younger, I'd snap him up and you wouldn't stand a look-in…"

As the strains of a popular Greek dance song began to pulsate around the garden, Captain Vasos sashayed towards Violet Burke, his hips moving in time to the music. Grabbing her hand, he said, "*Ela Violet, chorepse mazi mou,*" inviting her to dance with him.

"You daft 'apeth," she chuckled, allowing Vasos to lead her in the popular *syrtaki* dance. The couple were joined by Marigold and Doreen who had perfected their moves during endless Greek dance classes, and by Kyria Maria who stole the show, a vision in twirling black.

Renowned for having two left feet, I rolled up my sleeves and headed indoors. Since Violet Burke had been swept off her swollen feet, someone had to take responsibility for washing the dishes and scouring the kitchen.

Chapter 26

A Rose behind the Ear

"Finally," I said, my relief palpable as my mobile phone trilled beside me.

"About time." Barry's words echoed my sentiments exactly, his patience visibly wearing thin. "Is it them? Tell me it's them."

"It is indeed," I said, stepping onto the apartment balcony to take the call.

Having been on tenterhooks for the last six hours, Barry and I had practically given up on Felicity and Toby ever arriving, the two of us almost convinced the whole thing had been an elaborate prank, our entrepreneurial venture into the holiday letting business a disastrous flop before it had even begun.

"Mr Bucket, it's Felicity here. So sorry for the late hour. Our flight was delayed for hours. We left the airport half-an-hour ago and we've just hit the road to Meli. Toby thinks we should be with you in about another ninety minutes."

"As you pull into the village, you'll see a sign directing you to the Sofia Apartments," I said. "Better yet, I'll wait for you on the side of the road outside the taverna and personally direct you. I don't want to risk you getting lost."

"Fabulous. It's not easy negotiating these mountain roads in the dark. How will we recognise you?"

"I'll be the one holding a hair dryer, with a rose behind my ear." Admittedly, since I would be the only person hanging around outside like a lemon at close to midnight, the rose was a tad over the top, particularly as they'd met me before. Perchance the impression I'd made had been insignificant.

"They've landed," I informed Barry. "You might as well get off. There's no point in both of us hanging around any longer."

"Fair enough." Barry attempted to stifle a humongous yawn. "I'll stop off at yours and grab Marigold's hairdryer and drop it back here."

Earlier it had belatedly dawned on me that Felicity had complained about the lack of a hair dryer in the *apothiki*. Marigold had grudgingly agreed to hand over her own for the benefit of our paying guests.

"I'll walk down with you, Barry, and wait on the patio."

Taking a last look at the upstairs apartment, Barry grinned. "We did it, Victor. The place looks mighty fine."

"Well, you must take most of the credit…"

"It was a team effort. I could never have got it just so without everyone mucking in."

To parrot John Macey, in my modest opinion, the apartment was everything the discerning traveller could wish for; comfortable with more than a hint of luxury, the décor finished to perfection. Although it was too dark to appreciate the views at this late hour, Toby and Felicity would be in for a veritable visual feast when they threw the shutters open the next morning.

"Fingers crossed that it meets with their approval," I said, recalling the disparaging reception the Squires had given the place. Checking to ensure the welcome book was prominently displayed in the hope that our first couple would add a glowing endorsement to the review section, I realised there was nothing more we could do.

Waving Barry off, I took a seat on the new patio furniture, the new solar lights illuminating the garden and the newly tiled patio. The setting was much improved without the wooden structure that had housed the outside lav, thoughts of said lav suddenly reminding me that Spiros still had possession of the gun that had almost blasted Blat into oblivion. I made a mental note to find out what Spiros planned to do with the shotgun.

The carefully selected *nychtolouloudo*, or night flowers, released the most glorious scent, the night air heady with the intoxicating fragrance. My imagination went into overdrive as something rustled in the undergrowth, the silence of the night so all-encompassing that every small sound was magnified to the nth degree.

Fearing a snake may slither into view or a wild boar might be on the prowl, I exhaled in relief when Cynthia's vile cat Kouneli appeared: the irony of the much-loathed mutant cat being a welcome sight didn't escape me. Shooing the scraggy grey Tom off the property, I briefly considered the wisdom of investing in an ultrasonic cat deterrent. The calibre of guests we hoped to attract were hardly likely to welcome the patio furniture becoming infested with cat hairs. On the other hand, English tourists often had a tendency to come over all soppy at the sight of a Greek feline, even encouraging them to feed from their plates in the coastal tavernas.

"Cooee, Victor. Are you out here?"

"I'm on the patio, Marigold," I called back, delighted my wife had chosen to put in an appearance.

"Barry dropped me off with my hair dryer. I thought I'd come over and keep you company. The garden smells just divine." Dropping a kiss on the top of my head, Marigold began unloading her bag. In addition to the hair dryer, she had arrived with a bottle of wine and two glasses. "I thought it would be romantic for the two of us to share some wine under the stars and raise a toast to the Sofia Apartments."

"I like your thinking," I said.

"I didn't like to think of you waiting all alone. I knew you'd be getting anxious and worrying that everything is up to scratch."

"I think I'm beyond that. Either our business gamble pays off or we'll be living on bread and cheese for the foreseeable."

Taking my hand, Marigold assured me, "It wouldn't be the end of the world if it comes to that. Last night's dinner party made me realise just how lucky we are. There we were in an idyllic setting, surrounded by people whose marriages had failed: John Macey, that awful Bessie woman, Norman and Doreen. They all moved to what they thought were brighter pastures in Greece, but even after upturning their lives, they couldn't plaster over the cracks in their marriages. Yet, I never have any doubts about us."

"Feel free to divorce me, darling, if I ever become obsessed with collecting traffic cones."

"As if…"

"Well, I did say 'I do' again in the vow renewal service." Rather rashly, I added, "And I'd do it again."

I hastily crossed my fingers, hoping Marigold wouldn't take me up on it. The thought of being suited and barefoot on the beach again, held little appeal. Sipping the wine, I realised that Marigold hadn't spoken lightly; we really did have much to be thankful for.

Basking in the moment, the minutes slipped by quickly until it was time to make tracks and head down to the road to greet Toby and Felicity. Snipping a couple of red roses from the luxuriantly lush rosebush, I presented one to my wife as a romantic gesture before slipping the other one behind my ear at a jaunty angle.

"You look as though you've stepped out of a bad spy novel." Marigold's tinkling laughter followed me as I set off on foot to the meeting place.

I wish that I could have bottled the moment when Toby and Felicity first stepped into the apartment, their sheer delight at the accommodation surpassing my wildest expectations, their enthusiasm so genuine that I could have kicked myself for allowing Barry to miss the moment. As I showed them around, the couple raved over the apartment and how fabulous it was to be able to stay in Meli, saying the village had captured their hearts on their last visit, encapsulating everything that made them love Greece with a passion.

Leaving them to it, Marigold and I strolled home hand in hand, elated with the reception the apartments had received. "Do you suppose that if we'd discovered Meli when we were their age, we might have made the move back then?" Marigold asked wistfully.

"It's a moot point. We discovered it when we did. Let's just look forward and embrace the future we have yet to live."

"And we'll live it out together right here. Right here in our very own piece of Greek heaven."

"It sounds perfect."

Leaning in close, Marigold plucked the rose from behind my ear, whispering, "I've got a special treat for you when we get home."

Thinking it sounded like it could be my lucky night, I laughed out loud when Marigold revealed, "I've done a proper Hungarian trifle with rum and raisons…it's even got a dusting of chocolate sprinkles on top."

A Note from Victor

I hope you enjoyed the latest volume of the Bucket saga.

All Amazon reviews gratefully received, even a word or two is most welcome

Please feel free to drop me a line if you would like information on the release date of future volumes in the *Bucket to Greece* series at
vdbucket@gmail.com
or via Vic Bucket on Facebook.

I am always delighted to hear from happy readers.

Printed in Great Britain
by Amazon